HOLOCAUST ODYSSEYS

SUSAN ZUCCOTTI

Holocaust Odysseys

THE JEWS OF SAINT-MARTIN-VÉSUBIE AND
THEIR FLIGHT THROUGH FRANCE AND ITALY

YALE UNIVERSITY PRESS   NEW HAVEN & LONDON

Set in FontShop Scala and Scala Sans type by Duke & Company, Devon, Pennsylvania.

Printed in the United States of America by Vail-Ballou Press, Binghamton, New York.

Library of Congress Cataloging-in-Publication Data

Zuccotti, Susan.

Holocaust odysseys : the Jews of Saint-Martin-Vésubie and their flight through France and Italy / Susan Zuccotti.

p.   cm.

Includes bibliographical references and index.

ISBN 978-0-300-12294-7 (clothbound : alk. paper)

1. Jews—France—Saint-Martin-Vésubie—Biography. 2. Jewish children in the Holocaust—France—Saint-Martin-Vésubie—Biography. 3. Holocaust, Jewish (1939–1945)—France—Personal narratives. 4. Holocaust, Jewish (1939–1945)—Italy—Personal narratives. 5. World War, 1939–1945—Deportations from France—Personal narratives. 6. Holocaust survivors—Biography. 7. Saint-Martin-Vésubie (France)—Biography. I. Title.

DS135.F89Z83 2007

940.53'1809224494—dc22

2007000431

A catalogue record for this book is available from the British Library.

The paper in this book meets the guidelines for permanence and durability of the Committee on Production Guidelines for Book Longevity of the Council on Library Resources.

10 9 8 7 6 5 4 3 2 1

To Nicholas, Emma, Sophie, and Robby

Contents

France, 1940–44. The map shows the line of demarcation and the location of some of the principal internment camps (Map reproduced courtesy of Serge Klarsfeld. Used with permission.)

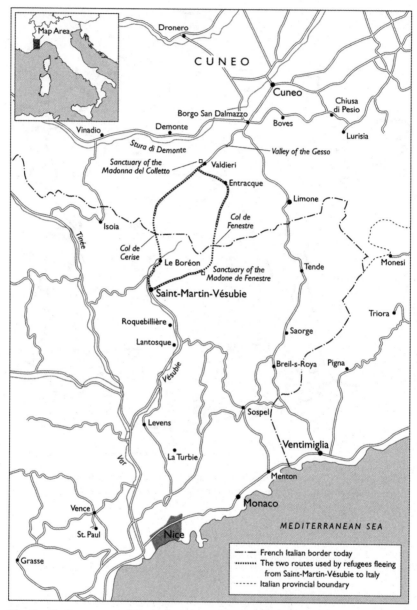

The French department of Alpes-Maritimes and part of the Italian province of Cuneo, where the Jews of Saint-Martin-Vésubie arrived after crossing the Maritime Alps in September 1943

Preface

ON SEPTEMBER 8, 2003, the sixtieth anniversary of the Italian armistice with the Allies, I attended a reunion in Saint-Martin-Vésubie of Jews who had lived there for a time during the Second World War. In the shadow of the Maritime Alps north of Nice, I watched as they found the hotels and pensions where they had stayed, met old friends, and gazed at photographs of themselves as teenagers. Their memories of this episode in their wartime experiences were pleasant. From November 1942 to September 8, 1943, the Italians had occupied Saint-Martin-Vésubie, and Jews there had been relatively safe.

The highlight of the reunion was the bus trip to the sanctuary of the Madone de Fenestre, twelve kilometers from the village in the direction of the Italian frontier. From there and from another point on a second trail to Italy, the Jews of Saint-Martin-Vésubie had scaled the mountains exactly sixty years earlier, to escape from the Germans. After the Italian armistice, the Germans had seized Italian-occupied France and had immediately begun to arrest the Jews.

From the sanctuary of the Madone de Fenestre, many visitors at the reunion in 2003, including a few of the now elderly Jews themselves and many of those who came to honor them, climbed the steep, rocky path to the summit. Gazing down into Italy from the ruins of an old barracks once used by Italian Alpine troops, we saw another group coming up from the other side. Those young people had left from Valdieri, the Italian village where most of the Jews of Saint-Martin-Vésubie had found temporary shelter so long ago. The Jews had stayed in and around Valdieri until they discovered, a few days after their arrival, that the Germans were there, too.

Before coming to the reunion, I had already met Charles Roman, Lya Haberman Quitt, Walter Marx, and William Blye, four of the Jews of Saint-Martin-Vésubie, now living in the New York metropolitan area. I had come to the reunion because of them. In Saint-Martin-Vésubie, I met Menahem Marienberg and Miriam Löwenwirth Reuveni from Israel and Jacques Samson and Paulette Samson Grunberg from Paris. I would meet Sigi Hart from California and Boris Carmeli from Rome a few months later. As I talked with these people and gazed on the mountain track that they had followed in their flight for life, I realized that theirs was an exceptional story. It involved not only a few months of respite in Saint-Martin-Vésubie but a broad range of experiences as Jewish refugees in France and Italy. I resolved to tell that story.

A word about my citations of the names of these ten principal witnesses is in order here. I generally refer to the three women among them by their maiden names, even though all three married after the war. Thus, Miriam Löwenwirth Reuveni is Miriam Löwenwirth in the text (friends from the war period may also have known her as Léa or Leah); Lya Haberman Quitt is Lya Haberman; and Paulette Samson Grunberg is Paulette Samson. These maiden names were the ones the women carried during the war and were the names of the families who suffered with them.

Several witnesses changed their family names after the war. For example, Sigi Hart was originally Sigi Begleiter and then Sigi Hartmayer; William Blye was Wolfgang or Wolf Bleiweiss; Jacques and Paulette Samson were Samsonowicz; and Boris Carmeli was Norbert Wolfinger. I have generally referred to these men by the names they bear today while occasionally reminding the reader of the original family names. Thus, I may write that Sigi Hart or William Blye say this or that (today), but the Hartmayer family or the Bleiweiss family did this or that (during the war). It is an imperfect solution but better than referring throughout to Sigi Beglieter or Hartmayer, Norbert Wolfinger, or Wolf Bleiweiss, for example, names that today have little relevance to those who once bore them.

I wish to express my profound gratitude to these ten principal witnesses, from nine families, for their time and patience in telling me their stories and answering my endless questions on so many occasions. This book could never have been written without their enthusiastic cooperation. I am also deeply grateful to Alberto Cavaglion, an Italian historian from Cuneo. Dr. Cavaglion was the first scholar to examine local archives both in Saint-Martin-Vésubie and in northwestern Italy and to introduce the drama of the Jews' flight over the Maritime Alps from France to Italy to Holocaust historians. His groundbreaking book *Nella notte straniera* has been invaluable to me.

I am also grateful to many others for their help and suggestions: Diane Afoumado, Danielle Baudot Laksine, Georges Borchardt, Mitch Braff, Manya Breuer, Don Francesco Brondello, Michele Calandri, Carlo Spartaco Capogreco, Vicki Caron, Enzo Cavaglion, Éric Charamel, David Cushman, Miriam Dubi-Gazan, Rakefet Elisha, Alfred Feldman, Régine and Jacky Gerhard, Eric Gili, Judah Gribetz, Stanley Hoffmann, Werner Isaac, Marion Kaplan, Robert Katz, Serge Klarsfeld, Massimo Longo Adorno, Eugenio Meinardi, Sergio Minerbi, Emanuele Pacifici, Mordecai Paldiel, Liliana Picciotto Fargion, Inge Roman, Chaya Roth, Miriam Rotondo Michelini, Marco Ruzzi, Jean-Pierre Samuel, Michele Sarfatti, Paola Severgnini, Dekel Sherman, Stanlee Stahl, Mario Toscano, Klaus Voigt, and Giovanna and Andreina Zuccotti. Laura Jones Dooley, my editor at Yale, saved me from many mistakes. I greatly appreciate the kind assistance, generosity, and patience of these many friends and colleagues.

Last, I thank my family, and especially my husband, John Zuccotti, for his unwavering patience, constant support, and thoughtful suggestions. His reading of the manuscript, combined with the perceptive advice of my agent, Georges Borchardt, enabled me to mesh the stories of nine families into a coherent whole.

Introduction

IN THE EARLY SUMMER OF 1943, Jews still alive in German-occupied Europe had little reason for optimism. The most destructive war in history, raging for nearly four years, showed little sign of abating. True, the Allies had landed in North Africa in early November 1942 and the Russians, after a titanic 125-day battle, had turned the German tide at Stalingrad three months later. But if the vise was slowly closing around the Third Reich, its progress was barely perceptible to most Europeans. The military front remained far away, scarcely in Europe at all.

Meanwhile, by the summer of 1943 nearly four million Jews had already been murdered—starved to death in the ghettos of Eastern Europe, shot by German SS Einsatzgruppen in the Soviet Union, or gassed at Chełmno, Treblinka, Sobibór, Majdanek, Bełzek, and Auschwitz. Most of the ghettos of Poland had been leveled or converted to other uses after the last of their Jewish occupants had been exterminated. The Third Reich and its Czech Protectorate, Slovakia, Serbia, and German-occupied areas of Croatia and Greece were nearly *Judenrein*—cleansed of Jews, in the hideous German terminology. Freight trains jammed with human cargo still left regularly from assembly points near Paris, Amsterdam, and Brussels. Jews hiding in private houses and barns, churches and monasteries, schools and hospitals, lived in mortal fear of the knock on the door that would mean death for them and perhaps for those helping them. Even those fortunate enough to have escaped into neutral Switzerland or Spain often lived in assigned residences or internment camps.

There were some relatively brighter spots, but those lights too were about to be extinguished. In Denmark, the German occupying forces would demand the arrest and deportation of the country's eight thousand Jews in the autumn of 1943, prompting the Danes to ferry most of them to safety in neutral Sweden. In Italy, an independent ally of the Third Reich and hitherto unoccupied, some ten thousand foreign Jews had been ordered to leave the country while forty-seven thousand native Jews had lost jobs, property, and the right to attend public schools as the result of Prime Minister Benito Mussolini's racial laws in 1938, but there had as yet been no deportations. That too would change in the autumn of 1943, after Mussolini's fall from power at the end of July, Marshal Pietro Badoglio's armistice with the Allies on September 8, and the German occupation of Italy that promptly followed. In Hungary, more than six hundred thousand Jews would be safe a little longer but would be more thoroughly annihilated than those in either Denmark or Italy when deportations finally began in April 1944. Meanwhile in Bulgaria and Romania, many of the Jews in border territories that had been lost at an earlier period but regained with German support in 1941 had already been murdered in one way or another. Most of those who lived in the historic centers of those two countries would survive.

Given the stark realities of wartime Europe, visitors arriving in the summer of 1943 in the remote French mountain village of Saint-Martin-Vésubie, about sixty-seven kilometers north of Nice on the border of Fascist Italy, would have been astonished. They would immediately have noticed more than a thousand foreign, not French, Jews—almost as many as the local French Catholic population of 1,650. Jews were resting in the shadows of the Maritime Alps, exchanging gossip in the central square, lingering in the local cafés, shopping or playing chess in the parks. A babel of languages echoed in the crisp mountain air. Heavily accented French mixed with the local dialect, but one could also hear German, Czech, Polish, Ukrainian, Romanian, Hungarian, and, especially startling, a Yiddish that was by then no longer heard in public places in occupied Europe. It had rarely ever been heard in the French Alps. Jewish children tumbled in the streets and parks. Jewish teenagers studied English or the piano, organized boxing clubs and choral groups, and invited local Catholic youngsters to their parties and dances. Occasionally one or two of the local authorities even came to the newly established synagogue to appreciate the cantor. But those authorities were not French, as one might expect in southeastern France, or German, as was the case in most of Europe, including most of France, in 1943. In the village of Saint-Martin-Vésubie that summer, the occupying forces were Italian, and that made all the difference.

Who were these Jews in Saint-Martin-Vésubie, and where had they come from? Apart from their Jewishness, their most important shared characteristic was their status as recent immigrants or refugees in France. Nearly all had come to the country after 1937 or 1938, often with temporary entry visas or with none at all. Many had arrived even later, in May or June 1940, when several thousand Jews had been among the million or so refugees from Belgium, Luxembourg, and the Netherlands who had poured into France by train, bus, truck, automobile, bicycle, or foot, just ahead of the invading German army. This shared characteristic was key, for it meant that these Jews lacked valid French identification cards and permanent residence permits. As semi-legal or illegal aliens in France, they were viewed by the authorities with suspicion and treated differently, not only from Jewish citizens but also from longtime resident Jewish (and non-Jewish) immigrants.

When arrests of Jews began in German-occupied northern France in 1941, French police seized mostly foreigners, with little regard for their dates of arrival. However, when those same police in the unoccupied southern zone, or "Free France," began delivering some eleven thousand foreign Jewish men, women, and children to the Germans in the north in August 1942 for deportation to Auschwitz, they deliberately focused on the most recent immigrants and refugees, who were the most economically dependent, legally insecure, and unpopular of all the Jews in the country. Most of the Jews who made it to Saint-Martin-Vésubie a little later had narrowly escaped arrest during that terrible August, and many had lost parents, grandparents, and siblings then or soon after. They arrived in the tranquil village with a heavy burden of personal sorrow and fear.

Apart from their similar status as recent immigrants and refugees, the Jews in Saint-Martin-Vésubie were extremely diverse. They included men and women from all occupations: doctors and lawyers, engineers and accountants, teachers and students, businessmen, salesmen, artists, tailors, furriers, shoemakers, leather workers, horse dealers, and more. All ages were represented, from newborns to the very elderly. Some Jews in the village were strictly observant while others were not observant at all. They came from the cities, towns, and shtetls of nearly every German-occupied country in Europe, but especially from Germany itself, Austria, Czechoslovakia,

Hungary, Poland, and the Eastern European region once called Galicia, today mostly in Ukraine. In the cafés and shops of Saint-Martin-Vésubie, there were sophisticated former residents of Vienna, Warsaw, and Berlin and rural folk from villages difficult to find on a map, then and now. Some had lived in Belgium since the 1920s, and perhaps learned a little or a lot of French there. Others, particularly the young, had learned French after their arrival in that country in 1939 or 1940, before moving to Saint-Martin-Vésubie in 1943. Many of their elders spoke only German, Polish, or Yiddish. But in the tiny French village in the shadow of the French Alps, these differences meant little. The Jews were there because they were Jews, and the freedom to reveal their identity without fear created an exuberance and a hope that drew them together and superseded all superficial diversity.

Regardless of their exuberance and hope, however, the interlude of Jews in Saint-Martin-Vésubie was, in the words of one of them, "too good to last." After the Italian armistice with the Allies on September 8, 1943, the Italian army abandoned its occupied territories in southeastern France (and elsewhere) and retreated back across the Alps. After some discussion, most of the Jews of Saint-Martin-Vésubie chose to follow them, expecting to find the American and British troops in Italy, and safety. Instead, after a harrowing three-day exodus over the mountains, they ran into the German army and the SS, busy occupying and terrorizing most of the country. The Allies, it seemed, were stalled well south of Rome, where they would remain until the early summer of 1944. More than a third of the refugees from Saint-Martin-Vésubie were arrested within a week and died at Auschwitz two and a half months later. The other two thirds went into hiding, mostly in mountain huts in the Alps, Catholic schools and convents in Florence, and inns and pensions in Rome. Their wartime odysseys resembled an hourglass. From all over Europe, they had come together in Saint-Martin-Vésubie, only to spread out again in Italy in their desperate struggle for survival.

This book tells the story of the Jews of Saint-Martin-Vésubie and their flight through Vichy France and German-occupied Italy. The format, however, is not that of a traditional historical narrative. Instead, the story is told primarily through the experiences of nine families, as related by survivors from each. Born in the second half of the 1920s, these survivors were all teenagers during the war, old enough to have understood much of what was happening to them and their families. When they spoke with me, they were in their mid- to late seventies. Although they often did not recall the precise dates of the events that affected them during their journeys through France and Italy, they remembered the experiences themselves with impressive clarity and detail.

While this book focuses on nine families, the experiences of many other survivors of the French mountain village and the flight over the Maritime Alps to Italy are described, including those of Harry Burger, Alfred Feldman, Régine and Jacky Gerhard, Louis Goldman, Ludwig Greve, Bronka Halpern, Werner Isaac, and Leopold Neumann. Several of these individuals have written memoirs of their wartime experiences, and some, including Alfred Feldman, Werner Isaac, and the Gerhards, have spoken with me. The information they provided complements that given by the nine families. For my aim is not only to describe a few individuals or families but also to paint a broad picture of experiences shared by all of the 1,100 to 1,250 Jews of Saint-Martin-Vésubie.

This book does not consist *only* of personal testimony; it is not solely an oral history. Several of the survivors discussed here have provided videotaped testimony for various institutions. Their stories are presented differently here. For as is often recognized, human memory is an imperfect tool. In *The Drowned and the Saved*, Primo Levi, the masterful memorialist of the Holocaust, wrote of his own craft, "The memories which lie within us are not carved in stone; not only do they tend to become erased as the years go by, but often they change, or even grow, by incorporating extraneous features." He added, "A memory evoked too often, and expressed in the form of a story, tends to become fixed in a stereotype, in a form tested by experience, crystallized, perfected, adorned, installing itself in the place of the raw memory and growing at its expense."

In addition to being imperfect, human memory is also inevitably incomplete. Holocaust survivors with the most reliable memories remember much of what happened to them before, during, and after the war, but they often do not know the exact dates or chronology of the events they experienced. Also, unless they have consulted other witnesses or written sources (and in so doing, diluted or distorted their own memories), they understand little more about the broader picture today than they did at the time of the persecutions. Thus, for example, survivors have no special expertise regarding the reasons for the rise of Nazism in the Third Reich. They cannot list every Vichy French anti-Jewish law or regulation, or explain the reasons for the escalating anti-Jewish policies in France after 1940. They know little about the delicate relations between the German and Italian occupiers of France or between the occupiers and Vichy French officials. They do not know statistics of overall populations, deportation, and survival. But they know very well what happened to them.

The tensions between witnesses and historians, so ably described by Annette Wieviorka in *The Era of the Witness*, can usually be resolved. Avoiding insult, cruelty, and arrogance, not to mention the tragic loss of rich sources of information and understanding, the historian can find several ways to deal with the limitations of human memory. With regard to imperfection and the possibility of error, the historian can evaluate each individual's testimony, balancing it against existing documentary evidence. In this book, therefore, all testimony has been checked against archival documents and reliable secondary studies. Survivors' descriptions of roundups, arrests, and internment have been confirmed by written prefects' orders and police reports. The deportations of specific individuals have been verified by lists of deportees composed by prison guards at the time. After careful verification, all testimony is presented in a historical context.

In addition, the historian must ask whether an individual testimony is consistent with that of other survivors, perpetrators, rescuers, or bystanders at the same events who are unknown to the person in question. With regard to this book, a few of the men and women interviewed knew each other during the war, and one or two others became friends afterwards. Most, however, lived apart from the others. Yet all the testimonies were consistent and compatible.

The date on which testimony is recorded is of course relevant to its value. Testimony provided during or soon after the war may be considered "purer," less influenced by subsequent knowledge and experience. But the skillful historian can extract valid insight and understanding from more recent testimony as well, again judging it against other sources of information.

Concerning the issue of incompleteness, as Donald Bloxham and Tony Kushner wrote in their book *The Holocaust: Critical Historical Approaches*, "It is essential not to expect the impossible from survivor testimony." The historian must scrutinize testimony and extract from it only what it can best provide. Survivors cannot be expected to supply precise dates and chronologies or describe events that they did not personally witness. Nor can they provide broad generalizations about behavior or explanations of motives and causation. Their personal experiences were too narrow for sweeping statements. For material of that nature, the historian must look elsewhere.

What, then, does survivor testimony offer? Is it useful only to illustrate what we think we know about the Holocaust, to humanize a terrible narrative of death and destruction? The question is best answered with precise examples connected with this book. Even though the interviewed survivors have no special expertise regarding the reasons for the rise of Nazism in the Third Reich, they describe the immediate impact of Nazism on particular Jewish communities—on middle-class Jews in Germany in the 1930s, for example, or on Jews in Vienna at the time of the Anschluss—providing details that might not otherwise be known. Although they cannot fully define or explain Vichy's anti-Jewish policies, they describe the impact of the laws on recent immigrant and refugee Jews and relate the confusion and pain that the escalating harshness caused. They recall some conditions in the French internment camps they were actually in that are not otherwise recorded and recollect important changes in the attitudes of camp guards that are not mentioned in official documents or noticed by subsequent historians. And for Italy, they speak of thousands of refugees pouring into the country about whom virtually nothing is known. They describe police arrests of mostly foreign Jews in Florence about November 6, 1943, and in Rome about May 1, 1944, of which there are almost no records. Not even the precise dates and the numbers of victims are known, much less the names of those arrested.

In addition, survivors can describe clandestine activities that even the most astute police reports might have missed. In France, witnesses for this book tell of evasions and escapes from internment camps and hospitals; of the spiriting of Jewish youngsters out of camps and into special children's homes operated by French Jews for their foreign brethren; of dealing with the French and Italians in the village of Saint-Martin-Vésubie; and of fleeing over the Alps to Italy when the Germans threatened them there. In Italy, they speak of traveling illegally from Cuneo to Rome; of hiding in mountain huts, convents, and secret apartments; of using false papers and joining the Resistance. In both countries, they remember official anti-Semitic policies and unofficial anti-Semitic attitudes. They also recall courageous men and women, Jews and non-Jews, French and Italian, who helped them. Little of this material was recorded in official documents at the time. On the contrary, invaluable written records of the Jewish assistance Comité Dubouchage in Nice, the Jewish rescue organization Delasem (Delegazione per l'assistenza agli emigranti ebrei) in Italy, and the Italian occupation authorities in southeastern France were destroyed in 1943 to avoid capture by the invading

Germans. Witnesses like those interviewed here are sometimes the only source of evidence about rescue activities.

In all these ways, survivor testimony can add to what we know about the Holocaust. But it is also precious in its own right, as an account of individual human experiences. For what men, women, and children personally went through just before, during, and immediately after the war is as much a part of the history of the Holocaust as the description of government policies, roundups, deportations, and extermination. We can learn of the policies and their enforcement from the documents, but only the survivors can tell us what it felt like to be on the receiving end of persecution, to be constantly hungry, dirty, and cold; uncertain, terrified, lonely, and bored all at the same time; deprived of all the amenities of civilization yet grateful to be alive for yet another day. Unless they wrote memoirs or diaries at the time, most Jews who experienced the persecution can tell us nothing because they were murdered. The survivors speak for them as well, revealing the essential humanity of men, women, and children struggling to live.

Each of the nine families interviewed here also makes an important contribution to the story of the Jews of Saint-Martin-Vésubie. Thus, we meet Jacques and Paulette Samson from Poland, who, unlike the others, remained in Paris, in German-occupied northern France, without parents, during the roundups of foreign Jews in 1941 and 1942. Young Charles Roman from Vienna crossed the border illegally with his mother late in 1938 and lived in Jewish children's homes in the châteaux of Chabannes and Montintin until it became too dangerous. Fourteen-year-old Miriam Löwenwirth, from a village in what is now Ukraine, convinced the German occupiers of Belgium, where she was living, to let her go to France in 1941 to join her mother, and traveled there with two younger siblings in her charge.

Most of the nine families lost loved ones or had narrow escapes when the Vichy authorities arrested Jews in the unoccupied zone in August 1942 and delivered them to the Germans for deportation. Warned by a sympathetic Frenchman, seventeen-year-old Sigi Hart from Berlin, who had already escaped with his family from the French internment camp of Agde, led his parents and siblings up into the Pyrenees to avoid arrest. Boris Carmeli, from a Polish family formerly living in Magdeburg, Germany, and then Brussels, was also warned at the last minute and able to hide. But Charles Roman lost his father and was nearly lost himself; Menahem Marienberg, born in Brussels of Polish parents, lost his mother and two siblings; William

Blye from Leipzig lost his father and two brothers in Nice. Others lost loved ones later: Walter Marx's father from Heilbronn was arrested in a massive roundup in southern France in February 1943; Lya Haberman from Berlin lost her mother and sister when the Germans seized Nice from the Italians in early September 1943. And later in Italy, Walter Marx's mother and Menahem Marienberg's father were arrested in the province of Cuneo, and Miriam Löwenwirth's father was caught in Florence. None of these family members returned from deportation. Meanwhile, Boris Carmeli and Sigi Hart were caught in Italy and deported to Auschwitz but survived.

Each of these nine stories is unique. Together they capture the essence of the Jews of Saint-Martin-Vésubie. They define the particular situation of recent Jewish immigrants and refugees in wartime France and Italy—a situation that has not often been examined separately from that of other Jews in those countries. They indicate the necessity of making choices, of playing an active role in the struggle for survival despite the terrifying lack of information about perpetrators' intentions and the absence of certainty that a given choice would ensure success. They illustrate the amazing resiliency and optimism of young people, often in distinction to their more burdened and devastated parents. They show the independence and capacity of women to take charge, make decisions, and lead their families to safety. They demonstrate the dilemma of Jews caught between increasingly hostile authorities in both France and Italy and sometimes sympathetic local populations. And they reveal the often overlooked role of Jewish assistance agencies, usually working closely with non-Jews, in rescue operations. In a sense, finally, these nine stories also capture the essence of the Jews in the Holocaust more generally—a tale of perfidy and heroism, courage and determination, tragedy and miraculous survival.

PART I

The Journey through France, 1933–1943

CHAPTER ONE

Jewish Immigrants and Political Refugees in France, 1933–1939

Jacques and Paulette Samson, Lya Haberman, William Blye, and Charles Roman

AFTER THE END OF THE First World War in 1918, the Treaty of Versailles provided for the restoration of a united and independent Poland. Poles in the postwar period were proud of their country, uneasy about the status of minorities, and frightened by Russian Bolsheviks threatening from the east. In a climate of political and economic insecurity, anti-Semitism in Poland soared. The situation became so bad that in July 1937, thirty-four-year-old Rywka-Rajzla Samsonowicz (the name would later be shortened to Samson) insisted that her husband, Szlama, immigrate to France with their two oldest children, twelve-year-old Jacob Joseph (Jacques) and ten-year-old Hinda Perla (Paulette). Szlama had a small business in Rawa Mazowiecka, near Łódź, buying and selling horses, but there did not seem to be much of a future for him there. Relatives had been living in Paris since the First World War, so he had contacts and a place to stay in the city. Following the time-honored practice of immigrants everywhere, he and the older children moved but Rajzla remained behind with their two younger daughters, Chana and Malka, then eight and five. When Szlama was more established, she and the girls planned to join him. Jacques and Paulette were delighted to accompany their father, but Paulette vividly remembers seeing her mother for the last time, weeping, at the railroad station in Warsaw.[1]

As a legal immigrant in Paris, Szlama was able to obtain residence and work permits, but life was difficult nevertheless. By making deliveries for an aunt who had arrived in 1900 and established a furniture and clothing business, he was barely able to support his children. He found a two-room apartment without running water in Pantin, a poor neighborhood on the northeastern edge of the city where his aunt's shop was located and other relatives lived. Paulette remembers that water and toilets, shared by multiple tenants, were on landings between the floors. She also recalls that the apartment was so cold in winter that she and Jacques entertained themselves by scratching designs into the frost on the inside of the windows. Less amusing were the monotonous evening suppers of bread and milk.

Szlama, Jacques, and Paulette had lived better in Poland. Desperately trying to bring his wife and other two daughters to France, Szlama regularly gave his meager savings to a *passeur,* a smuggler. But the man, Paulette says, was "not honest." The German invasion of Poland on September 1, 1939, caught Rajzla, Chana, and Malka still there. After the war, a neighbor told Jacques and Paulette that the three had been packed and waiting in front of their house for a clandestine escape to France when German police came to arrest them. They were murdered by the Nazis, probably in 1942.

In September 1937, soon after their arrival in Paris, Jacques and Paulette began school. They did not speak any French at first, but their teachers were helpful, assisting with the language and explaining the pronunciation. The brother and sister were known to be Jewish, but they had no problems with the other children. They worked hard in school and were soon at the top of the class, but when their father came to the award ceremony at the end of the school year, he could speak no French at all.

Except for being among the more recent arrivals, the Samsonowicz family typified most of the roughly seventy thousand Eastern European Jews who immigrated to Paris after the First World War.[2] Some families were more strictly observant; some report more experiences with anti-Semitism in France; others were not in the country legally and had to worry about expulsion. But like the Samsonowicz family, nearly all had immigrated to seek greater economic opportunity and to escape the anti-Semitism of Eastern Europe. Nearly all were poor. Many were helped by family members already in France but left loved ones behind in the old country, they hoped temporarily. Adults worked hard and long for little pay, lived in inadequate housing, had few contacts outside their Jewish immigrant circle, and learned French slowly. Their children went to French public schools, where they worked hard and often excelled. They soon spoke French better than their parents and felt more comfortable in their new world. It was the old story of immigrants everywhere.

Jews who arrived in France from the Third Reich between Hitler's rise to power in January 1933 and the outbreak of war differed from the Eastern Europeans. Less economic immigrants than political refugees unwilling or unable to live under the new Nazi regime, they tended to be better educated and relatively more affluent. Their experiences in depression-era France were not necessarily easier, for jobs were scarce and antiforeign sentiment, especially anti-Jewish and anti-German feeling, was high. Also, political refugees usually lost most of their possessions and savings when they emigrated. In part for those reasons, most Jewish refugees from the Third Reich did not stay in France but left to seek a better life elsewhere.[3] Those who remained were resourceful, and some lucky individuals were able to transfer their business skills to their new places of residence.

Two men from the nine families profiled in this book belong to that category. Lya Haberman's father, Oscar, who was born in Poland in 1901 and moved to Germany soon after the First World War, left his wife, Chana, and his daughters, Hilda and Lya, behind in Berlin when he emigrated again in 1933. This time he settled in Paris, where he established a successful import-export business in felt for making hats. Chana, who preferred to live in Palestine, moved there with their daughters for a time but finally joined her husband in Paris in 1938.[4] William Blye's father, Chaim Bleiweiss (William would assume the name Blye years later, in the United States), also an immigrant from Poland to Germany after the First World War, eventually established a thriving clothing business in Nice. His journey to Nice, however, was indirect.

Chaim Bleiweiss and his wife, Maria, actually emigrated three times. They married in 1919 in Warsaw, where their first child, Ruth, died at age three. The heartbroken parents were on their way to the local Jewish cemetery when they heard a Polish passerby remark loudly, "Good, there's one less Yid." At that moment they decided that they could not raise other children in Poland. They moved to Leipzig, Germany, where their three sons were born. The middle child, William, or Wolfgang (Wolf) as he was known until he moved to the United States after the war, was born on April 7, 1924. William's brother Bernhard preceded him by a year. Leo was born two years after William.

"My father, a furrier, was very good at business," William relates with admiration. "Everything he did turned out well." But after Hitler took power in 1933, life for Jews in Germany became increasingly difficult. The anti-

Semitism Chaim and Maria had known in Poland seemed to catch up with them and grow worse. In March 1937, Chaim was forced to walk through the streets of Leipzig with a two-faced sandwich board on his shoulders that said, "Do not buy from the Jews; buy in German shops." Slurs like *schmutziger Jude* (dirty Jew) and *Schweine Jude* (Jewish swine) were commonly heard. William, who readily admits that he cannot recall all the details of his subsequent odyssey through wartime Europe, vividly remembers one incident in Nazi Germany. "My mother had sent me to the store to get some milk, which in those days was dispensed into a pot. While walking home, I was surrounded by some kids from my school. 'Schweine Jude!' they yelled. Then they grabbed the pot and, laughing, poured the milk over my head. When I came home, I asked my mother what 'Schweine Jude' meant but she did not answer."[5]

The Bleiweiss boys attended an elementary Volksschule in Leipzig, but like their lives in general, school became ever more unpleasant. The other students tormented them. A teacher named Horst was especially cruel to William, beating him with a bamboo cane for the slightest infraction. On one occasion, the boy came home with large welts on his back. Later, when Jewish children could no longer attend public schools, the Jewish community established its own, called the Karlebach Schule. That was a great improvement. According to William, even some non-Jewish children attended the Jewish school for a while because the quality of the education was better and less ideological.

Shortly after the sandwich-board incident in 1937, William's father decided to leave Germany. After much consideration, he chose Italy, which placed him in a definite minority among Jews wishing to leave the Third Reich and Eastern Europe. Although Fascist Italy was not yet officially anti-Semitic, it had been an authoritarian state since Mussolini's March on Rome in 1922 and a nation at war since its brutal invasion of Ethiopia in 1935 and its support of Generalissimo Francisco Franco in the Spanish Civil War a year later. Still more ominous, Mussolini, by agreeing to a "Rome-Berlin axis" for the coordination of foreign policy on October 25, 1936, was increasingly identified with Hitler and the Third Reich. The Anti-Comintern Pact with Germany followed, and Italy withdrew from the League of Nations in December 1937. Throughout these developments, Italian Jews remained good patriots and, in some cases, even loyal Fascists. Jews elsewhere, however, if planning to emigrate, usually preferred to take their chances with democracies like France, Great Britain, or the United States.

Firm in his choice of Italy, Chaim Bleiweiss sent his three sons to a special camp for youngsters in Milan. William recalls the date, April 1937, because it was soon after his Bar Mitzvah. With the children safely out of the country, Chaim and Maria left home, taking nothing with them. "They even left the dishes on the table," William declares, "so that no one would suspect that they were not coming back." They entered Italy with tourist visas, but they intended to stay. Without speaking a word of Italian, Chaim started another fur company.

Although he was resilient and courageous, Chaim's timing was terrible. In September 1938, less than a year and a half after the Bleiweiss family arrived in Italy, Mussolini initiated his anti-Jewish program. One of the first provisions demanded that the more than ten thousand foreign Jews in Italy leave the country within six months or face expulsion.[6] Chaim, Maria, and their sons had to move again. This time they chose Nice, in France but barely forty kilometers from the Italian border. Of their journey, William says, "There was no country in the world that wanted to admit us, but our family, together with a group of Jewish friends, conceived of a plan. We went to the border and hired a guide to smuggle us over the Alps into France. After a day and night of climbing, with no roads to speak of, the guide abandoned us in the middle of the night. At daybreak, the French border guards caught us all, marched us to an outpost, and arrested us. Those with some money [including William's family] were given a six-month [renewable] permit to reside in France. The others spent a few days in confinement and were then released," presumably without the coveted *permis de séjour.*[7]

Many Jewish and non-Jewish refugees in the 1930s, including several Jews described in this book, recall being treated badly by French immigration authorities. They describe long waits for the renewal or refusal of documents by harassed and overworked bureaucrats who addressed them with contempt.[8] It must be remembered, however, that many of these refugees were illegal immigrants, often stateless, trying to stay in France during a period of economic depression, high unemployment, and, around the time William Bleiweiss arrived, increasing unease following Hitler's takeover of Austria in the spring of 1938 and his seizure of the Sudetenland the following September.[9] The mistreatment of illegal aliens in France before the war was arguably no worse than that in many other countries in times of stress. In any case, for William and his family, all went well. William thinks that they were able to stay because his father started another business, making uniforms for the French army. Because of his temporary residence permit,

Chaim provided the money but arranged to share the business and use the name of a non-Jewish Frenchman. With identity papers, a six-month renewable permis de séjour, and a source of income, the talented Chaim Bleiweiss established himself in a remarkably short time.

In Nice, William attended the Lycée du Parc Impérial. It was difficult in the beginning because he did not speak French. The teacher put him in the back of the room and treated him, in William's words, "as if I was retarded." But with a French tutor at home, the boy learned quickly. After that, Nice became a pleasant place to live. William went to school in the morning, to the beach for a swim at lunchtime, and back to classes in the afternoon. He does not remember that there were any other Jews in the school, but he readily made friends with the non-Jews.[10] The French treated him and his family well, without hostility. "They were totally different from the Germans," he says, "who many times cursed me."

The economic achievements of Oscar Haberman and Chaim Bleiweiss were exceptional among Jewish political refugees from the Third Reich to France after 1933. Probably more typical were Charles Roman and his mother, Marianne Uhrmacher Roman, who arrived in Paris from Vienna in 1938 after several harrowing attempts. Born in 1927, Charles grew up in Vienna's middle-class second district, where he attended grammar school for four years, took an examination at the age of ten for admission to an eight-year engineering program, and enrolled at the Realschule Wien II in Josef Gall Gasse. After his parents divorced in 1936, Charles remained with his mother, but his father lived nearby. Leopold Roman was a self-employed manufacturer and salesman of rubber heels. Marianne had two jobs, one as a secretary for a lawyer at a patent office and the other as a researcher and copier of patents.

Charles well remembers when his secure and comfortable world fell apart. On March 11, 1938, German chancellor Adolf Hitler sent his army into Austria and annexed it to the Third Reich. Charles watched in silence as the Führer passed through the Taborstrasse in his own neighborhood amid wild cries of "Heil, Hitler!" from thousands of ecstatic Viennese. A few days later, the eleven-year-old boy watched again as pro-Nazi Austrians made Jews scrub the sidewalks in his neighborhood on their hands and knees. Charles explains that before the Anschluss, some Viennese who opposed unification with the Third Reich had painted the slogan "Heil Osterreich," or "Hail Austria," on the sidewalks.[11] Now the Jews were expected to scrub it off. Nazi sympathizers picked out Jewish-looking pedestrians, especially men with long black coats and beards. When these were too few to suit them, they demanded that concierges in nearby apartment buildings identify their Jewish residents. Of course the paint did not come off with scrub brushes and buckets of water, so the tormenters kicked their victims ferociously. Along with the men with beards, their favorite targets, says Charles, were plump women. After kicking and beating them, they insisted, "Go on, Saujude, continue."

In addition to evoking his horror and disgust, the Anschluss affected Charles in practical ways. When the lawyer who was his mother's boss was denied the right to practice because he was Jewish, Marianne lost both her jobs. Charles was dismissed from the Realschule that he had so proudly entered a few months before and was obliged to enroll in a high school set up in 1938 for Jews only. The Anschluss also unleashed a wave of anti-Semitism unlike anything Charles had experienced before. A teacher at a nearby school, for example, deliberately dismissed his students early so that they could harass and torment the Jewish students at Charles's school when they left the building. Charles and other Jewish students were regularly beaten up.

Charles and his mother began trying to leave the Third Reich soon after the Anschluss. They were helped by several German and Austrian Jewish committees, composed of dedicated, self-sacrificing people whom Charles remembers to this day. At first, mother and son tried to leave legally. For weeks they waited for visas for Palestine that never came. The French refused them visas, while Switzerland and Britain were too expensive. In despair, they decided to emigrate illegally. On their first attempt, they crossed the border on foot from Germany to France with a group led by a passeur. They were caught and sent back. Next, they made a similar attempt to reach Switzerland. Because it had been raining for the past three days in the mountains, the water in the river they had to wade across was higher than usual. A Swiss guard caught them in midstream, holding their luggage over their heads. Charles still remembers his hostile greeting, "Seid Ihr Deutsche Juden?"—"Are you German Jews?"—and when they answered in the affirmative, he sent them back. In a third attempt, Marianne sent her son on a train to Basel without her. To avoid German controls at the exit of the Basel train station, the eleven-year-old boy was supposed to squeeze through a small opening in the fence. After doing so, he was stopped by two Swiss railroad workers, turned over to the Gestapo, searched, and sent back.

Marianne Roman must have been an indomitable woman, because she did not give up. Alone and without help, she and Charles made their way to a bridge leading over the Moselle River from Germany to Luxembourg. Quite by chance, Marianne began an animated conversation with a woman with a baby carriage who, it turned out, made the crossing daily and was known to the guards. No one bothered to stop her new companions—another woman and a young boy. They arrived safely in Luxembourg, but then their luck failed them again. The hotel where they spent their first night in freedom was frequented by prostitutes. When it was raided, Marianne and Charles were caught without proper papers. After two or three days in prison, they were expelled back to Germany.

Marianne still had her apartment in Vienna, so she and her son returned there. Thus they were in Vienna on Kristallnacht, November 9, 1938, when the Nazis launched an anti-Jewish pogrom throughout the Third Reich. Charles remembers that several synagogues in the city were burned. His grandmother's relatives had contributed to the original construction of one of them, which was totally destroyed. They felt its loss keenly.

After Kristallnacht, Marianne Roman knew she had to try again to leave. In December 1938, traveling alone at night without a guide, she and Charles followed the same route that they had taken on their first attempt to enter France. This time they succeeded, but again their luck did not hold. A Jewish assistance committee in Germany had referred them to a Jewish family in a small French village near the border. After a rest and a meal there, their host telephoned members of the French Jewish committee in Strasbourg who were to help them further. They arranged a meeting in the Place Kléber in Strasbourg, and their host drove them there. But the family's phone had been tapped, and the police were waiting for them at the rendezvous place. Marianne was imprisoned and Charles was sent to a local hospital for children whose parents could not care for them. The hospital was operated by strict nuns who confiscated their patients' clothes so that they could not escape.

Unable to speak a word of French, Charles remained at the hospital for four weeks with no news of his mother. In desperation, he finally planned an escape with another boy. They took their clothes from a closet and went out a window and down into the garden. They had intended to climb up a stone wall and shimmy down a lamppost, but they were obliged to wait because there were police in the area. Since there were bed checks every hour in the hospital, they realized that they would have to return their clothes to the closet and go back to their room. It was just as well. Their idea had been to steal bicycles and go to Paris, 490 kilometers to the west, to ask for help from a Jewish assistance committee there. It would have been quite a trip for an eleven-year-old boy.

Marianne was sentenced to thirty days in prison for crossing illegally into France. Once Charles learned of the sentence, he was able to wait. When his mother was finally released, however, she was refused a permis de séjour to remain in France. Instead, she and her son received a short-term permit that allowed them only a few days before they had to leave the country. After all their efforts to get there, they were not about to obey. Instead, in January 1939 they went to Paris where, like so many other refugees, Jewish and non-Jewish alike, they lived on the fringe of legality, dependent on continual renewals of their short-term residence permits. Every few days, according to Charles, they went to a police office to beg for more time. In the meantime, supported by Jewish assistance committees, they lived in Montmartre and Charles went to school. Because he spoke no French, Charles was placed in the second grade and teased mercilessly by boys who were much younger, but he learned the language quickly. Then the war broke out, and he and his mother were no longer in immediate danger of expulsion.

Jewish Immigrants and Political Refugees in Belgium and Luxembourg before the War

Menahem Marienberg, Miriam Löwenwirth, Sigi Hart,
Boris Carmeli, and Walter Marx

JEWISH ECONOMIC IMMIGRANTS and political refugees from Central and Eastern Europe in the 1920s and 1930s did not settle only in France. Thousands moved to other countries in Western Europe and South America, to the United States and Canada, and elsewhere. Those who made it to Great Britain or the western hemisphere escaped Hitler's clutches and do not figure in this story. Those who found refuge in Belgium, the Netherlands, and Luxembourg, however, were only temporarily out of danger. When the German army invaded on May 10, 1940, thousands fled to France without visas or permits of any kind. There, because of their status as undocumented illegal aliens and their poverty and unfamiliarity with the French people and language, they became the most helpless, vulnerable, and intensely persecuted Jews in the country. Five of the nine families profiled in this book fall into that category.

Two of the families emigrated from Eastern Europe to Belgium, largely for economic reasons, in the first decade after the First World War. Wolf and Simone (Sima) Marienberg moved from Poland to Brussels in the mid-1920s with Wolf's mother, Sara, and four of his brothers. Elena and Eliyahu Löwenwirth, from Iršava in what is now western Ukraine, chose Antwerp in 1929. The Marienbergs' four children were all born in Brussels, Menahem in 1927, Mina (Malka) in 1929, Léon (Arie) in 1933, and Maurice (Moshe) in 1938. In that French-speaking city, they learned to speak French well.

Miriam Löwenwirth was born in 1926 in Iršava, as were her sister Zehava and her brother Shlomo a couple of years later. Three more children, Dalia, Aryeh, and Moshe-Herschl, were born in Antwerp, where the local people spoke Flemish. Unfamiliar with French, they would be less well prepared for their wartime odyssey.

Both Menahem Marienberg and Miriam Löwenwirth describe life in Belgium before the war as difficult but secure, free from anti-Semitism.[1] Wolf Marienberg was a skilled leather worker who specialized in making wallets; Eliyahu Löwenwirth was a shoemaker. Both men worked hard. Both families were "not orthodox, but very traditional," according to Miriam; Menahem's granddaughter described his family as "traditional but not religious." Both families went to the synagogue for services on the high holidays and celebrated those same special days at home. Menahem prepared for his Bar Mitzvah, which was scheduled for May 1940. All the children went to public schools in Brussels or Antwerp, where relations between Jews and non-Jews were excellent. Miriam recalls that her teacher in Antwerp allowed her to be absent for the half-day session on Saturday. When this exemption ended during the German occupation of Belgium, the teacher quietly arranged that she would not have to write on the Sabbath.

Both families were also on good terms with their Christian neighbors. Menahem remembers that they even exchanged gifts on their respective holidays. He adds that one day a school friend gave him a picture of Jesus. His mother told him that he could not keep it because he was Jewish, but that he could not throw it away because it was a sacred object for Christians. He returned the picture.

As seen in the case of France, Jews who left Germany for other countries after Hitler came to power were usually political refugees rather than economic immigrants. Some left early, in 1933 or 1934, in anticipation of anti-Semitism to come. Still more emigrants experienced some direct anti-Semitic trauma in the Third Reich in the later 1930s that convinced them to abandon relatives, possessions, savings, and an entire way of life. All of our three families who left Germany for Belgium and Luxembourg after 1933— the Begleiter (later Hartmayer and then Hart), Wolfinger (later Carmeli), and Marx families—emigrated for the same reason. Their final decisive trauma occurred in November 1938 and was known as Kristallnacht.

Sigi Begleiter was born in 1925 in Berlin, where his parents, Hermann and Adela, had moved in the early 1920s. Sigi's sister, Manya, was three years older than he, and his brother, Willy (Wolf), was younger. Originally from Galicia, Hermann had served in the Austro-Hungarian army during the First World War, been captured by the Russians, and spent three years as a prisoner of war in Siberia. Adela was from Oświęcim, in Poland, about fifty kilometers southwest of Kraków. Oświęcim was a little-known town of about twelve thousand people, more than a third of them Jews, on a swampy, unhealthy plain, important only as a major railroad junction. During the Second World War, the town was incorporated into the Third Reich along with Upper Silesia, and renamed. It would become far better known during and after the war by its German name, Auschwitz.

The Begleiter family lived in a comfortable two-bedroom apartment at 18–19 Grosse Hamburger Strasse, in a neighborhood in central Berlin replete with Jewish history. The large and imposing Neue Synagoge in Oranienburger Strasse, built between 1859 and 1866, was just around the corner. The family did not attend services there but went instead to an orthodox synagogue in the same neighborhood. The great Jewish philosopher Moses Mendelssohn was buried in an old cemetery at 26 Grosse Hamburger Strasse in 1786. Nearby is a memorial on the site of the first Jewish old age home in Berlin, used by the Nazis as a transit center for some fifty-five thousand Jews deported to Auschwitz and Theresienstadt.

Hermann's job as a salesman kept him away from home from Monday morning to Friday afternoon. But life was not unpleasant for the family until January 1933, when Hitler became chancellor of Germany. After that, everyone and everything, says Sigi, became politicized, and violent anti-Semitism flourished.[2] On April 1, the Nazis imposed a one-day boycott of Jewish shops and businesses. On April 7, the process of removing Jews from the civil service, the professions, and German cultural life began. But Sigi's memory focuses more on the violence. One Friday night in 1933, for example, the seven-year-old boy was walking to synagogue services with his grandfather and carrying the old man's prayer shawl (he could not carry it himself on the Sabbath). Four SS men approached them, two on either side of the sidewalk. Sigi and his grandfather immediately stepped off the curb into the street to let them pass, but the men nevertheless beat up the old man so badly that he had to be taken to the hospital. Soon after this event, Adela decided to take her children back to Oświęcim for safety. She was blissfully unaware of the irony later generations would find in her choice.

Sigi spent a year in Oświęcim with his mother and siblings. "It was pretty nice there," he recalls. "I learned some Polish. Many family members were there." But in late 1934, Hermann notified them that the worst seemed to be over in Berlin, and they should come back. Many Jews were acting similarly. Some thirty-seven thousand had emigrated from Germany in 1933, and another twenty-three thousand in 1934, but by early 1935, about ten thousand had returned.[3] Sigi explains, "We did not believe that it would grow to something big, this Hitler."

Back in Berlin, Sigi realized that under the influence of the Hitler Youth, German children were being taught to hate and torment the Jews. Before 1933, he says, Jewish and non-Jewish children had played games together in the streets—cowboys and Indians, hide and seek, footraces—but now that was impossible. The non-Jewish children would not play with the Jews. Jewish children learned to step off the curb if a group of boys came along, to avoid a fight. No street was safe for them, and they had no place to play. The big synagogue in Oranienburger Strasse tried to compensate, organizing afternoon activities for Jewish children. Sigi and his brother and sister went there after school to do their homework and play chess or table tennis.

Sometime around 1935, Sigi began to go to a Jewish school for boys. The situation inside the new school was easier, but getting there was a problem. There was no bus, so Sigi had a forty-five-minute walk. The Hitler Youth caused trouble, and fights were common. "We were taught not to make any noise in the street; not to be recognized as Jews," Sigi says. Meanwhile the restrictions gradually worsened. Even before the Nuremberg Laws of September 1935, Jews in many municipalities were forbidden, by national law, local ordinances, or private policy, to enter movie theaters, restaurants, swimming pools, or public parks.

Sigi also relates that around 1935, the German government imposed two humiliating conditions on his family. Because it refused to recognize marriages performed only in synagogues, Hermann and Adela had to go to city hall to be remarried. At the same time, they were required to abandon their name, Begleiter, and choose a more German-sounding one. They chose the name Hartmayer, which Sigi shortened to Hart many years after the war.

Sigi well remembers the reprieve for Jews that occurred in Germany at the time of the Olympic Games in 1936. Suddenly the anti-Jewish signs were painted over, and some restrictions were lifted.[4] For example, Sigi says, Jews could go to the parks again. "Berlin became a really clean, nice city for a few months in 1936," he adds, "and we really enjoyed it. We didn't think it would all come back." But the reprieve did not last.

At the end of October 1938, as part of a broader effort to rid the Third

Reich of foreign Jews, the Gestapo rounded up about seventeen thousand Polish Jews throughout Germany and expelled them back to Poland. It is not clear why they did not arrest the entire Hartmayer family, but they did come for Hermann. When they pounded on the door, young Sigi opened it and said, yes, his father was home. Then Adela went to the door and courageously informed the agents that Sigi was mistaken. Yes, Hermann was home *in Berlin,* but no, he was not at the house at the moment. Meanwhile Hermann was hiding in the bedcovers. The Gestapo agents ordered Adela to tell her husband to report to their headquarters as soon as he returned. The Jews they had already caught left Berlin the next day. Three days later, after considerable reflection, Hermann decided that he should obey the authorities and report to the Gestapo. When he did so, he was told that the action was over, and he could stay.

The expulsion of the seventeen thousand Polish Jews from Germany had drastic unforeseen consequences. The Polish government, which had provoked the situation by recalling the passports of its citizens abroad and then declining to process those of the Jews so that they lost their legal status, now refused to accept them. The expelled Jews languished in appalling conditions in a no-man's-land on the border between Poland and Germany until the Poles finally relented. Among the victims were the parents of seventeen-year-old Hershel Grynszpan, then in Paris, who retaliated by shooting Ernst vom Rath, the third secretary at the German embassy there. That assassination prompted the pogrom known as Kristallnacht throughout the Third Reich on the night of November 9–10, 1938, when Nazi fanatics looted and burned Jewish property, murdered ninety-one Jews, and arrested some twenty thousand Jewish men, imprisoning them until they could show that they had found a way to leave the country. For some reason, Sigi's father in Berlin was spared arrest.

Because Sigi was born on November 15, his Bar Mitzvah was scheduled for the Saturday after that date in 1938. Since many of his aunts, uncles, and cousins had been expelled to Poland in October, it was to be a small family affair, but it was nevertheless to take place in the orthodox synagogue where the Hartmayers attended services. But that building was one of the 267 synagogues throughout Germany destroyed by rioters during the November pogrom. Sigi's family had to rent space in a little house behind the synagogue. In the house were the scorched remnants of the Torah scrolls, being prepared for burial according to Jewish tradition. The weeping rabbi told Sigi never to forget. He never has.

For Sigi's parents, the November pogrom was the final blow. The man who had fought on the German side in the First World War, suffered for three years as a prisoner of war in the Soviet Union, and built his life in Berlin now knew he had to leave. The woman who had created a comfortable home and was raising three children now had to abandon every possession, every family heirloom, every cherished memory of normal life. Hermann and Adela were not alone. In 1939, seventy-eight thousand Jews left Nazi Germany—double or sometimes triple the number in any previous year.[5]

The Hartmayers chose Belgium as their place of immigration but moved there illegally. Sigi thinks this was because the Belgian government was giving few entry visas but was not expelling back to Germany those refugees who managed to enter. Hermann and Adela planned their departure secretly for fear that the children would talk about it outside the family. For the children, Sigi recalls, it all seemed like a great adventure, but for the parents it was deadly serious.

With help from a paid passeur, Hermann Hartmayer left Berlin alone. In January 1939, he sent his family a message from Antwerp. They were to meet the smuggler, taking nothing too heavy. Sigi remembers that his mother bought them all new boots. Such are the memories of childhood. Adela and the children took a train to Cologne and then to Aachen, less than ten kilometers from both the Dutch and the Belgian borders. In Aachen, Sigi and his mother transferred to a local train for the nearby village of Rothe Erde, where they met the smuggler. With him, they walked for five hours in freezing rain and snow. After crossing the frontier, the smuggler left them to try to get a car. They were terrified that he had abandoned them, but he returned. They drove the rest of the way to Antwerp.

Seventeen-year-old Manya and her brother Willy, age eleven, left Sigi and their mother in Aachen. They traveled in a different train car to avoid arousing the suspicions that might focus on an entire family moving together toward the border. But Manya missed the connection to Rothe Erde. Thinking quickly, she put Willy on the next regular train to Antwerp, on the theory that no one would bother a little boy traveling alone. She was right, and Willy arrived safely. Jewish committee representatives at the train station in Antwerp helped him find his family. Learning from Willy what had happened, the smuggler then went back for Manya. Together they bicycled to the border. At one point they were stopped by German soldiers engaged in army maneuvers. The Belgian smuggler said that they had been on an outing and had somehow crossed the border by mistake. They were allowed to proceed, and joined the family in Antwerp soon after.

Life was difficult in Antwerp, for the family had no permis de séjour and few resources. But the Belgians did not threaten them with expulsion and treated them decently. Sigi's father made a meager living by buying cigarettes wholesale and selling them retail at the Diamond Market. Manya worked as a nanny for a Belgian Jewish family. With additional help from the Belgian government and from local Jewish assistance committees, Sigi says, his mother, Adela, was able to make their simple apartment comfortable and cozy. Sigi and Willy went to school, where they learned Flemish easily. It is, Sigi explains, very similar to German. Sigi also earned five francs a week as a tailor's apprentice, a job he hated. Sigi and Willy made friends, sang at the temple, and enjoyed being able to play in the parks again. Willy had his Bar Mitzvah in Antwerp. "My brother and I were happy-go-lucky and optimistic," Sigi recalls wistfully. "We thought all this would last forever."

Norbert Wolfinger, whom we shall call by his current name of Boris Carmeli, also remembers Kristallnacht as the event that determined his family's emigration. Boris was born in Poland in 1928, the second child of Hermann and Rachel. His brother, Pinkas (later known as Peter Carmeli), was born in 1921. In religious matters, the family resembled those of Miriam Löwenwirth, Menahem Marienberg, and Sigi Hart. Boris describes his parents as "religious, but not too much."[6] They attended Sabbath services, kept the rules of Kosher, and observed the Jewish holidays.

Boris's parents immigrated to Magdeburg (Sachsen-Anhalt), about 151 kilometers southwest of Berlin, in 1932, because they believed that Germany had an economic future. Hermann moved first, went into the fabric and textile business, and brought his wife and sons there a bit later. Life in Germany was comfortable for about a year. All too soon, however, Hitler came to power and even Boris, then only five, began to suffer from the growing anti-Semitism. The only Jewish pupil in his class during the winter of his first year at school, he was placed in the center of a circle in the snow in the playground. The other children exercised by marching around him and making fun of him. In later years, he had to go to a Jewish school.

In November 1938, suspecting violence against the Jews, Hermann took his family for a short trip to Berlin, where they were not known. The four stayed there until the trouble passed. At that point, Boris's parents realized that they would have to leave Germany. Boris relates that while the family was in Berlin, his father went to a shop and invested most of his assets in jewelry. When the family left Germany about nine months later, Rachel sewed the jewelry into their clothes.

Like Hermann and Adela Hartmayer, Boris's parents decided to take their family to Belgium, but they chose Brussels rather than Antwerp. They traveled there by way of Cologne just before war broke out in September 1939. They too had a terrible journey, traveling largely on foot with the help of smugglers and dogs. "The story of that trip alone could fill a book," Boris says. His mother fainted during the trip, which must have terrified her eleven-year-old son. But once in Brussels, Boris recalls that they "were happy, as much as refugees can ever be happy." Boris attended public school without incidents. While still in Germany, however, at the age of five, he had announced to his startled family that he wanted to be an opera singer. In Brussels, therefore, he was able to enroll in the prestigious Conservatoire. But despite this great treat, life was hard. Boris remembers the boring, repetitive diet, with the cheapest cuts of meat.

Like Sigi Hart and Boris Carmeli, Walter Marx also remembers escalating anti-Semitism in the Third Reich, culminating in Kristallnacht. Walter's family was not from Eastern Europe but was German through and through. All four of Walter's grandparents were born in Germany, and he has traced his paternal grandfather's German ancestry back to the seventeenth century. His mother, Johanna Isaac, was born in Fremersdorf, in the Saarland. His father, Ludwig, was born in Heilbronn (Baden-Württemberg), about sixty kilometers north of Stuttgart. Ludwig was a partner with his father in a wholesale paper company in Heilbronn. Of his parents, Walter recalls that they "had many Jewish and non-Jewish friends, but the social life of the family revolved mainly around the almost 1,000-member-strong Jewish Community."[7]

Walter was born in Heilbronn in 1926. Like Boris Carmeli, his first experience of Nazi anti-Semitism occurred at school. He explains, "I attended school in [Heilbronn], but when in fourth grade in 1935 my Christian schoolmates insulted me by calling me a 'dirty Jew' and beat me and just not talked to me anymore, my parents decided to send me out of Germany to live with an uncle and aunt in Luxembourg and to attend school there. I was nine years old then."

Walter went to Luxembourg with Werner Isaac, a cousin about his own age who was living with Walter's family because his father had died and his mother had immigrated to Britain to work as a maid. Walter, an only child, and Werner were like brothers. The two boys returned to Germany three times a year to spend their holidays with Walter's parents. Their last visit was in the summer of 1938. By that time, many of Walter's parents' Jewish friends had already emigrated, but Ludwig, decorated for military service in the First World War, believed that the Nazis would not bother him. "Little did he know," Walter remarks. Ludwig's business was forcibly "Aryanized" in 1938. Kristallnacht soon followed. In Heilbronn, Walter's parents' apartment was ransacked, and Ludwig was one of the estimated twenty thousand Jews throughout the country to be arrested without cause. Sent to Dachau, he was forced to stand with other inmates for hours in the cold and rain. His hands froze, and because he was not allowed to remove his wedding band, his ring finger developed an infection requiring amputation. Like most of the Jews arrested on that occasion, Ludwig was released after he produced the documents required to leave Germany. He and Johanna joined their son and nephew in Luxembourg in 1939, just before the outbreak of war.

CHAPTER THREE

Flight to Southern France, May and June 1940

Sigi Hart, Menahem Marienberg, Boris Carmeli,
Miriam Löwenwirth, Lya Haberman, and Walter Marx

THE GERMAN ARMY ATTACKED Belgium, Luxembourg, and the Netherlands on May 10, 1940. Until then, Jews in Western Europe had worried
about their relatives and friends in the East but hoped that they themselves
would escape the ravages of war. As Sigi Hart, then a fourteen-year-old lad in
Antwerp, explains, "It all started on a Friday. We had heard what happened
to the Jews when the Germans arrived in Austria and Czechoslovakia [in
1938] and, after the war broke out in September 1939, in Poland. And we
had heard that Hitler made a speech threatening to 'clean up' the Jewish
refugees in Belgium—to clean up Pelican Street, the main street of the
Diamond Market in Antwerp. So when the Germans invaded Belgium in
May 1940, my father never hesitated. My parents were prepared. Each child
had a rucksack, filled with as much as he could carry. My parents each had
a suitcase. We headed for the train station and asked for any train going
west. In Germany in 1939, we had locked the door of our apartment and
thrown the key out of the train window. Now, a little over a year later, we
did the same thing again."

Sigi and his family took a local train from Antwerp to Brussels, where
they ran to catch a bigger one for France. The big train was crammed with
terrified refugees, both Jewish and non-Jewish. The conductor never asked
for tickets. At the border with France, passengers saw British and French

soldiers standing around, looking confused. "We all leaned out of the windows and shouted, 'Vive la France!'" Sigi remembers.

The parents of Menahem Marienberg and Boris Carmeli in Brussels were equally determined to leave. Menahem remembers that the German attack on Belgium came just before his Bar Mitzvah. His mother and aunt had all the food ready for the celebration, but his father, Wolf, and Uncle Isaac decided that the family must flee immediately. The ceremony was cancelled, and Menahem and his family ate the food on the train. Boris recalls that it was his father's birthday. He gave his father a birthday gift, a pair of suspenders, on the train. But the memories are not always so benign. Menahem also remembers seeing the first results of German bombing at the train station, including dead bodies on the ground. Boris saw British soldiers advancing eastward.

These three families were lucky to have found places on a train. Roughly a million people from the Benelux countries, including between ten thousand and forty thousand Jews, were frantically trying to reach France just ahead of the German army.[1] They were fighting for every vehicle that moved—train, automobile, bicycle, horse cart, wagon, wheelbarrow, or baby carriage. Many simply walked. Reports differ on what happened to them at the French border. Some refugees declare that they were held up by French customs officials who lacked orders and were uncertain about what to do with undocumented aliens. Others claim that the French admitted them all. Undoubtedly, in the confusion, different officials responded differently.

In the confusion, many families split up and others had to turn back. Miriam Löwenwirth's large family, forced to travel in two groups, had both experiences. Her mother, Elena, finally made it to southern France with two of the children, but Miriam and her father, Eliyahu, and two other siblings progressed only as far as Lille, in northern France. There they discovered that the Germans had already arrived. There seemed to be nothing to do but return to Antwerp. It would be nearly a year before the family was reunited. In the absence of her mother, fourteen-year-old Miriam ran the household while Eliyahu resumed his work and all three children went back to school. But her father was "a different person," says Miriam, "more serious and quiet. He made a point of attending the synagogue more frequently." These role shifts were not unusual among Jewish families during the war. Male heads of households were sometimes shattered by the humiliation of no longer being able to protect their families. Older adolescents, including normally sheltered girls, often assumed leadership roles within their disoriented families.

The trains from Belgium headed for southern France with no apparent destination. Nearly all the passengers stayed on board for several days, hoping to get as far from the war as possible. The Red Cross provided food and water. "We all felt increasingly secure," Sigi says. "France is a big country." The refugees had their own problems but were blissfully unaware of the havoc they were wrecking with the French bureaucracy. As elsewhere in Europe then and now, French local authorities were expected to know who was living in their areas of responsibility, demand identity cards from everyone as well as entry visas from foreigners, and issue residence and work permits to newcomers. Refugees without documents were supposed to be expelled, but expulsion was impossible in wartime. French officials had to organize, categorize, document, register, and sustain about a million refugees at first. That number would quadruple as the German army approached Paris during the second week of June.

Although it seemed haphazard to the refugees from Belgium, the trains usually left them in French towns especially designated by harassed authorities. For the most part, the towns were in what would become the unoccupied zone, or Vichy France, after the armistice with the Germans was signed on June 22. After meandering through the countryside for two days, for example, Menahem Marienberg's train finally stopped in Revel (Haute-Garonne), a small town about fifty-four kilometers southeast of Toulouse.[2] There local officials requisitioned lodgings for the refugees, Jews and non-Jews alike, registering their names and addresses and paying a small subsidy for their support. In addition, the Marienbergs met a local family named Fournier who befriended them and helped them get settled.

After nine days, Sigi Hart's train stopped, he says, where "there were no more rails. It was the end of the line." But this too was not by chance. By order of the departmental prefect, the refugees were disembarked in Bagnères-de-Luchon (Haute-Garonne), a beautiful resort town in the Pyrenees just a few kilometers from the Spanish border.[3] With government authorization and all kinds of committees to help, the local people opened hotels, pensions, private rooms, and schools to provide shelter. Sigi's family received a one-bedroom apartment owned by a printer named Jean Gazave, whom Sigi describes as very nice. Under the circumstances, no one thought it unusual when the town caller—a man with a drum who marched through the streets, making the same announcement on every corner—informed the refugees, "Avis! Avis! The mayor of Bagnères-de-Luchon requests that all Jews are to present themselves to city hall." Most of the Jews, terrified of being arrested if they ignored the demand and were caught, obeyed. They received identity cards along with the ration coupons essential for survival, but their Jewishness was now on record. Non-Jewish refugees were also registered, and for a time, all refugees were treated similarly. "It was not so bad at first," Sigi says. But that would not last.

Boris Carmeli's train took him and his parents and older brother Peter to Bordeaux, a city already so jammed with refugees that few services were provided. On June 10, the French government left Paris to reestablish its capital first in Tours and soon after in Bordeaux. A difficult situation eventually became worse, and foreign refugees in Bordeaux were required to leave. Boris and his family were ordered to take a particular bus to the interior, but nineteen-year-old Peter was not with them. He had been arrested by the French police a few days earlier for making a false document for himself, in the name of Pierre Laffont, so that he could go dancing at a local nightspot. His parents must have been in despair. The bus, like the train that had brought them to Bordeaux, was crammed with people. Boris recalls that he climbed in through the window. As the bus pulled out, his mother realized that the family had left two suitcases on the platform. She fainted, just as she had done on her flight from Germany to Belgium the year before. The response was understandable. After losing most of her possessions when she left Germany, those two suitcases probably represented much of what she still owned.[4]

The bus took Boris and his parents to an assigned residence in the little village of Buziet (Basses-Pyrénées; Pyrénées-Atlantiques today), roughly sixteen kilometers southwest of Pau. On arrival, they learned that Peter had been interned at Saint-Cyprien (Pyrénées-Orientales), on the Mediterranean coast south of Perpignan, about three hundred kilometers from Buziet. With no money to buy passage on a bus or train, and with no legal documents and no ability to speak French, Boris's father, Hermann, immediately boarded a train for Saint-Cyprien without a ticket. When the director of the camp refused to see him, Hermann camped on the doorstep of his house and tearfully intercepted him whenever he came in or went out. "Mon fils, mon fils," was about all he could say in French, over and over again for several days. Peter was released and traveled back to Buziet with his father, again without tickets.

Miriam Löwenwirth's mother, Elena, and two siblings were settled by the French government in Quarante (Hérault), in the Massif Central about twenty kilometers west of Béziers and twenty-five from the Mediterranean coast. Back in Antwerp with her father, Eliyahu, and the other two children, Miriam learned where her mother and siblings were from the International Red Cross eight months later. Immediately her lifelong courage, initiative, and imagination came into play. Without hesitation and without telling her father, she went to the German authorities to request official permission for herself and her two siblings to leave Belgium. "To this day, I do not know how my legs took me there," she says, "I felt as though I was in a cage. I only knew one thing; I must succeed in reuniting our family." To her surprise, she received permission to travel, but only as far as Paris. Once in that city, she and her sister and brother, ages thirteen and eleven, simply boarded a train for the south, crossed the heavily patrolled demarcation line between German-occupied and unoccupied France without trouble, and passed through Lyon and Béziers before reaching Quarante in February 1941. Eliyahu, more at risk in crossing the line, traveled alone with the aid of paid smugglers, but he too managed to join his family in a government-assigned residence two weeks later.

With some exceptions, like Miriam Löwenwirth, most of the wartime refugees who fled from Belgium, the Netherlands, and Luxembourg after the Germans invaded on May 10 arrived in France within a few days. By the end of the month, most were settled in assigned residences in the south. Throughout May and June, however, every day brought devastating news of French, British, and Belgian retreats. On May 14, the German army broke through the French lines at Sedan; the French First Army abandoned Belgian territory the following day. Men, women, and children from north-eastern France now joined foreign refugees on the road. The British began their withdrawal from Dunkirk on May 26, the Belgians surrendered on May 28, and the Italians declared war on France and threatened Nice on June 10. Four days later, the Germans entered Paris. As they approached the city, hundreds of thousands of Parisians joined the frantic flight to the south and west. Terrified people clogged highways and trains, filled hotels, depleted local resources, and strained the patience of residents of southern France. Families slept in barns or fields, suffered air attacks from German fighter planes, and ate what little they could buy from local peasants. Eventually, at least four million refugees, French and foreign, non-Jews and Jews, descended on unprepared towns and villages in southern and western France.[5]

Among the refugees from Paris was Berlin-born Lya Haberman, her mother, Chana, and her sister, Hilda. Her father, Oscar, was not with them. Like thousands of other male immigrants in France, Oscar had volunteered for military service when Germany invaded Poland in September 1939, or perhaps even before. Though motivated in part by his anti-Nazi and pro-French sentiments, he had also come under great pressure to enlist by a decree law of April 12, 1939, which declared that stateless male immigrants and those enjoying the right of asylum in France were, if between the ages of twenty and forty-eight, subject to the same military obligations in wartime as French citizens. Within three days of the decree law, some ten thousand foreigners had enlisted, many under the impression that military service would hasten their naturalization.[6]

Lya does not know what kind of unit her father served in. She was, after all, barely eleven at the time. Foreigners, however, usually could not serve in regular line formations of the French army. The decree law of April 12 had implied that the policy would change and that immigrants who had resided in France for a given period would be accepted in the regular army. Most of the thousands who enlisted because of the decree acted on that assumption. Fearing subversion and espionage, however, army officials did not want the enlistees. As a result, few made it through the deliberately obstructive bureaucratic process. Like most foreign volunteers, therefore, Oscar Haberman was probably directed to the French Foreign Legion, which most immigrants distrusted as a harsh mercenary organization. He was most likely enrolled in one of the special legion units created on September 16, 1939, for foreigners who volunteered for the duration of hostilities. With officers and noncommissioned officers from the professional Foreign Legion in North Africa, most of those special units remained in metropolitan France, saw considerable action there, and sustained high casualties.[7] Lya knows only that her father "came and went" and may have seen combat in 1940.

Lya remembers her flight to southern France much better. With so many people competing for places, she and her mother and sister were lucky to catch a train moving south. "We traveled like cattle," Lya says, "with no destination—just trying to get away." When asked why her mother decided to leave Paris in the first place, she replies quickly, "Because we knew what the Germans were all about. So did the others, but especially the foreigners knew." The three women ended up in Villenouvelle (Haute-Garonne), about twenty-six kilometers southeast of Toulouse. Lya estimates that about five hundred other fugitives from Paris were with them. Oscar was still with the military, but he somehow found his family after the fall of France. As Lya remembers it, "We were all together again." But she is the only one from our nine refugee families who notes that the French during this early period were sometimes unpleasant to foreigners and, especially, to foreign Jews. "As refugees in Villenouvelle," she says, "we were offered housing in a private château, but the owners asked us to leave when they learned we were Jews."

The refugees described so far in this chapter—Sigi Hart, Menahem Marienberg, Boris Carmeli, Miriam Löwenwirth, and Lya Haberman—all chose to flee to France, although they had little choice about where to settle on arrival there. The story of Walter Marx and his parents Ludwig and Johanna, German immigrants in Luxembourg in May 1940, is somewhat different. When the Germans invaded the Low Countries on May 10, Walter's father, Ludwig, was determined to join the struggle against them. Leaving his wife and son in Luxembourg, he bicycled to France to volunteer for military service. He seems to have been unaware that German immigrants, even if anti-Nazi, were unwelcome in France.

Already in September 1939, when the German army invaded Poland, the French government had arrested about twelve thousand German and five thousand Austrian immigrants and political refugees throughout the country, both Jews and non-Jews, mostly men under fifty but including some women, and interned them as enemy aliens. About half were soon released or allowed to join special units associated with the French Foreign Legion, the Czech or Polish Legions, or companies of foreign workers attached to the French army, described below.[8] When the Germans invaded the Low Countries and France in May 1940, the French government again ordered internment, this time of *all* immigrants from the Third Reich between the ages of eighteen and fifty-five, later raised to sixty-five.[9] Many of those released in 1939 were rearrested, along with tens of thousands of others, including at least nine thousand women accompanied by their children. Although most of those arrested had immigrated to France before the German invasion, about six thousand German, Austrian, and Polish wartime refugees from Belgium, not all of them Jewish, were interned at Saint-Cyprien at the end of May.[10]

Ludwig Marx, German-born but residing legally in Luxembourg, was not arrested when he arrived in France, but neither was he accepted in a regular line unit of the French army. Instead, at Châlons-sur-Marne

(Marne), southeast of Rheims, he was enrolled as a *prestataire volontaire,* an army auxiliary who did not bear arms. Like other prestataires, he was assigned to a Compagnie travailleurs étrangers (CTE), a company usually of about 250 foreign workers attached to a French military unit.[11] His participation was chosen freely, but many other immigrants from the Third Reich had "volunteered" as a way of getting out of the wretched French internment camps. By the summer of 1940, there were more than one hundred thousand prestataires, including fifty-five thousand Spanish Republicans and sixteen hundred former soldiers in the International Brigades who had fought against Franco's troops in the Spanish Civil War. They had been interned when they fled to France at the end of that conflict in early 1939. The balance consisted of about forty-six thousand German, Austrian, and stateless men, many of them Jews, who had been interned in the same camps in September 1939 or May 1940 because they were enemy aliens.[12]

Ludwig served as a prestataire at the front until the Germans overran his unit. Filthy and exhausted, he then managed to escape and make his way back to his family in German-occupied Luxembourg. His respite there was brief. On September 12, 1940, the German civilian administrator of occupied Luxembourg, anxious to clear his territory of Jews before the policy of deportations "to the East" had begun, ordered the expulsion of all Jews. By the end of 1940, he had forced at least 521 Jews from Luxembourg into southern France.[13] Ludwig, Johanna, and Walter Marx, along with about fifty-one other Jews, were among the first victims. On November 7, they were sent by bus to the demarcation line forming the border between occupied and unoccupied France. South of Dijon, they were forced onto a train that crossed the line and left them at Mâcon (Sâone-et-Loire), about seventy-five kilometers north of Lyon. From there the Marx family traveled to Montpellier (Hérault), a few hundred kilometers to the southwest.

Walter believes that his parents, once in unoccupied France, were free to go anywhere they wished and chose Montpellier because they had distant relatives there. This may be true, but it is also possible that they were only permitted to go to Montpellier because their relatives there could vouch for them. In any case, they were treated very differently from the roughly 6,500 German Jews from Baden-Württemberg and 1,150 from the Palatinate and the Saarland whom two other zealous German district leaders also forced into unoccupied France toward the end of October 1940.[14] With deportees from Luxembourg and a smaller group from Belgium, these were the only

Jews to be deported to the *west*. Vichy officials, angered at seeing what they considered their "Jewish problem" aggravated by these expulsions, interned all the deportees from Germany. Most languished in wretched French camps until they were delivered to the Germans in Paris in August 1942 and eventually deported to Auschwitz.

CHAPTER FOUR

Jewish Refugees in the Unoccupied Zone, May 1940–August 1942

Sigi Hart, Charles Roman, Menahem Marienberg,
Walter Marx, Miriam Löwenwirth, and Boris Carmeli

AS THE FRENCH GOVERNMENT wavered and military resistance faltered in early June 1940, the nation literally fell apart. Shortly after noon on June 17, three days after the fall of Paris, the newly appointed French prime minister, eighty-four-year-old Marshal Henri-Philippe Pétain, announced by radio that France must cease hostilities. Five days after that, on June 22, French delegates signed an armistice with the Third Reich. France was now divided. About three-fifths of the country north of the Loire River and extending south in a narrow strip along the Atlantic coast to the Spanish frontier was occupied by the Germans and cut off from the rest of the country by a strictly guarded demarcation line. Forty departments south of the line constituted "Free" or unoccupied France. The French government with headquarters in the resort town of Vichy, south of the line, enjoyed complete jurisdiction in the unoccupied zone but exercised authority in the German-occupied north only if it did not conflict with German wishes.

Also occupied and removed from the full jurisdiction of the Vichy regime was the city of Menton and part of the Vallée de la Tarentaise east of Bourg-Saint-Maurice, in southeastern France near the Italian frontier. This area was awarded to Mussolini, whose army had occupied it after the Italian declaration of war on the Allies on June 10. Mussolini had hoped to recover much more of the region of Nice and Savoy, controlled by the ancestors of the kings of Italy until 1860. In 1940, he had to be satisfied with less, but he continued to gaze toward France with greedy eyes.[1]

The French military defeat and armistice in 1940 were immediately followed by equally catastrophic political developments. On July 9 and 10, what was left of the senators and deputies elected to the Popular Front Parliament of 1936 voted by an overwhelming majority to revoke the 1875 constitution of the Third Republic and award Prime Minister Pétain full powers to promulgate a new one.[2] Within a few hours, Pétain declared that he was chief of the French state with a "totality of government power" and adjourned the Chamber of Deputies and the Senate. Roughly 330,000 Jews, including about 195,000 citizens and 135,000 foreigners, now found themselves in a divided, authoritarian, and increasingly anti-Semitic state.[3]

The Vichy regime lost little time before acting against those it considered not truly French. Its first measures were directed against foreigners in general. Laws in July, August, and September 1940 limited employment as civil servants, physicians, dentists, pharmacists, and lawyers to individuals born in France to French fathers, and called for a review and possible revocation of grants of French citizenship awarded since August 1927.[4] On September 3, a law directed departmental prefects to intern immigrants from the Third Reich considered "dangerous for the national defense and public security." Then on September 27, as government subsidies to refugees who were not French citizens were beginning to be terminated in many departments, another law authorized prefects to intern, at their own discretion, indigent male immigrants between the ages of eighteen and fifty-five regarded as "superfluous in the French economy" (*en surnombre dans l'Économie Nationale*). Alternatively, indigent male immigrants in those age brackets who could work could be forced into Groupements de travailleurs étrangers (GTE), or civilian labor groups for foreigners.[5]

The newly formed GTEs, now under the jurisdiction of the Ministry of Labor, were in fact a demilitarized version of the CTEs, the foreign labor companies formerly attached to military units. Those drafted for labor in the GTEs included some former French, Polish, and Czech soldiers unable to return to their homes, Indochinese workers, and former military prestataires and volunteers in units associated with the French Foreign Legion who had enrolled for the duration of the war and were now demobilized. The men worked on roads, construction, drainage projects, sewers, lumbering, mining, and other manual tasks for meager wages. They lived in miserable little camps throughout the country, while their women and children received a small subsidy and were often crowded into strictly supervised second-rate hotels in big cities. Only after a year of service did some workers receive a ten-day leave to visit their families. An estimated sixty thousand men, of whom about a third were Jews, were laboring in the GTEs at the end of July 1941.[6]

While these early Vichy measures were aimed at foreigners in general, several exclusively anti-Jewish measures soon followed. Already on August 27, 1940, the so-called Marchandeau decree of April 21, 1939, which prohibited attacks on individuals in the press based on race or religion, had been revoked, unleashing a flood of anti-Semitic publications. Then on October 3, the Vichy regime's first Statut des Juifs defined who was to be considered Jewish and excluded Jews from the public service, the officer corps of the armed forces, teaching, journalism, the theater, radio, and cinema. Unprompted by the Germans in the north, the anti-Jewish measures were applicable in both occupied and unoccupied France. A second Statut des Juifs on June 2, 1941, broadened the definition of who was to be considered Jewish, extended the list of prohibited occupations, and imposed a census on Jews in the unoccupied zone.[7] For reasons of pride as well as fear of the consequences of disobedience, some 140,000 Jews, representing perhaps as many as 80 or 90 percent of the total in "Free France," registered for the census.[8] The authorities now knew exactly who they were and where to find them.

The two Statuts des Juifs were accompanied by other oppressive measures aimed at all Jews in France. The Vichy government ordered the confiscation of Jewish property; Jews could no longer publish their written work or serve as publishers or editors; Jewish painters could not exhibit at the Salon d'Automne; the performance of plays and music by Jewish authors and composers was strongly discouraged and reduced to a minimum on the radio; and a *numerus clausus* of 3 percent was imposed on Jewish university students and of 2 percent on Jewish lawyers and doctors. Jews were also subjected to much petty harassment. National decrees or local ordinances prohibited Jews from going to public beaches, parks, swimming pools, theaters, cinemas, libraries, and cafés. Jews in Paris had to ride in special cars in the métro, respect a strict curfew, and shop during limited hours. Those caught ignoring the regulations could be arrested and imprisoned.

Despite their harshness, Vichy's anti-Jewish measures could have been worse. No law ever prohibited intermarriage or the attendance of Jewish

children in public primary and secondary schools in either zone. Both prohibitions, it might be noted, existed in Fascist Italy by the end of 1938 and
were scrupulously enforced. Also, Jews in unoccupied France did not ever
have to wear the Star of David, imposed by the Germans in the north on
May 29, 1942. Nor, until the Germans occupied southern France in November 1942, did they have to bear the large stamp on their documents
identifying them as "Juif" or "Juive," as required in the north.

Devastating as the Vichy regime's anti-Semitic legislation was on French
Jews, the measures aimed exclusively at Jewish immigrants and refugees
in the unoccupied zone were even more repressive. Most threatening was
a law on October 4, 1940, that gave French prefects the discretionary authority to send any foreigners "of the Jewish race" in their departments to
internment camps, forced labor groups, or assigned residence, without
cause or justification and regardless of nationality. By the end of 1940,
some twenty-eight thousand to thirty-five thousand Jewish immigrants and
refugees had been interned in the unoccupied zone. The number increased
to forty thousand by the end of February 1941.[9] It would drop significantly
in the months that followed, as women and children were moved out of
camps into supervised "welcoming centers" or Jewish children's homes,
and as thousands of men were transferred to forced labor units. But these
individuals were not free. On the contrary, an order to the prefects from
Vice-Prime Minister Admiral François Darlan at the end of June 1941 specifically stipulated that "no foreigner of the Jewish race" who had not lived in
France before May 10, 1940, should henceforth be freed from internment
camps or forced labor groups.[10]

During the second half of 1941, Vichy decrees specified that *all* destitute
male Jews (but not all destitute non-Jews) between the ages of eighteen and
fifty-five who had entered the country after January 1, 1936, were to be put
into forced labor groups. Many groups that had previously included both
Jews and non-Jews were reorganized at this time, with special so-called
Palestinian units established for the Jews. Even foreign Jews with jobs useful to the national economy were to register for forced labor but could be
released under supervision. Other measures established obligatory professional training centers for all foreign Jewish boys younger than eighteen.
Jewish refugees and recent immigrants not in camps or forced labor units
were also reminded that they must register for assigned residence.[11]

Though perhaps not intended in 1941, internment and forced labor
came to be the equivalent of a death sentence. When Jews who had arrived

in France after January 1, 1936, were delivered from the unoccupied zone to the Germans in the north in August 1942 for subsequent deportation to Poland, those in internment or forced labor were the first to go. Those living in assigned residence had a slightly better chance, but they too were primary targets.

Sigi Hart

How did our nine refugee and immigrant families fare under the anti-Jewish measures of 1940 and 1941? Only the Hartmayers were affected as an entire family by the October 1940 law permitting prefects to intern foreigners "of the Jewish race" without cause or justification. Sigi explains that he and his parents, Adela and Hermann, his sister, Manya, and his brother, Willy, remained in Bagnères-de-Luchon during the summer of 1940. Then one day in October, the drummer came through the streets with another important message for them. "Avis! Avis! In two days, all Jews are to report to the local train station with all their belongings." Sigi relates, "We had been treated well so far. We were harmless civilians. What would they do to us? And what choice did we have?"

When the Hartmayers arrived at the train station, they were encircled by gendarmes and crammed into open cattle cars. They began to panic, but the gendarmes assured them that there was no reason to worry. Sigi describes the scene. "They told us, 'We have to move you because we don't have the supplies here to sustain you.' They said that we would go to a nearby place with white sheets and good food. Instead, we traveled for four or five hours. We arrived at a camp with open barracks, no beds, nothing, surrounded by barbed wire and Senegalese guards. The men and older boys were separated from the women and children under fifteen or sixteen. They gave us fresh straw to put on the floors for sleeping." Sigi remained for a while with his mother and siblings, but one day the guards decided that he was too old to stay there. He was transferred to the men's section, where his father was.

The Hartmayers had arrived at Agde (Hérault), an internment camp about fifty-seven kilometers southwest of Montpellier. Located on low, swampy land on the Mediterranean coast, Agde had begun as a camp for refugees from the Spanish Civil War before 1940. By the end of November of that year, it held 5,700 people, of whom at least 1,300 were Jews, most of them refugees from Belgium like Sigi and his family. The camp was divided into several parts, and only a barbed wire fence separated the Jewish sections from that of Indochinese workers. Sigi recalls that the presence of the Indochinese frightened the Jewish women and children for a while. He explains, "We didn't know anything about Indochina. But we soon realized that the Indochinese were very nice, and tried to help us. They were prisoners too." Others in the camp included demobilized Czech soldiers, other non-Jewish foreigners, and some French civilians. All lived in atrocious conditions, without sufficient food, heat, or blankets, in barracks often without finished floors and with roofs that leaked.[12] Sigi observes, "For me it was all an adventure, because we [children] didn't realize the trouble we were in. Our parents knew."

The Hartmayer family remained at Agde for four or five months, probably until around February 1941. Slowly they made slight improvements in their living conditions. "I was a specialist in building ovens," Sigi says, referring to little makeshift ovens cut into the earth for cooking. Later there was a communal kitchen. But twelve-year-old Willy became seriously ill and was taken to a hospital in Béziers, twenty-four kilometers to the west. When Sigi also developed a high fever, he followed him there. Sigi remembers that Willy was on the second floor and he was on the third. From time to time, their parents were allowed to see them, in separate visits but without guards. Security was not tight. Without residence permits or language skills and dependent on government ration cards, subsidies, and housing allocations, many internees perceived no alternative other than to remain in the camps where they were sent. They had no reason to suspect that internment in 1940 or 1941 would mean deportation and death in 1942.

Adela and Hermann Hartmayer, however, were determined to get out of Agde. Because of her organizational skills, Adela had been elected chief of the women's barracks. As a result, she was allowed to leave her section of the camp and talk to Hermann in the men's section through the barbed wire. At this point, the two saw an opportunity to escape, and they made a simple plan. Sigi and Willy were feeling better, but the doctor was allowing them to remain in the hospital because he knew that conditions in the camp were terrible. Hermann arranged to visit the boys at the same time that Adela did. Adela arranged to take Manya with her. A tailor in the camp made pants for Sigi and Willy from an old blanket. When Adela arrived at the hospital with the pants, the boys went into the bathroom, got dressed, and, looking like visitors, walked out and joined their parents.

Because the Hartmayers were now living outside the system, the problem became where to go. The only place where they knew anyone was

Bagnères-de-Luchon, so they took the train there. It was tricky. They had no identity cards or travel permits, and the gendarmes were checking everyone. To avoid the suspicious appearance of a family of five arriving in a small village together, Hermann and Sigi decided to get off the train one station before Bagnères-de-Luchon and walk the rest of the way, a hike of about five kilometers on a major road. In retrospect, says Sigi, that decision was crazy, because they were equally likely to be checked on the road by police who knew everyone in the area and could immediately recognize strangers. In fact, that nearly happened. Two gendarmes on bicycles passed them on the road. Of French gendarmes in general, Sigi declares, "They were terrible. . . . They helped a lot to make the misery greater." These two gendarmes, however, knew perfectly well that Sigi and his father were strangers in the area yet did not stop them.

Jean Gazave, the Hartmayers' friend in Bagnères-de-Luchon, literally cried from joy at seeing them again. But since they had escaped from Agde and were known in the village, the family could not stay with him. Jean therefore sent them to his son, Clément, who lived with his wife, Berte, and their two teenaged children, Henriette and Jeannot, in an even smaller village four or five kilometers away. Juzet-de-Luchon, says Sigi, was a place where "everyone knew everyone, and their birthdays." Nevertheless, Clément and Berte accepted the Hartmayers into their little three-room house and gave them an entire room for themselves. Clément later even built them a separate kitchen.

During the first winter in Juzet-de-Luchon, Jeannot, about Sigi's age, taught Sigi to ski. Though entertaining, this new skill was not for sport but for the practical purpose of working and moving around in the snow. Like most of the young people described in these pages, Sigi had to assume adult responsibilities during the war years and help support his family. Sigi worked unofficially in the village for anyone who needed a hand. With their sons in prisoner-of-war camps, many farmers found him useful. Propped up on a little one-legged stool that he moved from cow to cow, he did the milking for one neighbor. He chopped wood for another, cut hay, and plowed the fields with a draft animal and a wooden plow. "I loved to work in the fields," says this Berlin-born man, "and they were glad to have me. I was paid only with food, but that was what we needed."

Sigi and his family would gladly have remained in Juzet-de-Luchon for the duration of the war, but that was not to be. After about a year there, the mayor of the little village, who knew they were Jews, began to pressure their hosts to make them leave. He said that it was too dangerous for all concerned for them to stay—that the whole village might be punished if they were caught. Not knowing where to go, the Hartmayers rejoined a group of Jewish refugees in supervised residence. This time they were sent to Aulus-les-Bains (Ariège), a small vacation spa with about four hundred inhabitants in a valley at the foot of the Pyrenees, near Andorra. Hermann was uncomfortable because there were at least 375 Jews assigned to residence in the village.[13] He always believed that many Jews in a single place attracted dangerous attention. But conditions seemed safe enough in this quiet town in the summer of 1942. French Jewish organizations were providing rent and food subsidies, a soup kitchen, and religious and social support. Sigi worked for a while in a quarry, but the labor was so hard that he could not continue. He resumed working for the peasants, which he loved, and cultivated the small plot of land allotted to his family for a vegetable garden. The terrible events of August 1942 caught up with him there.

Charles Roman

Charles Roman and his mother, Marianne, as we saw, had escaped from Vienna late in 1938, after many previous attempts, and lived precariously in Paris until the outbreak of the war. Realizing in November 1939 that she could no longer support or protect her young son, Marianne sent Charles to a children's home for Jewish orphans, refugees, and others whose parents could not care for them. She remained in Paris until the German army approached in June 1940. At that point, she fled south, made her way to Bordeaux, and was arrested there, perhaps as an enemy alien rather than as a Jew. Like Sigi and his family, she was interned at Agde. There she developed pneumonia and was sent to a hospital in Béziers. As seen in the case of the Hartmayers, surveillance was not strict at this early date, and internees were often released from the camps for health reasons or if they could demonstrate that they were not a security risk and could support themselves. Thus, after her recovery, Marianne was able to leave the hospital and live in the town of Agde but outside the camp, presumably in some form of supervised residence.[14] While there, she applied for a position at the children's home where her son was living, but there was no opening. She remained in the town of Agde until the autumn of 1942.

Charles Roman, meanwhile, was at the Château de Chabannes, in a little farming village near Saint-Pierre-de-Fursac (Creuse), about forty kilometers northeast of Limoges. Operated by the Oeuvre de secours aux enfants (OSE), the château housed between sixty and a hundred Jewish children, according to Charles.[15] In terms of age, he was about in the middle. Despite his young age, Charles was useful there, for the château was badly in need of renovation. Charles Roman, the beginning engineering pupil in Vienna dismissed in 1938 at the age of eleven for reasons of "race," now helped convert the building from gas to electric lighting. The "assistant to the assistant" electrician, he moved up as both his superiors were drafted into the French army. Within a few months, he was the chief electrician, at the age of twelve. A few months later he turned thirteen, but he chose not to remind his supervisors of his birthday. Thus, he did not have a Bar Mitzvah.

School was critical for the children of Chabannes. Because their supervisors realized that they might someday have to blend into the French population to avoid internment, it was essential that they learn to speak good French. School also had the advantage of keeping the children out of trouble. With others from the château, then, Charles attended a public school in the village. Scores of lonely, often disoriented, and, above all, non-French-speaking children must have constituted an enormous challenge for the local teachers. Nevertheless, Renée and Irène Paillassou, then in their thirties, later testified to their pleasure at having such highly motivated pupils in their classroom. It was also beneficial, they said, for the local children to meet pupils from different cultural backgrounds.[16]

Not all the residents of Saint-Pierre-de-Fursac shared that view, and inevitably some parents complained that their children were in daily contact with foreign Jewish pupils. The Jews, however, remained. When the danger period came in August 1942, more benevolent residents of the village warned Félix Chevrier, the non-Jewish director of Chabannes, of pending police raids. He immediately hid the children among them.[17]

By August 1942, however, Charles Roman was no longer at the Château de Chabannes. Sometime in 1941, he and a companion were transferred to the Château de Montintin, another OSE home for Jewish children in the commune of Château-Chervix (Haute-Vienne), about twenty-five kilometers southeast of Limoges.[18] All went well for a time. After receiving his *Certificat d'études primaires* in June 1942, Charles was put into a program to learn a trade, first as a shoemaker and later as a carpenter. But as we shall see, this quiet life was too good to last.

Menahem Marienberg, Walter Marx, Miriam Löwenwirth, and Boris Carmeli

Other Jewish refugees lived quietly in their places of assigned residence in the unoccupied zone for more than two years, from the summer of 1940 until August 1942. Despite restrictions on foreigners working, some even had paying jobs. Menahem Marienberg's father, Wolf, and Uncle Isaac found work in a factory in Toulouse, making wallets. The non-Jewish owner, desperately in need of skilled leather workers, obtained work permits for them. Walter Marx's father, Ludwig, found an unofficial job with the president of the local Jewish community in Montpellier. As we saw with Sigi Hartmayer, some teenagers also found low-paying odd jobs to help support their families and keep them out of internment camps. Fifteen-year-old Walter Marx worked part-time as an errand and delivery boy for a florist. Miriam Löwenwirth in Quarante joined her father and older siblings in the vineyards for the autumn harvest. They were paid little but had plenty of grapes to supplement their meager diet.

Most imaginative in his search for earning a living was Boris Carmeli, in Buziet. Boris and a handful of other young Jewish refugees figured out that they could buy milk from the local peasants, turn it into butter, and sell it for a modest profit. Before long, they were traveling to Pau to sell fresh butter to wealthy French Jews there. "We were a factory of butter," Boris recalls gleefully. "We had a lot of fun." After about a year, Boris's family was reassigned to Lamalou-les-Bains (Hérault). There, thirteen-year-old Boris became a cowherd. He had a dog to help him and a long stick with a sharp point at the end to prod them. "On the first day," he chuckles, "the cows all ran away and I was almost out of a job." He soon learned to do better.

Like Sigi Hart, most of our witnesses report that life for Jewish refugees lucky enough to be outside the French internment camps during these early years of the Vichy regime was difficult but not unpleasant. They were usually poor, and ate badly. Miriam Löwenwirth remembers eating nothing but turnips, except during the wine harvest. But the French people with whom these witnesses had contact usually treated them well. Miriam Löwenwirth says, "Most of the people . . . were very good to us." Walter Marx comments, "The florist treated me very well, and the people in Montpellier were generally supportive." Miriam Löwenwirth and Menahem Marienberg, along with their siblings, attended public schools and report no anti-Semitic incidents there. Miriam's mother, Elena, was even allowed to go to the hospital in

Béziers in January 1942 for the delivery of her last child, Ben-Zion. "This is no time to be having a baby," Miriam heard her mother grumble at one point, but it proved to be otherwise. In August 1942, that child would save their lives.

Boris Carmeli's memories of the French people's treatment of him and his family are also favorable. He especially remembers the kind French farmers of modest means in whose large house in Bénéjacq (Pyrénées-Atlantiques today) he and his family were billeted after they had to leave Lamalou. As a youngster, Boris was impressed by the fact that the daughter's husband was a prisoner of war in Germany. Many of Boris's memories resemble those of any young boy growing up in a French town in the 1940s. He recalls, for example, that his twenty-year-old brother Peter, charged with looking after him, used to park him at the local cinema for the afternoon while he spent his time trying to meet girls.

These were not normal times, however. Our witnesses' memories are those of young people. Their parents would undoubtedly tell another story, of the constant terror of internment at the whim of the local prefect as indigent, or simply unwelcome, Jewish outsiders. They would speak of their anxiety about relatives left behind and of their own poverty, the loss of former savings and possessions, and the fear that they would not make ends meet and feed their families. And the children, too, suffered. As Walter Marx puts it, "I was an adult before my time. I'm not sure I can explain it. Having to work and help support the family, having been away from my family at a young age, these things helped to form my character. I didn't play with other children, or go to dances." For the young refugees, their childhood was over.

CHAPTER FIVE

Arrests in the Occupied Zone, 1941–1942

Jacques and Paulette Samson

EVEN BEFORE THE VICHY REGIME began issuing its antiforeign and anti-Jewish measures in the summer and autumn of 1940, the German occupiers of northern France and their French collaborators had begun to act. Newspapers like the *Paris-Press* and *L'Oeuvre* that had castigated Germany for atrocities in Poland in 1939 and early 1940, including those against the Jews, now blamed the Jews for France's troubles. Blue-shirted French Fascist militants began to put up anti-Semitic posters, picket Jewish stores, and break shop windows. In the cafés, restaurants, and streets, many Parisians began mouthing anti-Semitic slogans. Then on September 27, 1940, a week before the Vichy government produced its first Statut des Juifs, the Germans issued an ordinance applicable in their zone of occupation defining who was to be considered Jewish, prohibiting Jews who had fled south from returning, demanding that Jewish-owned businesses be identified by a sign in their windows, and ordering a Jewish census.[1] In the Paris region, 149,734 Jews of all ages—85,664 citizens and 64,070 foreigners—officially registered their names, addresses, professions, and places of birth at local police headquarters and received the requisite stamp on their personal documents identifying them as "Juif" or "Juive."[2]

The deadly vise tightened slowly. Weeks passed, allowing Jews to adjust, to reassure themselves that this was France, after all, and the German occupiers were still behaving "correctly." French Jews were affected by Vichy's laws depriving them of positions and property, but there were few arrests and internments of recent immigrant and refugee Jews, as was happening in the south. Indeed, most recent immigrants and refugees were already in the south, where they had fled in May and June 1940. A large proportion of the foreign Jews in the German-occupied zone fell into the category of longtime resident immigrants.

Throughout 1941 and 1942, however, conditions grew steadily worse for Jews in the occupied zone. The first roundup occurred between May 9 and 14, 1941, when 6,494 Polish, Czech, and stateless Jewish men throughout Paris received small hand-delivered green cards, ordering them to report to their local police headquarters. Although the men were all foreigners, they were not necessarily recent immigrants or refugees, as was the case for those being arrested and interned in the south. Some 3,747 recipients obeyed the summons and reported for what turned out to be internment at Pithi-viers and Beaune-la-Rolande, both about eighty kilometers south of Paris.[3]

A more public roundup of Jews in Paris began at 5:30 A.M. on August 20, when French police blocked all streets and closed all métro entrances in the eleventh arrondissement, north and east of the Place Bastille. Through-out the entire day, the police arrested about three thousand Jewish men, again most of them foreigners but not necessarily recent immigrants or refugees. When that number failed to satisfy the Germans who had ordered the roundup, French police in the days that followed arrested more than a thousand other Jewish men throughout the city. In a major exception to Vichy policy, about two hundred victims were French professionals and intellectuals, including, on specific German orders, forty prominent law-yers from the Paris Court of Appeals and the Council of State, the highest administrative court in France. By August 25, 4,230 men had been taken to Drancy.[4]

The internment camp at Drancy, just a few kilometers from central Paris in the direction of today's Charles de Gaulle airport, ultimately be-came the assembly point for nearly all the 75,721 Jews deported from France during the war.[5] It is best described by Roger Gompel, the director of the Trois Quartiers department store in Paris, who was arrested in December 1941, sent to Drancy in March 1942, and released the following September. Writing a few months after his release, Gompel explained, "the word 'camp' evokes an image of barracks or tents spread out in a rural setting. Here, nothing of the kind. In one of the most dreary suburbs of Paris, a huge lot has been set aside for cheap housing. Arranged in a horseshoe pattern around an immense courtyard covered with cinders, the constructions are still unfinished. The concrete-slab carcass is divided into seven strictly identical buildings, served by twenty-one stairways. It is an entire city which will sometimes contain up to six thousand internees."[6]

The four-story buildings on three sides of the courtyard contained a single large room on each floor, of concrete only. Prisoners could go up and down the separate stairways in each building but could not pass from building to building on any single floor. There were no sanitary facilities or heat in the buildings. Privies and water for washing were in the courtyard. The entire complex was surrounded by guardhouses and a double row of barbed wire. Conditions were so appalling that more than thirty people died in the camp by early November 1941, within two months of the opening and before the onset of winter. Prisoners at the windows on the top floor could see the outline of Sacre Coeur in Montmartre and the rooftops of Paris. Non-Jews from Paris were allowed to stand at the barbed wire and search for loved ones. But unlike the internment camps in unoccupied France, relatively few prisoners were released or escaped from Drancy.[7]

The third major roundup of Jews in Paris occurred when German rather than French police discreetly visited individual households in the early hours of December 12, 1941. This time, with the Germans making the decisions, the victims were 743 French rather than foreign Jewish men, many of them elderly and prominent. They included René Blum (the brother of former Prime Minister Léon Blum), the historian Jacques Ancel, the playwright Jean-Jacques Bernard, the physician Georges Wellers, and the husband of the novelist Colette, Maurice Goudeket.[8] These prisoners were quietly driven to nearby Compiègne, where they spent the winter freezing in a primitive internment camp.

As tensions rose and the attitudes of French police hardened during the first half of 1942, hundreds of Jews in the occupied zone were arrested for infractions, real or imagined, of the racial laws or for attempting to cross the demarcation line illegally. Worse still, the first six trains carrying about a thousand Jews each left the Paris area for "the East" between March 27 and July 17, 1942.[9] The destination was in fact Auschwitz, a name and a concept that would remain obscure for many months. Also devastating was the German ordinance on May 29, ordering all French and most foreign Jews over the age of six in the occupied zone to wear a six-pronged yellow Star of David printed with the word "Juif" clearly visible and solidly sewn to the upper left side of their outer clothing.[10]

◇ ◇ ◇

During the first two years of the war, Jacques and Paulette Samson, just fifteen and thirteen in 1940, found themselves in Paris without parents. Their mother and sisters, as we saw, had stayed in Poland in 1937 and were ultimately murdered by the Germans. Their father, Szlama Samsonowicz, meanwhile, had volunteered for French military service in Paris on January 19, 1940, a few months after Hitler invaded Poland. Possibly because of his experience as a buyer and seller of horses in Poland, he was enrolled in the Second Cavalry Regiment of the French Foreign Legion and served in Morocco and Algeria.

After the French defeat, the armistice with the Germans called for the reduction of the French army in metropolitan France to 125,000 officers and men. Foreigners were among the first to be demobilized, and thousands of immigrants who had volunteered to fight for France were virtually abandoned. Because the Vichy regime often refused to issue residence or work permits in recognition of military service, many demobilized foreigners could not prove their ability to support themselves and their families and were immediately interned or subjected to forced labor service. For a time, Szlama Samsonowicz, demobilized at Midelt in Morocco on September 22, 1940, was among them. Documents now in the possession of his daughter indicate that on the day of his release, he was enrolled in the Fourth Groupe de travailleurs étrangers. He was more fortunate than many, however, for he was apparently able to leave his work group after proving that he could support himself in Marseille. According to Jacques and Paulette, he found work with a cousin there. But because of the German ordinance prohibiting Jews from returning to the occupied zone, he could not visit his children in Paris.

Back in Paris, Jacques and Paulette had been evacuated to the countryside with their school groups as the German army approached Paris in early June 1940. After their return when things settled down, Jacques was obliged to leave school and go to work in his great-aunt's clothing store. There he sold clothes to German soldiers, among others. The workshop for making the clothing was behind the shop. Paulette says that her brother was charming and popular with the clients and often received tips. The two youngsters saved what they could to send to their father. They too had left their childhood behind.

Jacques and Paulette were certainly aware of the anti-Semitism emerging in occupied Paris, but it seems to have bothered them very little. In October 1940, however, they made the most important decision of their young lives when they chose to ignore the Jewish census. "It was not from fear or some sort of superior wisdom," Jacques explains. "We just had this fierce desire to integrate into the society—to be totally French." They were not alone in their refusal. An estimated 10 percent of the Jewish community in Paris did the same.[11] The percentage is in fact astonishingly low. Religion had not been recorded in French censuses since 1872. Thousands of French Jews were nonobservant and not otherwise identifiable as Jewish. Yet from motives of injured pride or a fear of disobeying the law, they registered when they could have avoided it. In doing so, many of them signed their death warrants. But not Jacques and Paulette. For a time, the decision made their lives considerably easier.

Jacques and Paulette may have been only vaguely conscious of the Jewish roundups of May, August, and December 1941. Jacques says that he does not remember them. Also, because they had not registered as Jews in the census, the brother and sister were not obliged to wear the Star of David after May 1942. And although the shop where Jacques worked was "Aryanized," the young man did not lose his job. Yet even Jews "passing" as Christians could not miss the roundup of 12,884 foreign Jewish women and children, as well as men, in Paris on July 16, 1942.[12] This event, carefully planned and conducted by French police, was new and different not only in its size but in its inclusion of women and children. For a day and a half, police with lists of specific Jewish names and addresses broke into apartment buildings and emerged in full public view with entire families. Scarcely a family of Jewish immigrants from Germany, Austria, Poland, Czechoslovakia, or the Soviet Union, regardless of the date of their arrival in France, was untouched.

Jacques and Paulette were spared arrest on July 16, again because they were not registered as Jews. But their fifteen-year-old cousin Annie Biner, the daughter of their father's sister, Rywka, was with them in their apartment when the French police came for her parents, her ten-year-old brother, Albert, and her. Annie's father, determined that the family must stay together, came to get her. Such a response was not unusual among Jews who believed that arrest would entail repatriation to Poland and perhaps internment and forced labor there, but not murder. Annie and her parents and brother were deported from Beaune-la-Rolande to Auschwitz on August 5, in a convoy carrying 1,014 Jews.[13] About 214 men and 96 women were selected to enter the camp for work. The other 704 were immediately gassed. Six people from the convoy are known to have survived. None of the four Biners returned. In the days before and after their departure, most of the other 12,884 victims of the July 16 roundup were also deported to Auschwitz, thousands of them children under fourteen separated from their parents. None of the children and few of the adults returned.

Jacques and Paulette remained in Paris after the roundup of July 16 but were increasingly uneasy. Arrests continued at an alarming rate: at least 5,277 more Jewish men, women, and children were seized in the city between July 20 and December 31, 1942, to say nothing of incidents outside Paris or after 1942.[14] Although not registered as Jews, in itself a serious offense for which they could have been imprisoned and deported, the brother and sister were known as such to many of their neighbors and schoolmates.

Jacques well remembers the incident that finally forced Paulette and him to move south. In late July or early August 1942, a *copain*, a pal, who lived nearby and had gone to school with Jacques stole some money from his father, a local butcher, to buy presents for a girl he had his eyes on. When the young man was caught, he said that he had stolen because Jacques had asked him for money. Jacques denied it. He and his buddy were taken to the police station, where the young man murmured to Jacques, "Admit that you asked me for money. Otherwise I will tell them you are a Jew who did not register in the census." He knew Jacques was Jewish from their schooldays. Overhearing this conversation, a policeman reported it to his chief. Everyone realized that Jacques was telling the truth about the stealing but not about his status as a non-Jew. He was allowed to go, but the police chief quietly advised him, "If I were you, I would go to the Free Zone." Jacques needed no convincing.

For safety, Jacques and Paulette traveled south separately. The trip was dangerous; unauthorized persons caught crossing the demarcation line could be arrested, and the Jews among them were interned and eventually delivered to the Germans for deportation. But both Jacques and Paulette had documents identifying them as non-Jews, and neither remembers the trip as particularly eventful. Jacques traveled by train without incident, arriving in Marseille sometime before the Germans occupied it in November 1942. Paulette took a more roundabout route, traveling with an aunt and the aunt's children in a group attempting to reach Spain. Her problems arose not with the crossing into unoccupied France but when the guide in Pau informed her group that they would have to pay him more and abandoned them when they could not. Paulette eventually managed to leave the group and join her father and brother.

In Marseille, Szlama had official demobilization papers proving his eight-month wartime military service for France. That status apparently saved him from arrest during the roundups of recent Jewish immigrants and refugees in August 1942.[15] It also helped Jacques when he went to the mayor's office in Marseille to secure ration cards and was about to be detained as an unauthorized foreigner. Somehow Szlama learned that his son was in trouble, came to the office, and informed the authorities that he was a veteran of the Foreign Legion. Jacques was released.

When the Germans occupied Marseille in November 1942, however, Szlama, Jacques, and Paulette were in enormous danger. The new occupiers were intent on arresting all Jews regardless of nationality, time in France, military service records, or any other possible criteria. The worst time came between January 22 and 27, 1943, when the Germans destroyed the city's Old Port and, for five days, combed entire neighborhoods for partisans, criminals, beggars, and Jews. During that terrifying period, Jacques and Paulette recall hiding with their father in a room on the top floor of a building at 25, rue Barbarou, totally silent and with all lights extinguished at night. Of the 5,956 people ultimately arrested, 3,977 were released, but 1,642 were promptly sent north to Compiègne in filthy, overcrowded freight cars without food or water. Among the 1,642 were at least 782 Jews.[16]

On March 9, the Jews from Marseille were transferred to Drancy, from where, on March 23, most of them were deported to Sobibór. None survived.[17] Others arrested around the same time were deported on other trains. But Szlama and his children were no longer at risk by then. Sometime in the spring of 1943, Paulette traveled to the village of Le Chambon-sur-Lignon, where Jews were being hidden by the local, mostly Protestant population. Around the same time, her father and brother learned that Jews were being treated better east of the Rhône River, in the area of southeastern France occupied by the Italians when the Germans seized the rest of the unoccupied zone in November 1942. Szlama and Jacques immediately left Marseille for Nice. After only a few weeks there, they were sent to enforced residence in Saint-Martin-Vésubie. Paulette was able to join them, although she was never officially registered there as an internee.

CHAPTER SIX

Arrests in the Unoccupied Zone, August 1942

William Blye, Charles Roman, and Menahem Marienberg

ONE MONTH BEFORE the deadly roundup of 12,884 foreign Jewish men, women, and children in Paris on July 16, 1942, Vichy officials agreed to deliver ten thousand additional Jews from the unoccupied to the occupied zone. The intention was to rid southern France of the economic, social, and political burden of recent immigrant and refugee Jews, especially those already in internment or labor camps. If the number already detained was insufficient to meet the quota, more Jewish newcomers were to be seized from among those in supervised residence or living freely. The details for this operation were finalized in July, as the victims in Paris were being arrested, imprisoned, and deported to Auschwitz. The actual order from Vichy police headquarters to the regional prefects for expulsions of Jews from the unoccupied zone was issued on August 5.[1]

According to the order, Jews in the unoccupied zone eligible for delivery to the Germans were to be immigrants and refugees from the Third Reich, Poland, the Soviet Union, and the Baltic countries who had entered France after January 1, 1936. They were, in other words, precisely those newcomers with whom we are concerned in this book. Specifically excluded initially were individuals over sixty; unaccompanied children under eighteen; parents with a child under five; pregnant women; sick people incapable of being moved; veterans (but not prestataires) who had seen combat or served for at least three months with the French army or former allied armies, and their families; men or women with French spouses or children, or with spouses from countries other than those eligible for expulsion; and adults with jobs in the national economic interest or with a record of special service to France. In addition, parents with children under eighteen could choose to leave them behind.

As a result of the order, about 3,436 recent immigrant and refugee Jews in the camps of Gurs, Récébédou, Noé, Rivesaltes, Le Vernet, and Les Milles were jammed into the filthy cattle cars of four different trains to Drancy, where they arrived between August 7 and August 14. Then it was the turn of Jewish men of similar nationalities and immigration dates in forced labor sites, along with their women and children being held in obligatory residence hotels. Assembled in mid-August, about 1,184 people in this category arrived at Drancy on August 25 on yet another wretched train. At least 4,394 of these 4,620 internees and forced labor workers and their families were deported "to the East" within a few days.[2]

But the horrors of August 1942 had barely begun. To fulfill the Vichy authorities' agreement with the Germans, French police with carefully compiled lists of names and addresses of Jews of specific nationalities and recent immigration dates began raiding homes throughout the unoccupied zone in the early morning hours of August 26. In an effort to obtain more victims, the date of arrival in France for male bachelors between the ages of eighteen and forty had been extended from January 1, 1936, to January 1, 1933, unless they had served in the military or rendered special services to the country. For the same reason, parents were now exempted only if they had a child under two, rather than five; unaccompanied minors were exempted only if they were under sixteen, rather than eighteen; and parents lost the right to leave their children under eighteen in France. Also, in the name of the "non-separation of families" police were instructed to find children not living with their parents, so that they could be sent north together.[3] In the days that followed, thousands were arrested. In the terrifying eight days between August 29 and September 5, seven trains from the unoccupied zone arrived at Drancy with about 5,259 newly arrested recent immigrant and refugee Jews. Another 1,135 arrived on five more trains between September 15 and October 22. Deportation within a few days of arrival can be traced for at least 4,989 of them. Of the total number of about 11,014 foreign Jewish men, women, and children expelled from unoccupied France to Drancy between August 7 and October 22, 1942, and the 9,383 known to have been deported from Drancy to Poland by November 6, roughly two hundred to three hundred survived.[4]

William Blye

William Blye's family, it will be recalled, had emigrated from Leipzig to Milan in 1937 and to Nice in 1939. Until August 1942, William and his parents and two brothers had a more pleasant experience in France than most other recent immigrants and refugees. With his successful clothing business, William's father, Chaim, made his family economically secure, and fifteen-year-old William was able to attend a local lycée. Not much changed when the Germans invaded Poland in September 1939 or even when they attacked Belgium, Luxembourg, and the Netherlands in May 1940. Probably because he was useful to the national economy as a manufacturer of uniforms for the French army, Chaim was not arrested as an enemy alien in the early days of the war.

Not surprisingly, William remembers little of the defeat and division of France and the new Vichy regime's anti-Semitic measures. He was a teenager, and his thoughts and fancies were undoubtedly elsewhere. Also, he speculates, "It could be that things were not that normal and my parents probably kept things from us." But William did not have to leave his lycée. Nor, because he lived in the unoccupied zone, did he have to carry the humiliating "Juif" stamp on his identity and ration cards or wear the yellow star. His father had no professional or artistic position to lose. The clothing business, of military utility and legally in the name of a non-Jew, was spared confiscation. As for prohibitions on Jews enjoying gardens, parks, beaches, theaters, and other public amenities, it is unlikely that William, with his blue eyes, Nordic good looks, and youthful insouciance, paid them much heed.

When William completed his studies at the lycée in June 1942, his father asked him what he would like for a graduation present. Without hesitation, he answered that he would like a ski vacation on an Alpine glacier. He chose the village of Pralognan-la-Vanoise (Savoie), near the well-known ski resort of Courchevel, northeast of Grenoble and not far from the Italian frontier. Since his family's documents were in order, he did not have to obtain a special permission for travel. William recalls, "My father took me to the railroad station to send me away. When I waved from the train, I saw my father wipe his eyes. Maybe he had a premonition that he would not see me again." On arrival in Pralognan-la-Vanoise, William was disappointed to discover that summer skiing was not good that year, but he joined other guests who were hiking and had a grand time. Only later did he realize that "the ski trip saved my life."

When Chaim Bleiweiss saw his son off from the railroad station in Nice, he probably knew about the arrests and internment of thousands of Jewish men in Paris in May, August, and December 1941. He may even have heard that deportations of Jews from the Paris region had begun in March 1942 and that 12,884 Jewish immigrants, including for the first time women and children, had been arrested on July 16. But terrible as these events were, they remained, in Chaim's eyes, far away in the German-occupied zone, virtually in another country. He was not necessarily surprised. Jewish refugees from Germany had few illusions about the Nazis, and Chaim may not have understood that, for the most part, the arrests in Paris had been made by French police. But that such events should occur in the unoccupied zone was inconceivable.

And yet, while William was safely in Pralognon-la-Vanoise, the inconceivable happened.

On or about August 26, 1942, seven French gendarmes possibly accompanied by one German in civilian clothes knocked on the door of William Blye's third-floor apartment in Nice.[5] When no one answered, they started to leave, but the concierge stopped them. The family was certainly in residence, he explained; he had picked up their garbage that day. The gendarmes returned, broke down the door, and, in the presence of William's mother and two brothers, ransacked the apartment. They then took away the two boys, Bernhard, age nineteen, and Leo, sixteen. Their mother Maria feigned illness, telling the police that she needed surgery. William writes, "A sympathetic gendarme believed it. He had her brought to the hospital in Nice. She had herself operated on for a hernia that she did not need. Maybe the doctor wanted to help."

William's father was not at home when the police came for his family. He wrote to William to warn him not to return to Nice. He told him that he would try to get his sons released but that if he failed, he would go with them to wherever they were going. William comments, "He said that he knew the Germans, and that [he and his sons] would work [in deportation] and with God's will, they would return. He lost his head, because he could have saved himself." William's mother later told him that his father had hoped to bribe the French officials to release the two boys. The plan failed, and William never saw or heard from his father or brothers again. Until the end of the war, he and his mother believed that they would come back—that they had only been taken to a labor camp.

With about 557 other newly arrested Jews, Chaim, Bernhard, and Leo

Bleiweiss were expelled from Nice to the German-occupied zone on August 31. Their train arrived at Drancy the following day. The day after that, September 2, 1942, the three men were among the 1,016 Jews deported to Poland on convoy 27. Some thirty men survived deportation and returned in 1945, but the Bleiweiss men were not among them. Their precise fate is unclear. As with a number of other Jewish transports from Drancy, their train stopped at Kosel, a work camp not far from Auschwitz, where an unknown number of men were selected for labor. William's brothers were young and strong. They may have been selected at Kosel and died there or at another work site in Poland or the Third Reich. Or perhaps they were not selected for labor at Kosel but died instead after their train arrived at Auschwitz. Records indicate that ten men and 113 women from the French convoy of September 2 were selected to enter that camp. William's father, born in 1894, was forty-eight at the time of his deportation. Unless he looked exceptionally fit for his age, it is unlikely that he was among them. He was most probably murdered on arrival at Auschwitz.[6]

Like all the men and women interviewed for this book, William Blye finds it difficult to discuss certain subjects. Of this most tragic memory, he says only, "On my return to Nice after the war, in April 1945, I went to see the concierge. There was a new man there who said that he just got the job recently. I saw some of our apartment's furniture there. I guess the [former] concierge stole everything. Maybe this was always his plan." William then turns to the subject of Pierre Laval, the prime minister of Vichy France during much of the war who agreed to the expulsion of recent immigrant and refugee Jews from the unoccupied to the occupied zone in August 1942. "You know what they did to him after the war?" he asks. "How he took poison the night before he was to be executed, so they had to tie him to a chair to shoot him?" William Blye, a gentle, reticent man who, when in the Resistance in Italy, was unwilling to execute two German prisoners, says only, "I would have done it."

In an irony not uncommon in wartime France, although a French concierge betrayed William's family and French police arrested them, a French woman saved William's life. Madame Guttin, "née Monge," as she always presented herself, owned the hotel in Pralognan-la-Vanoise where William was staying. When word came that his brothers had been arrested and that the police were presumably looking for him, Madame Guttin closed her little hotel and accompanied the young man to the apartment of friends in Grenoble. After a brief period of hiding there, she helped him travel to Nice.

As William puts it, "My mother was being guarded by a French gendarme while she recuperated from her operation. Then, she was also scheduled to be deported. With the help of Madame Guttin, I went to the hospital in Nice and saw my mother sitting on a bench in the hospital garden. A gendarme was standing nearby. I secretly showed myself to my mother and signaled her to take a casual walk toward me. She did so. I ran with her to a horse-drawn carriage (those were the only taxis at that time) and we escaped." Perhaps the gendarme was not enthusiastic about his assignment guarding a Jewish invalid and looked the other way.

William and Maria did not return to their apartment in Nice. Instead, they chose the hazardous option of living illegally in hiding, uncertain what to do next. Two months later, their problem was solved by the arrival of the Italian army.

Charles Roman

In the summer of 1942, fifteen-year-old Charles Roman from Vienna was still at the OSE children's home called the Château de Montintin. His mother, Marianne, had left him with OSE in November 1939 when she realized that she could not support and protect him. Charles's quiet life was interrupted after August 26, when Vichy police launched their roundup throughout the unoccupied zone. By then, as we have seen, French police orders had changed, so that unaccompanied minors sixteen or over, rather than eighteen, could be deported without parents. Young people in Jewish institutions were technically unaccompanied minors. Also, according to the new principle of "non-separation of families," French police were taking children under sixteen from Jewish institutions to unite them with their families for expulsion. These changes drastically affected the Jewish children's homes. Charles and hundreds like him were now at great risk.

Under these circumstances, police came to Montintin several times in late August. At first, probably on August 26, they came for unaccompanied minors sixteen or over. Charles Roman's friend Ludwig (Lutz) Greve, born in Berlin in 1924, recorded that he was arrested on that date with all his friends over eighteen. He may have been unaware that the cut-off age was actually sixteen. Lutz writes without detail that he managed to escape and was hidden by the directors of Montintin in the surrounding woods for five weeks until he received false papers and was directed to a Resistance group.[7] Charles does not remember a large raid on August 26, but he recalls that at a certain point, the older boys at Montintin were no longer there. He remembers that the younger boys were moved into the now-empty rooms of the older ones. But then the police began to come for younger boys, to be reunited with their arrested parents.[8]

Initially caught off-guard by the change in Vichy's exemption policies and not clear about which children were eligible for arrest and expulsion, Montintin's directors after August 26 made escape plans for all their remaining immigrants and refugees. One or two youngsters were stationed where they could hear any cars approaching the house. Almost all cars carried officials in those days, Charles explains, so cars meant trouble. If a car drew near, the young watchmen were to sound an alert, and the children most at risk would run to hide in the woods.

When the police came again to Montintin one day in late August 1942, Charles made his way to the woods as fast as he could. After a few minutes, however, a young girl came from the house to tell him that the police were not looking for older children or for many children. This time, two police detectives were asking specifically for him. Charles assumed that his mother, Marianne, had sent for him, because she had recently written from Agde that she expected to be taken to a camp soon. Reluctant but believing that he had no real alternative, he presented himself to the police. He traveled with them to Limoges, Perpignan, and then Rivesaltes (Pyrénées-Orientales), the site of an internment camp about ten kilometers north of Perpignan. Originally a center for fugitives from the Spanish Civil War, Rivesaltes held male immigrants arrested as enemy aliens after May 1940 but became increasingly known as a camp for Jewish families in 1941 and 1942. After August 26, 1942, it was a center for "family regrouping"—a place where Jewish husbands, wives, and children were brought together so they could be deported as a unit.[9]

Only after his arrival in Rivesaltes did Charles learn that his father, not his mother, had sent for him. Divorced from Marianne, Leopold Roman had left Vienna for Belgium in November 1938. When the war began, he was interned as an enemy alien in Belgium. From there he was forcibly expelled to France in May 1940, along with some eleven hundred other German and Austrian men, both Jews and non-Jews, regarded as spies. In France, he was imprisoned first at Saint-Cyprien and then at Gurs, near the Spanish frontier. Somehow he managed to remain at Gurs in early August 1942, when most German and Austrian Jewish internees there were expelled to the occupied zone. Charles believes that around August 26, when Vichy police were instructed to bring in the children of Jews eligible for expulsion, they tricked Leopold into giving them his son's address. They told him that he would not be deported if he were accompanied by a child under sixteen. This would have been a deliberate lie, for police orders stated clearly that recent immigrant and refugee parents would be exempt from expulsion only if they were accompanied by a child under five, an age soon lowered to two. The lie was almost certainly motivated by the desire of the police to gather in as many children as possible, to fill their quota. But Leopold believed it, and he gave the police his son's address at Montintin.[10] He was then sent from Gurs to Rivesaltes to be reunited with Charles.

Leopold was not even to have the pleasure of a little time with his son. Charles was in Rivesaltes for several days before he finally found his father. The reunion occurred about 6:00 A.M. on September 4, at a roll call on a truck taking them both, with some 620 other Jewish men, women, and children, to the local railroad siding.[11] They were being delivered to the Germans in the occupied zone. At the siding, there was a second roll call, with a guard calling last names only. When the name "Roman" was called, Leopold answered "present" and walked up the plank into a waiting freight car. When the same name was called a second time, Leopold answered "present" again. To this day, Charles does not know if he did it deliberately, to give his son a chance to escape, or whether he thought both calls were for him. He had been in internment for a long time, Charles says, and he was used to roll calls. Perhaps he answered automatically. In any case, Charles, on the platform, did not move. He was still there when nearly all the prisoners had boarded. When a guard asked him his name, for reasons he still cannot explain he said that it was Rosenberg. Not on the list, he was sent back to the camp.

Leopold Roman arrived at Drancy the next day and was deported on convoy 31 on September 11, nine days after the father and brothers of William Blye. Of the thousand prisoners on Leopold's train, at least 570 were from Rivesaltes. Many were parents with children. Like the trains carrying William Blye's loved ones, Leopold's convoy stopped at Kosel to unload an unknown number of the strongest men for labor. It then proceeded to Auschwitz, where two men and seventy-eight women were selected for work. The others, including all the children and their mothers, and all the elderly, were gassed. Thirteen men from the convoy are known to have survived.[12] Leopold Roman was not among them, but his son does not know where or how he died.

Fortunately for young Charles in Rivesaltes, a French Jewish Red Cross worker named Emma Lederer, formerly an OSE educator at the Château de Chabannes, recognized him and was determined to help him escape. She crammed him under the back seat of a car, where he was nearly smothered. With Red Cross commissioners sitting on him and the springs of the seat in his chest, he was driven out of the camp. Emma then sent Charles to Solange Zitlenok, the OSE regional representative for southeastern France, based in Perpignan. Solange gave him a document confirming his release from Rivesaltes and placed him with a French Jewish family not yet at risk of arrest.[13]

But Solange had a task in mind for Charles. After August 26, Jewish immigrant and refugee families continued to be arrested and brought to Rivesaltes every day. Because parents no longer had the option of leaving their children under eighteen behind, hundreds of children entered the camp. There, desperate social workers, both Jewish and non-Jewish, tried to persuade camp officials to release them, usually to no avail. OSE representatives obtained the liberation of about twenty children, while other organizations had similar slight success.[14] Camp officials were firm—orders were orders, and the children must be delivered to the Germans along with their parents.

But then, according to OSE representative Andrée Salomon, "Once again, everything changed—suddenly. Hearing no response from Vichy [to the prefect's request for more precise orders], the *préfecture* of Perpignan assumed the responsibility to liberate children under sixteen years of age in the [department of] Pyrénées-Orientales, as long as we submitted their files to the officials."[15] Immediately, social workers moved among the interned families, trying to persuade parents to give up their children. Others met newly arrested families just arriving at the camp and talked to them even before they were admitted. Solange was among the social workers with that assignment. Charles's role, as a young lad rescued and being cared for by OSE, was to give Solange credibility. The two of them were able to save about twenty-five children in this way. Charles has a photograph of them. Altogether, according to Andrée Salomon, 427 children were separated from their parents and placed in institutions and private homes in the area of Perpignan. Most of them survived. Their parents did not.

After helping Solange, Charles lived in the area for about a month before returning to Montintin. The directors were uneasy about sheltering a young man his age, for they were never certain whether the French police would return. Tensions increased further when the Germans occupied southern France in early November 1942, following the Allied landings in North Africa. Nevertheless, Charles stayed at the château until late January, when he left to visit his mother.

Menahem Marienberg

Like the families of William Blye and Charles Roman, Menahem Marienberg and his parents and siblings precisely met the criteria for Jews whom the French police were to arrest and deliver to the Germans in August 1942. They had fled from Brussels in May 1940 and registered as Jewish refugees, but been permitted to live freely in Toulouse because Menahem's father Wolf was needed in a local factory. As rumors spread that Jews already in internment or in forced labor brigades were being sent north, they became increasingly uneasy. They had no way of knowing if Jews living freely or in supervised residence would be arrested or who the targets would be. At first they thought that only men would be taken, which seemed logical if the deportations were for labor.

Under these circumstances, the Fournier family who had befriended the Marienbergs in 1940 offered to hide Wolf, and he accepted. The three eldest Marienberg children then planned summer camping trips with the Éclaireurs israélites de France (EIF), the Jewish scouts of France. Thirteen-year-old Mina went first, returning just as Menahem and Léon, ages fifteen and nine, left. Around August 26, the two boys were on a train returning from their own vacation when the French police came to the apartment to arrest their family. Menahem's mother, Simone, and two of her children, Mina and four-year-old Maurice, were taken. Menahem learned from the neighbors after the war that his mother had tried to resist arrest, but in vain.

Simone, Mina, and Maurice were first interned at Noé (Haute-Garonne), about thirty-five kilometers southwest of Toulouse.[16] They were then among the 960 Jews from the area of Toulouse to be sent north to Drancy, where they arrived on September 2. Two days later, they were deported on convoy 28. Their train carrying 981 men, women, and children arrived at Auschwitz two days later. Along the way, like convoy 27 from Drancy on September 2 with the father and brothers of William Blye and convoy 31 on September 11 with Leopold Roman, the train stopped at Kosel to disembark men capable of hard work. At Auschwitz, only sixteen men and thirty-eight women were admitted to the camp. Accompanied as she was by two young children, Simone Marienberg was almost certainly not among them. Those not admitted, including all the children, were gassed on arrival. About twenty-seven people from convoy 28 returned to France or Belgium after the war.[17] Menahem's mother, sister, and brother did not return.

Of this terrible tragedy, Menahem states, "I couldn't cry when my mother and sister and brother were taken. I never cried. It didn't seem real. I was just astonished. Why would they take a four-year-old boy?" It is a question without an answer.

While still on the train returning from their camping trip, Menahem and Léon learned of the ongoing arrests of Jews in Toulouse. Their scout leaders were advised not to let the refugee children return to their homes. After much debate, the group divided, with each leader assuming responsibility for three or four children. In the railroad station, they all began to sing the "Marseillaise," the French national anthem. When the French guards stood briefly at attention, the children went past them. Once past, they broke and ran, each child with his assigned leader. The EIF scout leaders were French Jews, not liable for arrest at this time. The children stayed in their homes for a few days. Menahem found his father during this period. "His eyes were completely different," Menahem recalls. "His hair was gray. He was an old man."

Like so many foreign Jewish families in France at that point, Menahem's father and his two remaining sons split up for safety's sake. Menahem's scout leaders sent him to the village of Lautrec (Tarn), about seventy-six kilometers northeast of Toulouse and thirty-one kilometers south of Albi. The EIF ran a children's center in Lautrec where mostly non-French teenage Jewish scouts lived full time, studying, farming, and learning a trade.[18] Most were youngsters like Menahem, whose parents had been interned or could not support them for other reasons. Léon, not old enough for Lautrec, went to a similar place for younger boys. Moissac (Tarn-et-Garonne), seventy-one kilometers northwest of Toulouse and at least a hundred kilometers west of Lautrec, is a charming town of about twelve thousand people on the Tarn River. There, in an old patrician house at 18, quai du Port, on the banks of the river, and in adjoining buildings, the EIF established a home for Jewish orphans and needy children. The center included a children's residence, synagogue, school, library, document center, and artisan workshop.[19] Like Charles Roman but a little later, Menahem and Léon had found their way to two of the many remarkable institutions operated by French Jews to help their young and needy coreligionists, most of whom were in a strange country.

As we saw in the case of Charles Roman, however, immigrant and refugee children were no longer safe in Jewish institutions like those in Lautrec and Moissac when Menahem and Léon arrived at the end of August 1942. The directors of Jewish institutions had no way of knowing when another raid might occur or which children would be targets. As a result, they were beginning to search for non-Jewish families or Catholic institutions willing to take in foreign Jewish children. For those who remained, they planned escape routes in the event of a police raid.

To the relief of their supervisors, Menahem and Léon did not need to stay at Lautrec and Moissac for more than a few months. With his brother Isaac, sister-in-law Eva, and nephew, also named Menahem, the boys' father, Wolf Marienberg, made his way to Nice, under Italian occupation after November 1942. From there, the four were sent to enforced residence in Saint-Martin-Vésubie. This village, Wolf immediately realized, was the place for his sons. He promptly contacted them at Lautrec and Moissac, and they embarked on yet another dangerous journey.

Narrow Escapes and Subsequent Arrests in the Unoccupied Zone, August–November 1942

Miriam Löwenwirth, Boris Carmeli, Sigi Hart, Charles Roman, and Walter Marx

Miriam Löwenwirth

Miriam Löwenwirth and her large family, Czechoslovakian war refugees from Antwerp, were in Quarante on August 26, 1942, when the Vichy police came for recent immigrant and refugee Jews. The Löwenwirths seemed to meet the criteria for arrest, with one vital exception. Little Ben-Zion, whose mother had declared at his birth that it was no time for a baby to be born, was eight months old. The police had been instructed to spare all families with infants under the age of two. Ben-Zion saved the lives of his entire family.

After that narrow escape, the Löwenwirth family was ordered to leave Quarante. Miriam is not certain of the date, but surviving documents indicate that Jewish refugees in the Hérault were ordered to transfer to the departments of Aveyron or Lozère or to the region of Limoges on November 12, soon after the Germans occupied southern France.[1] Miriam, now sixteen years old, undertook the task of traveling to those areas to find a place to live. She chose the village of Chirac (Lozère), which she describes as "a little town surrounded by beautiful countryside, four kilometers away from Marvejols." Chirac is perhaps more easily understood as being in the Massif Central about seventy-five kilometers southwest of Le Puy. The family moved in, officially registered again in "supervised residence." "The townsfolk were simple good people," Miriam recalls. "The person to whom I had spoken originally [about finding a house], who was the head of the town council, visited us occasionally, always with something in his hand for us."

Unfortunately, this pleasant interlude was not to last. Two or three months after their arrival in Chirac, French police came to the village and arrested Miriam's father, Eliyahu, and a few other Jewish men. Miriam believes that no Germans were involved in the actual arrests. As soon as her father left with the police, however, she responded with her usual courage and imagination. The friendly head of the town council informed her that the arrested men were being held temporarily in a small military barracks near the railroad station in a nearby village, pending transfer to a more established camp. Traveling alone to the barracks, Miriam arrived after dark and asked to see the commanding officer, a Frenchman. Told that she could not see the officer until the next day, she sat down on the nearest bench and refused to move. Surprisingly, the man received her.

Miriam explained to the commander that her father had six children, her mother was ill, and the family was desperate. She asked him to grant her father a twenty-four-hour leave. At first he said it was impossible, but after Miriam insisted, he seemed to reconsider. Miriam says, "He began to ask me all sorts of questions, and then suddenly he looked at me intently, I remember that look, and asked me where I was born. He said: 'You are a brave little Czechoslovakian.' He gave me a twenty-four-hour permit even though he must have understood that he was not free to do so." One might also ask whether he understood that Eliyahu would not return in twenty-four hours, or ever.[2] Perhaps the commander took pity on the young girl before him. Or perhaps he was not happy with his assignment in the first place. Or both.

With a twenty-four-hour pass, there was no time to return to the family. Eliyahu and Miriam had heard the same rumors as the other survivors described in this book. The Italians had occupied the southeastern corner of France and were treating the Jews decently. Father and daughter immediately boarded a bus for Nice. Miriam still remembers her terror when two German soldiers entered the bus and began to check documents. Somehow, she says, they passed right by her father and her, "as if they never even saw us." Miriam and Eliyahu arrived safely. Leaving her father at the synagogue in Nice, Miriam returned to Chirac for the rest of the family. Within a few days, the Löwenwirths were reunited in Nice. Despite her gender and her youth, or perhaps because of them, Miriam had saved her family. After a week or two, the Italian authorities sent them to Saint-Martin-Vésubie, where another pleasant but brief interlude awaited.

Boris Carmeli

The Wolfinger (later Carmeli) family was at Bénéjacq just before August 26 when a secretary at the local mayor's office warned them that the police would come for them the next day. They left immediately, traveling on foot to a nearby village, where they knocked on the door of total strangers. The peasants instantly agreed to help them. The Wolfingers hid in their hayloft for about two weeks, until a group of young French Jews, still safe from arrest and able to move about, came to their rescue.

Boris describes his rescuers as "Zionists." They may have been affiliated with the Mouvement des jeunesses sionistes (MJS), which was the most Zionist of the French Jewish youth groups, or with the Éclaireurs israélites de France (EIF), French Jewish Boy Scouts particularly involved with helping Jewish children. Not much older than Boris himself, these young people took him to Pau, bought him a train ticket to Toulouse, and instructed him to go to the offices of a particular Jewish committee there. The fourteen-year-old lad did as he was told. In Toulouse, the committee sent him on to the same EIF children's home in Moissac that we have seen in connection with Menahem Marienberg. Boris stayed there for about two months, study-ing bookbinding. He was also part of a group of Jewish children at Moissac scheduled to immigrate to the United States—a plan that fell apart when the Allies landed in North Africa in November.

With Boris in apparent safety at Moissac, his parents moved to Tou-louse. There, for the first time, they did not register with the authorities. Always fearful of another French police raid, they lived on the edge of the city, on a quiet street at the end of the tram line where they could see or hear the police arriving. When the Germans occupied Toulouse in November, their terror intensified. After word reached them that the Italians occupying the southeastern corner of the country were treating Jews better, they asked Boris to join them and gratefully made the hazardous trip to Nice. They did not stay there long but were promptly sent to Saint-Martin-Vésubie.[3]

Sigi Hart

Like the family of Boris Carmeli, Sigi Hart's father, Hermann, was warned by a sympathetic villager shortly before August 26 that the French police were going to arrest Jews in Aulus-les-Bains that night. As in Antwerp more than two years before, Hermann did not hesitate. Sigi, now almost seventeen, knew the mountains well because he had been working there. Hermann and the family followed him upward for about half an hour and spent an uncomfortable night in the forest. The next morning, Sigi returned to the village to see what had happened. The police had not come and everyone was laughing at his parents for their fears. Somewhat chagrined, they returned to the village for the day. That afternoon, the same man warned them again, and they went back to the same mountains for the night. "We probably don't have to do this," they thought, and took fewer supplies. But when Sigi walked down to the village the next morning, he learned that the gendarmes had indeed come and had taken away the Jews.

Sigi believes that he and his family lived in the mountains for about six weeks. They slept out in the open, and he remembers that it was already cold at night. Twice a week he went down to the village to harvest the tomatoes, potatoes, and other vegetables ripening in their allotted garden. They could not have a fire in the daytime, but at night Adela made a small fire for cooking. They had to ration their food carefully. Spain was not far away, but they had been told that the mountains were too steep and treacherous to cross without a guide. They did not know how to get a guide.

The Hartmayers' life in the mountains ended abruptly in mid-October, when a French patrol of gendarmes caught them and took them back to Aulus-les-Bains. After spending the night there, they were taken to Le Vernet (Ariège), in the same department but farther from the Spanish frontier. Le Vernet had already acquired a fearful reputation in the autumn of 1939, when more than two thousand Spanish Republicans, French political dissidents, common criminals, and German nationals, both Jewish and non-Jewish, were interned there under dreadful conditions.[4] Still an exceptionally harsh punitive camp in the autumn of 1942, it also served as a transit camp for recently arrested Jewish families.

After two or three weeks at Le Vernet, the Hartmayers were sent to Gurs, in the town of Oloron (Basses-Pyrénées; Pyrénées-Atlantiques today), about thirty-five kilometers southwest of Pau and not much more than that from the Spanish border. Gurs was the largest and most notorious camp in southern France. Thousands of foreign Jews had been interned there as enemy aliens in September 1939 and May 1940, but many had eventually been released. After the fall of France, however, the Vichy regime had interned thousands of recent immigrant and refugee Jews there. To the Hartmayers, arriving at Gurs toward the beginning of November 1942, it must have looked as if they had lost the battle for survival. Although they could not have known it at the time, however, the six weeks they spent in the mountains saved their lives.

Between August 6 and September 1, 1942, more than two thousand men, women, and children in Gurs had been sent north to Drancy, from where most were deported. These included at least five children from Aulus-les-Bains, with parents.[5] Had the Hartmayers been in the camp during that period, they would surely have been among them. After September 1, only 820 Jews remained in Gurs, most of them ineligible for expulsion by reason of nationality or date of immigration to France. But in November, the number of prisoners in Gurs began to rise again. Some 1,380 newcomers, of whom about seven hundred were Spanish non-Jews, were transferred there from Rivesaltes after that camp's unhealthy location and miserable facilities were aggravated by a severe storm. An additional 240 Jewish refugees who, like Sigi's family, had managed to elude the French police in August, were arrested throughout southwestern France in November and sent there. By March 1943, the number of prisoners at Gurs had risen to 2,920, and the camp was crowded.[6] In part for that reason, according to Sigi, Jewish youngsters were sent from Gurs to live in supervised residence in various children's homes and schools. With other boys up to the age of about seventeen, Sigi and Willy were sent to the farm school of La Roche (Lot-et-Garonne), operated by the Organisation pour la reconstruction et le travail (ORT) to teach agricultural skills.

Hermann Hartmayer escaped from Gurs at the end of 1942. Around the same time, his wife, Adela, Sigi's mother, became ill with either typhus or typhoid fever and had to be transferred to an infirmary. Because Sigi's sister, Manya, was now alone in the women's section of Gurs, social workers with access to the camp and a handful of permits to distribute tried to move her to a more congenial supervised residence, just as they had moved Sigi and Willy. Unexpectedly, Manya resisted. "My biggest fear," she says, "was to be separated from my parents." When she visited Adela in the infirmary, however, her mother was furious, insisting that she agree to leave Gurs. Manya was finally placed in a home for Jewish girls in Vic-sur-Cère (Cantal), in the mountains of the Massif Central.

Vic-sur-Cère was one of several *centres d'accueil,* or reception centers, set up by a committee of private Jewish and non-Jewish charities in 1940 and 1941 for Jewish adults and children who had been arrested and interned but were then allowed to live under supervision outside the camps. It was founded by Abbé Alexandre Glasberg, the colorful vicar of Notre-Dame in

Saint-Alban, one of the poorest parishes in the suburbs of Lyon. A Ukrainian immigrant and Jewish-born convert to Catholicism, Glasberg was described by those who knew him as a big, rumpled man, "spontaneous to the point of anarchy."[7] Before Manya's arrival, Glasberg had been able to hide and save girls living at Vic-sur-Cère who were summoned by the police for "family regrouping" and expulsion to Drancy at the end of August 1942, although he was less successful at two other centers. On August 29, he also helped save some eighty-four to 108 children slated for expulsion with their parents from the camp of Vénissieux, outside Lyon, to Drancy. In that case, the order from Vichy on August 18 ending the right of interned parents to leave their children behind never reached the camp commander because Abbé Glasberg intercepted it.[8] He was truly a hero, and now, one of the institutions he founded helped Manya Hartmayer.

By the end of 1942, most recent immigrants and refugees lucky enough to have escaped the expulsions from southern France in August understood that it was just a matter of time until their turn would come. At present, the Germans were busy tightening their hold on the newly occupied south, but the reprieve would not last. Thus, as seen, Menahem Marienberg's father got his two sons out of Moissac and Lautrec. After escaping from Gurs, Sigi Hart's father set about to do the same. Hearing that conditions might be better for Jews in the Italian-occupied zone in southeastern France, he promptly made his way to Nice to see for himself.

Sigi and his brother, Willy, also realized that they were living on borrowed time. Fearing arrest by French police, most of the Jewish boys over sixteen had left La Roche in August. Equally insecure, the younger boys who remained rigged up an effective alarm system, just as the friends of Charles Roman had done at Montintin. By running an electrified wire from the front gate to the school building itself, a distance of about half a mile, two or three boys on guard at the gate, in three-hour shifts around the clock, could trip the wire and ring a bell in the house if the police approached. On the other hand, the boys were not carefully guarded at La Roche, which was, according to Sigi, twelve kilometers from the nearest village. Government authorities expected the directors of the school to keep them there until they were recalled for internment, but the directors themselves were committed to saving their lives. The directors consequently gave the boys much freedom of movement, while the police assumed that they were isolated and had nowhere to go.

From Nice, Hermann was able to send a letter to his sons at La Roche.

It said, roughly, "My aunt is very sick, and may not live. Try to come and visit." He also sent them some money. Sigi understood this code immediately. As a result, he and Willy simply walked away one day in the spring of 1943, with no trouble. Far more dangerous was the train trip with no identity cards or travel permits. If caught, they would probably have been sent back to Gurs. But as Sigi recalls it, no one was interested in two boys. He remembers traveling to Marseille on a train with many German soldiers. He and Willy could understand everything they were saying but of course they did not let them know that. The boys arrived safely in Nice, as did Manya, whom Hermann also summoned from her institution. After two or three weeks in Nice, Hermann and his children were assigned to residence in Saint-Martin-Vésubie.

Charles Roman

Living in supervised residence outside the camp in the town of Agde, Charles Roman's mother, Marianne, had somehow escaped the wave of arrests of recent Jewish immigrants and refugees in August 1942. Charles does not know how she managed it, for she fit all the criteria for arrest. Soon after August, Marianne moved to Florac (Lozère), in the heart of the Massif Central about thirty-five kilometers south of Le Puy. Probably this was an assigned residence. In Florac she met and became engaged to Wilhelm Bauer, a Czech Jewish soldier who had fought with the Czech Legion in France in 1940 and had consequently been exempted from arrest in August 1942. She then wrote to Charles, back at the OSE children's home of Montintin after his narrow escape at Rivesaltes, asking him to come for the wedding on January 26, 1943. Charles did so, remaining with his mother and her new husband for about a month. Of this time, he especially remembers the struggle to find food. Every day he rode his bicycle through the countryside to visit farmers, hoping to buy a little meat.

The period of happiness for Charles, Marianne, and Wilhelm was short-lived. At 11:10 P.M. on February 13, 1943, two German Luftwaffe officers were assassinated by partisans in Paris as they were returning from their office to their hotel. In reprisal, the Germans demanded that French police arrest and deliver two thousand Jewish men between the ages of sixteen and sixty-five. Vichy authorities believed that they had little choice but to obey. In their determination to spare French Jews, however, they ordered that in every department, but especially in the former unoccupied zone, lists be prepared of a specific number of male Jewish immigrants from the Third Reich, Poland, the Soviet Union, the Baltic countries, Belgium, Holland, and Yugoslavia, with a preference for recent refugees.[9] But there was a problem, because thousands of recently arrived Jews had been arrested the previous August, while those who had escaped had gone into hiding. It was therefore necessary to seize men who had hitherto been exempt from arrest, either because they had been in France for a long time or because they had served in the military. French police thus found themselves preparing lists of unsuspecting Jews who had risked their lives for France in wartime.

Once their lists were prepared, the police launched their roundup on Saturday, February 20. Wilhelm Bauer was among the thirteen foreign Jewish men arrested in Florac at this time. The thirteen were among forty-one men arrested in the departments of Lozère and Gard.[10] Of this tragic incident, Charles says, "I was there. . . . In the afternoon [following Wilhelm's arrest] the group of approximately twenty-five persons guarded by two gendarmes was marched to the train station through local streets with onlookers on both sides of the street. In this confusion I rode my bicycle next to [Wilhelm] and told him to ride off on it. He said, 'I don't do this. I was a French soldier and I will get out on my own merit.'" Wilhelm was under the impression that foreign Jews who had fought for France would be spared deportation. He was wrong.

Wilhelm Bauer, born in Brno, Czechoslovakia, in 1901, was sent to Gurs, where Sigi Hart and his family had been a few months before. But for Bauer and most of the other men arrested that February 1943, there was to be no escape. Some 957 Jewish men were shipped north from Gurs to Drancy on February 26, 1943. At least 770 others followed on March 2. Most were deported "to the East" on March 4 and 6, on convoys 50 and 51. Bauer was on convoy 50. From the train, he was able to send a card that found its way to his new wife, Charles's mother. "We are on our way to Germany," he wrote, "Nothing to do." In an exception to the general rule in France, Wilhelm's train delivered its 1,008 victims to the death camps of Sobibór and Majdanek rather than Auschwitz. It is not known how many were admitted to the camps and how many were gassed on arrival. Wilhelm Bauer was not among the four from his convoy who survived.[11]

Charles had lost two fathers before he was sixteen. After Wilhelm's arrest, he returned to Montintin, but he did not stay long. It was increasingly apparent that none of the Jewish children in OSE's care were safe, and Charles made preparations for leaving. He received a false identity card with no Jewish stamp. He kept his name, not identifiable as Jewish, and his date of birth. His red hair made him convincing as a non-Jew, while his declared place of origin, the department of the Nord, explained his accent. Furthermore, his false card could not be easily checked because the Nord, along with the Pas-de-Calais, both in northeastern France, was under the administration of a German military governor based in Belgium. With that cover, in early spring 1943 Charles joined a rural unit of the Compagnons de France, a Vichy government youth organization for boys between the ages of fifteen and twenty, unaffiliated with the Catholic Church or the French Boy Scouts.[12] With his unit, Charles harvested potatoes—"they were heavy, those bags of potatoes"—and later worked as a mechanic in a bicycle and motorcycle shop in Saint-Pons (Hérault).

Charles never felt quite at ease in his new role. As far as he knew, there was only one other Jewish boy in his unit of the Compagnons de France, whom he recognized from Montintin but with whom he rarely associated publicly. One day, the chief of his unit asked Charles where his parents were. He replied that his father had died and that his mother had run off with another man but that he had an aunt who looked after him. But the question made him nervous. Charles knew from her letters that his mother had made her way to Nice and then to Saint-Martin-Vésubie, so in early August 1943 he decided to make the risky and illegal trip there.

Walter Marx

Like the families of Miriam Löwenwirth, Boris Carmeli, and Sigi Hart, Walter Marx and his parents, German Jews expelled from Luxembourg in November 1940, were lucky in August 1942. They were among the 1,010 Jewish refugees in the department of Hérault who met the Vichy criteria for arrest and expulsion to the occupied zone in August 1942, and among the 140 eligible Jews who lived in Montpellier. But they were not among the departmental total of 419 people who were seized and sent to Agde, from where they were expelled to the occupied zone and ultimately deported.[13]

It had been a close thing. Aware of rumors of the pending arrests, Walter and his parents, Ludwig and Johanna, and Walter's cousin Werner Isaac had hidden for a week or two in the apartment of a French woman who offered them shelter for pay. Walter says, "We were not allowed to walk outside or look out of the window or make any noise for fear that neighbors would become suspicious and question who was in the apartment aside from the landlady." But despite their precautions, French police knocked on their door one day and took them to the police station. Someone had denounced them, but they never learned who.[14] From the station, Ludwig contacted his employer, the president of the local Jewish community. In August 1942, French Jews not only were not being arrested but could sometimes protect foreign Jews who worked for French Jewish social agencies. Ludwig's employer sent him a certificate testifying that he worked for the Union générale des israélites de France (UGIF), the German-imposed coordinating organization of all French Jewish social welfare agencies. The fact that Ludwig had volunteered to serve in the French army as a prestataire during the early months of the war may also have given him an edge, but not a guarantee, for prestataires were not exempt from arrest and expulsion in August 1942. He and his family were released and returned to their own apartment.

Walter and his parents and cousin remained in Montpellier until November 2, 1942, when they departed for the interior.[15] It is not clear why they left at that time. The Allies did not land in North Africa until November 8, and the Germans did not reach Montpellier until November 12. Walter believes that his parents had heard rumors of a German occupation of at least the Mediterranean coast, which may have influenced their decision. He also remembers that the family did not have a clear destination. They traveled first to Millau (Aveyron) to look for a place. Then they heard that there were plenty of apartments available in Lamalou-les-Bains (Hérault), about seventy-nine kilometers west of Montpellier and more than forty kilometers from the sea, where the family of Boris Carmeli had earlier been sent for a short time. They may not have known that those apartments were available in part because some recent Jewish immigrants and refugees had been arrested there in August 1942, expelled to Drancy, and ultimately deported.[16] In any case, they went there, registering with the authorities as required.

Life for Jews in southern France became more difficult toward the end of 1942, for with the Germans came more anti-Jewish regulations. In November, foreign Jews were prohibited from moving outside their communes of residence without official permission. At the same time, Jewish refugees began to be ordered to move away from the Mediterranean coast and the Spanish and Italian frontiers. Like other Jews in the Hérault, those in Montpellier where the Marx family had been living were ordered to resettle in the departments of Aveyron or Lozère or in the region of Limoges on November 12. Some 233 people eventually left.[17] During the next few months, similar orders reached refugee Jews elsewhere. Meanwhile, in December all Jews were required to receive a stamp on their documents identifying them as "Juif" or "Juive." They did not know it, but they were being concentrated and labeled for more efficient arrest and deportation.

Around this same time, the Germans also initiated a series of round-ups of Jews in the former unoccupied zone. The terrifying and brutal raids in Marseille at the end of January 1943 were described in connection with Jacques and Paulette Samson. Then on February 9, German Gestapo agents raided a Jewish assistance center at 12, rue Sainte-Catherine in Lyon. Eighty-four French and foreign social workers and their clients were sent to Drancy after the raid. Nearly all of them subsequently died at Auschwitz. Throughout April and May 1943, hundreds of other Jews in Marseille, Toulouse, Nîmes, Avignon, Carpentras, Aix-en-Provence, Clermont-Ferrand, and elsewhere in southern France, to say nothing of the north, were arrested and shipped to Drancy. The fact that Jews who were citizens and longtime resident immigrants were increasingly among the victims was of little consolation to more recent immigrants and refugees. Life had become untenable for all.[18]

In February 1943, Walter's father fell victim to the same huge roundup in reprisal for the two German officers assassinated in Paris in which Charles Roman's stepfather, Wilhelm Bauer, had been caught. In the department of the Hérault, where the Marx family was living, the police were ordered to select and arrest seventy men as their contribution to the national quota of two thousand victims demanded by the Germans. They were instructed that all Jewish male immigrants of relevant ages and from specific countries were eligible for arrest, regardless of dates of entry into France, but that to fill their quota they should naturally begin with the most recent arrivals. They were also told that "Jews with French connections or who have rendered civilian and military services to France" should be placed at the bottom of the list. While the preferred targets, then, remained the same as those seized in August 1942, the parameters were extended to affect many who had not been in danger before. In the Hérault, forty-eight of the seventy men listed were caught and deported. One of them was Ludwig Marx, arrested in Lamalou-les-Bains on February 20.[19]

When he learned of his father's arrest, Walter sought help from the president of the Jewish Community in Montpellier. There he learned that his father had already been taken to Gurs. It was too late to intervene. Ludwig Marx was sent to Drancy on either February 26 or March 2, 1943. Although his name does not appear on the transport lists of convoys 50 and 51, which left Drancy for Poland on March 4 and 6, respectively, and are incomplete and in bad condition, Ludwig was probably among the passengers. Both trains stopped at the death camps of Sobibór and Majdanek, in the Lublin district of Poland, rather than Auschwitz. Ludwig was not among the four men from the first train or the five from the second who returned.[20] After the war, Walter received a death certificate from the German government, stating that his father died at Majdanek two days after his arrival there.

After Ludwig's arrest and expulsion to Drancy, Walter and his mother learned that the Italians occupying southeastern France were more hospitable to Jews than the Germans in the zone where they were living. They traveled, illegally but without much difficulty, to Nice. There they registered with the Italian occupying forces and were directed to enforced residence in Saint-Martin-Vésubie. A new life began for them.

PART II

Shared Experiences

CHAPTER EIGHT

Saint-Martin-Vésubie, November 1942– September 1943

THE VALLEY OF THE VAR RIVER leading north from Nice is broad and flat for several kilometers. Gradually, however, steep limestone hills appear, and both the valley and the road following it begin to narrow. After about thirty kilometers, at the point where the smaller Vésubie River flows into the Var from the northeast, the traveler to Saint-Martin-Vésubie forks right, entering a dark and gloomy gorge. The cliffs of the Gorges de la Vésubie now rise directly from the river and road, or even overhang them or yield to dank tunnels. Houses and entire villages seem to cling to the road to avoid hurtling down to the river below. In September, the month that is the focus of our story, the trees in the lower valley are rust and gold, but dark green conifers slowly dominate as the traveler climbs higher. To the northeast, bordering the Italian frontier, is the wild Parc National du Mercantour, once the hunting grounds of the dukes of Savoy and the kings of Italy. These are the southern Alps, or what the French call the Alpes Maritimes (the Maritime Alps) and the Mercantour range.

About sixty-seven kilometers north of Nice, the village of Saint-Martin-Vésubie (Alpes-Maritimes) lies at another confluence of waters. This time, two smaller streams, the Boréon from the north and the Madone de Fenestre from the northeast, join to form the Vésubie. The valleys are wider here, but the mountains are higher. The village stretches along a rocky promontory between the two streams. A beautiful central square shaded by plane trees occupies much of the available flat ground. Steep flagstone streets, alleys, and stairways flanked with ancient stone houses twist away from the square. Medieval drainage gutters still funnel fresh water down the middle of old streets, which widen at unexpected intervals into quiet little squares with ancient fountains. A medieval gate indicates one original point of entry. Mountain peaks tower in all directions. Locals call their region "La Suisse niçoise," the Switzerland of Nice.

The Italian influence is strong in La Suisse niçoise, as it is in Nice itself, and adds to the charm of the place. At least half of the surnames of residents in Saint-Martin-Vésubie have an Italian ring, as in Airaudi, Blanchi, Crenna, Gasiglia, Giraudi, Grinda, Morelato, and Vassallo. The local patois is a mixture of French and Piedmontese, the dialect spoken in northwestern Italy around Turin, and is understood on both sides of the mountains. After all, until 1860, the kings of Piedmont-Sardinia who presided over the unification of Italy controlled the city of Nice and the region of Savoy (today the two French departments of Savoie and Haute-Savoie south of Lake Geneva), as well as additional territory along the western slopes of the Maritime Alps that today form the border between Italy and France. Even after King Victor Emmanuel II ceded Nice and Savoy to Napoleon III in exchange for French support for Italian unification, he retained some of those western slopes, so that the border was several kilometers closer to the village of Saint-Martin-Vésubie than it is today.[1] Italians in search of work in France crossed the border easily, usually illegally. As a result, some eighty-three thousand people in the department of Alpes-Maritimes, or about 16 percent of the population, were of Italian origin on the eve of the Second World War.[2]

At an altitude of 928 meters above sea level, Saint-Martin-Vésubie offers a cool refuge in summer for hikers, climbers, and trout fishermen eager to escape the torrid heat of the Riviera. In the winter, frequent snowfalls invite skiing and other winter sports. Visitors arrive from the coast by bus or car in less than two hours and stay for a day, a weekend, or a season. Consequently, the village of about 1,650 inhabitants in 1943 has long been a popular resort, with numerous hotels, pensions, boarding houses, and, more recently, chalets outside of town. Before the Second World War, many English tourists came for the summer, staying in hotels like the Victoria, the Stéphany, the Londres, or the Châtaigneraie. They gave the village an air of elegance and sophistication, in marked contrast to the simplicity of the somber, hardworking local craftsmen, herdsmen, and peasants. But not all visitors were English. In the summer of 1939, Arthur Koestler wrote

Darkness at Noon in nearby Roquebillière. The elderly Italian Socialist leader Filippo Turati vacationed briefly in Peira-Cava, also nearby, during his period of exile from Fascist Italy. To the dismay of many locals, however, the tourist trade in the area died out during the war. Hotels in Saint-Martin-Vésubie remained vacant until the Italians temporarily occupying southern France east of the Rhône nearly doubled the local population by sending some 1,100 to 1,250 Jewish refugees up the mountain road from Nice to live there in the spring and summer of 1943.

The story of the Italian occupation of southeastern France began on November 8, 1942, when the Allies landed in North Africa. Three days later, the Germans in occupied northern France, declaring their intention to defend the Mediterranean coast, moved south and seized most of the rest of the country. As the Germans marched south, their Italian allies moved west from Menton, which they had controlled since July 1940. They occupied all or some of ten departments east of the Rhône River, including the cities of Nice, Cannes, Valence, Grenoble, and Vienne.[3] At last Mussolini regained the coveted territories lost to the French in 1860, and more.

While Italians rejoiced and the Germans and French grumbled, the Jews in southeastern France carefully assessed the situation. They were uneasy at first, for the new Italian occupiers were from a country that had been officially anti-Semitic since 1938. But within a few weeks, it became apparent that those occupiers would refuse to enforce the anti-Jewish policies of their German partner and the Vichy police on the scene. As early as December 1942, when the Vichy government ordered that all Jews in the formerly unoccupied zone must have their documents stamped "Juif" or "Juive," as had been done in the German-occupied north since the end of September 1940, the Italians refused to allow it in their area. Also in December, when Vichy police attempted to register or arrest foreign Jews in Italian-occupied France, pending expulsion to the German zone, the Italians ordered them released. Under no circumstances, the Italians declared, were Jews to be transferred out of the Italian zone. Within that zone, they could be arrested only by Italian authorities, except in cases of specific violation of the law.[4] Lya Haberman, who had been living with her family in Nice since the second half of 1940, says, "It was a paradise for us. The Italians even put carabinieri to guard the synagogue from the French police."

The Italians' refusal to enforce German and French anti-Jewish measures may be explained in part by their concern to assert their own authority against the demands of Vichy officials in the Italian-occupied zone, as well as by their resentment of their overbearing and often contemptuous German ally. But they also seem to have been genuinely sympathetic to the Jews and increasingly aware that deportation meant murder. After the Allied landings in North Africa and the German defeat at Stalingrad not long after, they also realized that the war might well be lost and did not want to incur responsibility for the Jewish genocide.[5]

The word spread like wildfire. The Italian zone was a good place for the Jews. Despite laws prohibiting movement without authorization, thousands of desperate people moved into southeastern France by train, bus, bicycle, or foot. Some were French citizens or longtime resident immigrants, but the majority were the most helpless—the recent immigrants and refugees who are the subject of this book. Some of these newcomers had false documents, while others had no papers at all. Some encouraged their children to travel separately, on the theory that the police would not bother with youngsters. Others traveled in large or small groups, with or without guides.

Most Jews fleeing into the Italian zone had little trouble crossing the Rhône. The German police, never numerous in France and now spread thin throughout almost the entire country, were increasingly concerned with partisans, while the Italians lacked the will to stop refugees. During the ten months of Italian occupation, southeastern France's Jewish population of some twenty thousand in March 1942 increased to at least twenty-five thousand, and perhaps to as many as forty or fifty thousand, most of them foreigners. Most newcomers initially settled in a thirty-kilometer strip along the Mediterranean coast on either side of, and including, Nice, where there had been only twelve to thirteen thousand Jews, including seven to eight thousand foreigners, in March 1942.[6] Because of the unofficial nature of the migration and the subsequent destruction of many Italian, French, and Jewish records when the Germans finally seized Nice in September 1943, more precise statistics do not exist.

Once in the Italian zone, the Jews again sorted themselves out along lines of national origin and length of time in France. French Jews, with their legal documents, friends, language skills, economic resources, and familiarity with the local scene, were usually able to settle in quickly without much help. Jewish immigrants in the country for many years found it more difficult, but most were able to get by as long as the Italians were in control. Recent Jewish immigrants and refugees, however, without papers, resources, and contacts, still needed assistance. For the most part, the Italian occupation authorities, understaffed, distracted, and often demoralized, allowed the Jewish community of Nice to deal with them.

Even before the Italian occupation, French and foreign Jews in Nice had organized a Centre d'Accueil, or reception center, under the direction of Ignace Fink, to help Jewish newcomers. Adjacent to the central synagogue at 24, boulevard Dubouchage, the center, also called the Comité d'Assistance aux Réfugiés, became popularly known as the Comité Dubouchage. As the trickle of newcomers turned into a flood after the Italians arrived, Italian occupation authorities encouraged volunteers from the committee to meet Jewish refugees in the bus and train stations and direct them to the boulevard Dubouchage. There, other volunteers urged the newcomers to destroy their false papers, if they had them, and accept new documents prepared by the committee on behalf of the Italians.[7] Copies of the resulting identification cards complete with photographs of the refugees were sent to the Italian police, who took the bearers under their protection.

Refugees with the new cards enjoyed many benefits. Above all, they could no longer be arrested by Vichy police as illegal aliens, a drain on the national economy, or violators of French laws against residence or travel without special permits.[8] In addition, the Italians issued ration books and housing permits to the card holders. Money for food and housing came from the Jews themselves. To support the poorest refugees, the Comité Dubouchage collected contributions from well-to-do French Jews along the Riviera, as well as from French Jewish organizations.[9] As long as the Italians remained in control, the system worked well.

Two of the witnesses interviewed for this book, William Blye and Lya Haberman, were already living in Nice before the Italian occupation. William and his mother, who had been there since 1939, had remained in hiding from the Vichy police in the city after the arrest of William's father and brothers in August 1942. They were no longer in danger after the Italians arrived, but they were without resources. In desperation, they turned to the Comité Dubouchage for sustenance. Lya, by contrast, whose father, Oscar, had immigrated to France in 1933 and was therefore not threatened with arrest in August 1942, lived at home for another year after that.

Most of our other witnesses, however, arrived in Nice soon after the Italian occupation. Among the first was Miriam Löwenwirth, who fled there with her father after securing his release from a French detention center near Chirac. Miriam then left her father with the Comité Dubouchage and returned to the German-occupied zone to fetch her mother and other siblings. Others arriving early were Jacques and Paulette Samson and their father, who traveled to Nice from Marseille, where the German occupiers had launched fierce roundups in January 1943. Jacques and Paulette had not registered as Jews in the census in German-occupied Paris, but now in Nice they declared their real identity. Walter Marx and his mother, Johanna, still reeling from the arrest of Ludwig in the reprisal roundup of February 20 and 21, 1943, in Lamalou-les-Bains, arrived a few weeks later. Boris Carmeli came to Nice from Toulouse with his parents, but he is not certain of the date. In other cases, parents arrived before their children. Sigi Hart's father, Hermann, for example, traveled to Nice and then summoned Sigi and his brother and sister from the Jewish children's homes where they were living.

Most of these newcomers would not remain in Nice for long. In meetings with German foreign minister Joachim von Ribbentrop in late February 1943 and with German ambassador to Italy Hans Georg von Mackensen on March 17, Mussolini came under intense pressure to do something about the "Jewish problem" in the Italian-occupied territories. As a result, he sent Guido Lospinoso, a former police chief of Bari, to Nice on March 19. According to Lospinoso, his mission was to placate the Germans by expediting the internment of *all* Jews in a camp one hundred kilometers from the coast. Instead, he worked with Angelo Donati, a prominent Italian Jewish banker living in France and a spokesman for the Jewish community there, and with the Comité Dubouchage of Nice to move Jewish refugees to supervised residence in the interior.[10]

The Italians had already begun the move in late February. Primarily a stalling measure, the relocation program nevertheless proceeded efficiently, with full cooperation from the Comité Dubouchage, which paid the expenses of the transfer and maintained the refugees in their new assigned residences. By the end of July, as many as five thousand people may have been relocated in resort villages in the hills and mountains of southeastern France such as Megève, Saint-Gervais, Castellane, Barcelonnette, Vence, Moutiers, Sainte-Marie, Venanson, and Saint-Martin-Vésubie, where rooms in hotels and pensions were available. By September 1943, there were about eight hundred refugees in Megève and almost six hundred in Saint-Gervais.[11] But Saint-Martin-Vésubie had the largest contingent. Already in early April, the village had received about five hundred refugees. By the end of August, that number had grown to between 1,100 and 1,250, and the Jews had spilled over into neighboring villages like La Bollène Vésubie, Roquebillière, Lantosque, Venanson, and Peira Cava.[12]

Most of the nine families discussed in this book moved from Nice to Saint-Martin-Vésubie during the late spring and early summer of 1943. Miriam Löwenwirth, Jacques and Paulette Samson, Walter Marx, Boris Carmeli, Sigi Hart, and William Blye were all sent there with their families. Charles Roman and Menahem Marienberg, however, followed a slightly different pattern, remaining in German-occupied France until a parent already settled in Saint-Martin-Vésubie summoned them. Charles Roman, still in his Compagnons de France uniform of blue shirt, shorts, and beret, simply climbed onto a train in July or August 1943 and traveled east. He had false papers but no special travel permits. He does not remember any particular problem crossing from German-occupied to Italian-occupied France. Generally speaking, that border was vague and much less heavily guarded than the demarcation line between occupied and unoccupied France had been.

Because Charles kept his false papers instead of exchanging them for documents from the Comite Dubouchage in Nice, he could not register for assigned residence in Saint-Martin-Vésubie. He became one of many Jews who lived there unofficially, always somewhat apprehensive that the Italians might make him leave if they discovered him. He did not, he says, join the social activities of the other young people.

When summoned by their father, Wolf, Menahem Marienberg in the EIF children's home of Lautrec and his brother, Léon, at Moissac also traveled to Saint-Martin-Vésubie, but separately. Léon, traveling alone, left first. When asked how it was possible for a nine-year-old boy to accomplish such a feat, Menahem, surprised by the question, replies, "But children were not children then. Léon was not a child anymore. The people at Moissac told him how to get there, and he did it. Only much later, in Israel, did I see him playing with marbles, and I saw that he was still a child after all."

Not long after Léon, Menahem also set off for the Italian-occupied zone. He traveled first to Nice, where he met his little brother, whom Wolf had sent to meet him and help him find a bus to Saint-Martin-Vésubie. In wartime France, even the buses and trucks were a challenge. Charles Roman describes them with a certain fondness. Most, he says, were *gazogènes*. Charcoal-burning units mounted outside the cabs, usually just behind the drivers' seats, produced a gas that powered the motors, barely. On steep mountain roads, passengers on the buses often had to get out and push. But Menahem and Léon arrived safely.

Fourteen-year-old Lya Haberman came to Saint-Martin-Vésubie from her home in Nice in yet another way. In December 1942, under German pressure to address alleged security problems, the Italians began interning several hundred politically suspect foreigners, mostly men but not only Jews, in their zone of occupation. Lya's father, Oscar, of military age, with military experience, and a potential candidate for the Resistance, was among those sent to a labor camp at Sospel (Alpes-Maritimes), on a winding mountain road about forty kilometers northeast of Nice, near the Italian frontier. The occupying authorities then suggested that Lya's mother, Chana, with Lya and her older sister, Hilda, go into supervised residence in the interior. According to Lya, Chana refused, and her refusal was accepted. It was apparently not Italian policy to force foreign Jews who had been residing legally in Nice before the Italians occupied it in November 1942 to move.[13] Chana did not want to take her daughters out of school. She was not well, and she did not believe that anyone would bother women and children.

After a few months at Sospel, Oscar was released and directed to Saint-Martin-Vésubie. His family remained in Nice until August 1943, when Lya had her school vacation. At that point, Chana sent her daughter to visit her father. Lya still remembers, "My mother went with me to the bus station. We had to wait for about three hours for the bus, which was very late. My mother cried and cried, and I did too. I never saw my mother again. That is my last memory of her."

While nearly all the refugees remember their arrival in Saint-Martin-Vésubie, none describe it better than Alfred Feldman, not from one of our nine families. Born in Hamburg in 1923, Alfred moved with his family to Belgium after Hitler came to power, like Sigi Hart and Boris Carmeli but slightly earlier. Like them and like the families of Menahem Marienberg and Miriam Löwenwirth, in Belgium since the 1920s, the Feldmans fled to France in May 1940. Directed to supervised residence in Montagnac (Hérault), Alfred lost his mother, Paula, and three sisters, Edith, Hella, and Jenny, in the roundups of August 26, 1942.[14] His father, Joachim, and grandmother Chinka then made their way to Nice and Saint-Martin-Vésubie, where Alfred joined them in the spring of 1943.

Of the village, Alfred has recorded, "I arrived in Saint-Martin toward evening and saw something that I had not seen for a long time: Jews walking peacefully through the streets, sitting in the cafés, and speaking in French, German, or other languages, even Yiddish. I saw carabinieri passing through the narrow streets of the village with their characteristic Napoleonic hats, and even a group of bersaglieri with their black plumes. Everything seemed to be happening freely, there were no particular regulations concerning relations between refugees. Discussion flourished with the greatest liberty."[15]

Walter Marx also remembers the elation brought on by the ability to speak his own language. He says, "The time in St. Martin was probably one of the best times of my life. It was like a paradise. After years of persecution by the Germans and the French, we could speak any language we wanted, publicly. In Montpellier, we had never been able to speak any foreign language at all. There was such an elated feeling of freedom."

Although the Italian occupation authorities requisitioned living quarters for the Jews assigned to Saint-Martin-Vésubie, the refugees themselves had some choice about specific assignments. Those with private savings could sometimes rent apartments more comfortable than any they had known for years, often sharing them with family and friends to ease the expense. For example, Alfred Feldman, who had been living in a simple stone house in Montagnac, declared, "My cousin . . . lived with others in an elegant villa, a bit outside of town. In the villa there was a piano: that is one of the things that impressed me the most, perhaps because it had been so long since I had heard the sound of a musical instrument."[16] Walter Marx also describes a comfortable apartment at 5, rue Kellerman. But even when living quarters were not elegant, the location was usually spectacular. Of his own apartment, Alfred recorded, "We had a marvelous view of the valley of the Vésubie." Sigi Hart must have been similarly impressed, for he says that his family nicknamed their apartment in a house across the river "Beau Soleil," or "Beautiful Sunshine." His family of five, it will be recalled, had lived in a single room in a French village for a year and had been in and out of three French internment camps, Agde, Le Vernet, and Gurs. Saint-Martin-Vésubie was luxury indeed.

Not all apartments offered comfort and views. Many refugee families, especially those who arrived a little later, were squeezed into single hotel rooms and obliged to take their meals in common. Some were not even in the village itself. Charles Roman recalls living with his mother in a room a half-hour's walk from town. But all were happy to be there, and most remember fondly where they lived. On September 8, 2003, for example, Menahem Marienberg returned for the first time since the war to celebrate the sixtieth anniversary of the Italian armistice and the Jews' flight over the Alps. With his two grandchildren Rakefet and Dekel, he walked straight to the Villa Ugo, where he had spent a brief but happy interlude. He also recognized one of the several still-functioning medieval gutters that had so intrigued him as a boy. He remembered his childhood fascination at the discovery that drinking water from the faucets in Saint-Martin-Vésubie was naturally "fizzy." And he recalled the terrifying road from Nice up to Saint-Martin-Vésubie, so narrow and full of curves that the buses had to stop to let the rare vehicles in the other lane pass. These were things that a sixteen-year-old boy would surely notice.

Food in Saint-Martin-Vésubie was expensive, rationed, and scarce, a condition aggravated by the presence of more than a thousand Jewish refugees. Charles Roman with his false papers remembers that his classification as a "Juvenile 3" entitled him, as a growing boy, to a larger sugar ration than many others received but that sugar was often not available. "You bought whatever you could," he says, but the queues for bread were long and shopping took hours. Hungry refugees scoured the surrounding countryside for food, feeding their families with trout from the local streams, vegetables purchased from peasants with cash or bartered goods, and wild mushrooms, strawberries, cherries, raspberries, and apples foraged during their respective seasons. It all sounds better than it was. Boris Carmeli still remembers his constant hunger and the monotony of a diet of beans in all varieties.

Charles Roman does not recall an extensive black market in Saint-Martin-Vésubie. He only remembers that a friendly butcher would occasionally slip him an extra lamb chop or two. Nevertheless, a black market clearly existed. Long before the Jews arrived, French and Italian smugglers had made a living by crossing the mountains between the two countries, carrying huge loads of Italian parmigiano cheese, rice, sausages, lard, and tobacco in one direction and French sugar, coffee, salt, and paper for rolling cigarettes in the other.[17] The trip, ten or eleven hours in each direction for those with "good legs," was extremely hazardous, involving the same steep, rocky unmarked trails that the Jews themselves would soon take. Torrential thunder storms and deadly blizzards could catch travelers unaware, as could the ever-present French and Italian border guards. But cordial relations between villagers on both sides of the frontier made the trip more pleasant, and the profits could be considerable. Jewish youngsters like Charles Roman may have been less aware of the resulting black market than their elders. But as they contemplated their uncertain future and the possibility that the Germans might one day arrive at Saint-Martin-Vésubie, they became increasingly conscious of trails leading to Italy.

◇ ◇ ◇

Unlike the situation in Italy, where internees and individuals in supervised residence were given small government subsidies, refugees in Italian-occupied France received nothing from the authorities. They were instead supported with great difficulty by the Comité Dubouchage in Nice. In Saint-Martin-Vésubie, consequently, many refugees took small jobs to help make ends meet. Most worked for self-help groups organized by the Jews themselves, such as a nursery school, kindergarten, and childcare center, a medical clinic, a communal kitchen, a laundry, and shoe repair and tailoring shops. Marianne Roman found work as a seamstress. Miriam Löwenwirth recalls, "For a period of time I worked with children in the home of a Jewish family. It was the first time that I had ever worked for payment. Afterwards, I worked in the laundry of a hotel. . . . I wanted to earn some money." A Viennese refugee named Frederick Thorn recorded that he worked as a teacher in the school set up for the youngest Jewish children, probably with help from OSE. Walter Marx's cousin Werner Isaac also had a job with a Jewish group. While still in Lamalou-les-Bains, Werner had taken a position as a *ravitailleur*, a purchaser of foodstuffs, for a small Jewish old age home. After the Italians occupied southeastern France, the entire home with some thirty to fifty elderly patients moved to Berthemont-les-Bains, just a few kilometers from Saint-Martin-Vésubie. Werner continued his job but often visited Walter and Walter's mother.[18]

Other refugees found work outside the Jewish community with local French residents. Sigi Hart, for example, the boy from Berlin who loved farmwork and had learned to milk cows, chop wood, plow fields, and cut hay while hiding in Juzet-de-Luchon, was delighted to help farmers in the surrounding area. Local manpower was short, for about one and a half million French soldiers, many of them agricultural workers, were prisoners of war in Germany in 1940; nine hundred thousand remained in 1944. Another 2,800 young men from the department of Alpes-Maritimes alone went to work in Germany between June and November 1942. Some 5,600 others did the same between December 1942 and August 1943.[19]

In addition to their work, the Jews in Saint-Martin-Vésubie had a wide choice of extracurricular activities. This was not by chance. The Comité Dubouchage in Nice appointed twenty-two-year-old, Polish-born Jacques Weintraub, an organizer of the Mouvement de jeunesse sioniste (MJS) and a Resistance activist, to act as a liaison between itself and the Jews in the village. Weintraub was based in Nice, but he designated two even younger refugee-associates, twenty-year-old David Blum and eighteen-year-old Ernst Appenzeller, to remain in Saint-Martin-Vésubie to ensure that the Jews there, and especially the young people, were kept busy. Blum was especially well prepared for the assignment, for he had organized educational and social activities in Agde while interned there with his family in 1941 and early 1942. A dedicated Zionist, he had also trained with a Jewish Resistance group near Lacaune (Tarn) in the Massif Central for a few weeks in 1943 before Jacques Weintraub sent him to Saint-Martin-Vésubie at the end of June.[20] Sigi Hart remembers Blum and Appenzeller, saying, "I mixed mostly with the Jewish boys of my age. There was an older group of boys, in their twenties. They organized things."

In addition to David Blum's group, other Jewish organizations, including UGIF, the Fédération des sociétés juives de France, OSE, and ORT also sent delegates to help the refugees. The results were impressive. With permission from the Italian authorities, a small synagogue was set up in the chalet Les Pervenches. According to refugee Harry Burger, the head of the carabinieri in the village frequently came to services there because he loved the voice of the cantor. Along with the nursery school and kindergarten, there were classes in Jewish history, Zionism, Hebrew, music, nursing, artisan skills, and farming. Also available were a chess club, a theater group, swimming parties, and a variety of sports. Sigi Hart, a gentle man today, enjoyed a boxing club. He also learned to play the mandolin. "It was wartime," he says, "and we couldn't get picks. Someone suggested that I use a tooth from a comb. It worked, and I still use that today." With the Italian soldiers, he played and sang Italian songs.[21]

Jacques Samson, practical and enterprising even then, remembers taking English lessons from a seventy-two-year-old English woman named Miss Mainehood. She had lived in Saint-Martin-Vésubie before the war and, like several other British citizens, was trapped there, or perhaps chose to remain, when hostilities broke out. Jacques also took piano lessons from a Madame Gorges, a Jewish refugee a little older than he.[22] But the most fortunate, with regard to music lessons, was fifteen-year-old Boris Carmeli, the boy who had informed his family at the age of five that he wanted to be an opera singer. Someone with influence in the Jewish community at Saint-Martin-Vésubie or Nice learned of his aspirations and convinced the Italian authorities to allow him to travel by bus to Nice once a week to take lessons at the Conservatoire. On each trip, Boris spent the night, so he actually took two lessons a week. It is not clear who paid for this training.

But for a lad who had been starved of music and education for more than two years, it must have seemed like a dream.

Nearly all refugees who were in their late teens in 1943 remember the joy of being together with youngsters of their own age in Saint-Martin-Vésubie. A few of them, like Charles Roman and Menahem Marienberg, had previously spent some time in homes for Jewish children, but others had lived almost exclusively with their families for several years, without even the outlet provided by going to school. Photographs of them from the Saint-Martin-Vésubie period are invariably of large groups of happy, healthy youngsters, cavorting with the carefree, zany abandon of teenagers everywhere. Nor were the groups always exclusively Jewish. Many young-sters made friends with their local French counterparts. Jacques Samson, particularly gregarious even today, especially remembers Carmen Giraudi (later, Parlarieu), the niece of the local baker. Carmen was a couple of years older than Jacques, but she liked him. She worked in the bakery, so she had access to extra bread coupons. Every night she left some for him in a letter box. Such indications of human kindness and consideration often meant more than the food itself. Jacques is still grateful.

As might be expected from a young woman who had essentially taken over responsibility for her entire large family, Miriam Löwenwirth's social relationships were more serious. Miriam pays special tribute to David Blum, like herself originally from Eastern Europe but a naturalized Belgian citizen after 1930. With David and his circle of friends, Miriam relished the luxury of long talks about Palestine. She also worked with David as a supervisor of Zionist youth groups.

Along with the parties, dances, and games, Walter Marx also remembers serious conversations with his peers. Much of the talk focused on the war and the deportations, of which most refugees knew very little. Walter had seen his father arrested in February, so the fate of deportees was very much on his mind, but he had not abandoned hope. Sometime during the summer of 1943, his mother had received from someone in the United States or Switzerland a notice that Walter's grandfather had died on January 15, 1943, in Theresienstadt.[23] But he had been seventy-seven years old, Walter says, so it seemed natural. Walter also recounts that at one point a strange man came into the office of the Jewish Committee at Saint-Martin-Vésubie, very excited and raving in Yiddish. Walter did not understand much Yiddish, but he understood "verbrennt Menschen" and "Oifen"—"burned men" and "ovens." But everyone thought the man was crazy.

Alfred Feldman, whose mother and sisters had been arrested in August 1942, has a similar version of this story. He relates that the Jews in Saint-Martin-Vésubie elected a committee to represent them in their dealings with the Italian carabinieri. Members of the committee also functioned as an information center. Alfred explains, "With press and radio censored, with foreign broadcasts jammed and few people having access to radio anyway, the tidbits of information the committee obtained from the carabinieri were invaluable." One day, Alfred's father told him that he had learned at the committee that two Jews who had escaped from a concentration camp in Poland had returned home to Nice to report that the Germans were murdering Jewish deportees. The information, Alfred adds, was unimaginable. "Not even living eyewitnesses could convey such depravity. Trusting that the absence of mail from my mother and sisters was due to the disruptions of the war, I did not relate their fate to the escapees' report, to which I gave no further thought."[24]

Alfred spent many hours visiting his grandmother Chinka Feldman at the old age home in Berthemont-les-Bains where Werner Isaac worked. The old woman watched the blood red sunsets caused by the summer haze and forest fires and insisted that a terrible battle was in progress and her children were in danger. Alfred assured her that the color of the sky had natural causes, but, he writes, she knew better.[25] Chinka lost three daughters and four grandchildren during the war before she herself died at Auschwitz.

Jacques Samson also recalls that the greatest hardship at Saint-Martin-Vésubie was being cut off from the rest of the world and having no news. He and his father and sister were tormented by their lack of information about the progress of the war and especially about the fate of Jacques's mother, Rajzla, and his two sisters, Chana and Malka, whom they had left behind in Poland when they moved to Paris in 1937. They would never learn exactly how or when they were murdered.

Many refugees mention the requirement that they report, morning and evening, to the Italian authorities in their office just off the main square of the village. Not only Jews had to report. Other foreigners in supervised residence in the village had to do the same. Frederick Thorn wrote of the routine, "It was an extremely interesting spectacle to see, next to Lady Butler and other elegant English aristocrats, some Jews in caftans with the characteristic curls, all of them gathered close together to respond, twice a day, to the roll call of the Italian carabinieri."[26] Scarcely a burden, the obligation was a welcome excuse for socializing for young and old alike. Public assembly had, for years, been dangerous and even illegal for Jews in occupied Europe. Increasing the pleasure of the occasion, the Italians seem to have been casual, friendly, and decidedly unbusinesslike. According to several witnesses, they simply checked off one's name on a list. In theory, refugees were confined to the village and the immediate surrounding area, but that regulation seems not to have been rigorously enforced.

Although the refugees' relations with the Italians were amicable, it is harder to determine the precise nature of their contacts with the local French villagers. Many Jews had come to Saint-Martin-Vésubie with favorable memories of the French men and women who had helped them at critical moments during the past few years. Sigi Hart, for example, was hidden in a small village for over a year and later warned in advance of the August 1942 roundup by a friendly French official. Boris Carmeli escaped arrest the same month because of a similar warning from a secretary of the local mayor. Jacques Samson was spared arrest for not registering in the Jewish census when a French policeman in Paris looked the other way. But other refugees had been scarred by French individuals who betrayed them. The fathers of Walter Marx and Charles Roman and the mother and two siblings of Menahem Marienberg were arrested by French, not German, police. Most refugees had both good and bad experiences. William Blye lost his father and brothers because a French concierge betrayed them, but he survived because a French woman helped him. Miriam Löwenwirth's father was arrested by the French but released when a French officer took pity on her. With this mixed background, the refugees were suspicious and sensitive when they arrived in Saint-Martin-Vésubie, and their accounts of their contacts with the French there differ.

Despite his earlier good experiences with the French, Sigi Hart's attitude hardened after his arrest and his time in Le Vernet and Gurs. He relates that he had little contact with the French in Saint-Martin-Vésubie. "They were neutral," he comments. "They knew they couldn't do anything to us. I was young, I didn't mix with them." He also recalls gleefully, "We used to walk by the French gendarmes, smiling. We knew that they couldn't do anything to us. The Italians had taken their guns away. Their holsters were empty, and they used them to carry cigarette butts. The Italians told us, 'If any gendarme tries anything, run away and come and tell us. Any Italian will help you.' We each had an identity card from the Italians for our rations. If I tell you there was one people that helped the Jews, it was the

Italians." But Sigi was speaking primarily about the French police. Relations with local civilians in Saint-Martin-Vésubie appear to have been friendlier on both sides.

Certainly there were reasons for tension, at least among adults who unfortunately are no longer alive to bear witness. Villagers viewed the Jews as protégés of the Italians, whom most French men and women resented as the occupiers of part of their country. Also, the Jews created an additional demand for scarce foodstuffs. With their subsidies from the Comité Dubouchage, they may have bid up the prices of some items in local shops and especially in the black market. They may also have undercut local wages by working for less money or simply for food. On the other hand, in the absence of tourists, many property owners in the village were overjoyed to rent rooms to the newcomers. In addition, the Jews lent a hand in the harvest of 1943, at a time when labor was short. They also brought a touch of the exotic to a remote village in wartime, where life for the local people was dreary. Some locals welcomed the influx, while others may have been suspicious and resentful.

The warmest French testimony about the Jews in the village comes from those who were teenagers at the time. Thus, René Gasiglia, son of the local banker Pierre Gasiglia, who had helped the Italian occupying authorities find living quarters for the refugees, says, "We [Jews and non-Jews] got along so well! For me, despite the war, what marvelous memories, what a beautiful vacation, that summer [of 1943]. Everything was beautiful, I experienced this urgent happiness with a sentiment of ephemerality because I dreaded, with the reopening of school, my departure for Monaco and my return to the severe discipline of the Christian Brothers." Jacques Samson's friend Carmen is even more eloquent:

> If you only knew what fun we young people, refugees and native villagers, had! We always had outsiders on summer vacations before the war, but with the exception of the sons and daughters of our few upper-class families, we young people never danced with the sons and daughters of the rich summer visitors. It was not even imaginable, while with the young Jewish refugees. . . .
>
> Most of them were very poor, but so rich in enthusiasm and new ideas! Even if it was for the worst, these unhappy people, forced out of their homes and sometimes separated from their

families, had at least traveled, seen the country, and they knew
so many things! Ah, with them, one was never bored for a
single minute . . . always on the go, always a project! There
was so much joy. We danced everywhere and every evening,
it was terrific![27]

Given the villagers' subsequent knowledge of the Holocaust and the
fate of many of the Jews who had lived among them, such positive postwar
testimony is not surprising. The spontaneous warmth and richness of the
language, however, make it convincing, as does the fact that it is confirmed
by many others.[28] But equally revealing is the fact that few refugees complain
about their contact with the villagers. Almost no Jews speak of price gouging
or nastiness at a time when most French men and women were suffering
from food shortages, the absence of their men, political repression, and the
humiliating foreign occupation of their country. Still more important, when
the Jews of Saint-Martin-Vésubie had to disperse in September 1943, some
villagers and peasants in the surrounding valleys hid those who chose not
to go to Italy. One of those hidden was sixteen-year-old Paulette Samson,
whose story will be told in chapter 10.

And so the summer of 1943 unfolded amid mountain peaks and glori-
ous, if ominous, red sunsets. The Jews in Saint-Martin-Vésubie were almost
at peace. In a kind of affirmation of life, Menahem Marienberg's Aunt Eva
gave birth to a daughter, Simone, on June 25. Named for Menahem's mother
who had been deported, Simone was one of twelve babies recorded as being
born to Jews in Saint-Martin-Vésubie during that spring and summer. There
may have been others who were never registered. In another indication of
a return to a semblance of normal life, there were also two marriages registered in Saint-Martin-Vésubie in August, and perhaps others not recorded.[29]
But blissful summers invariably come to an end. In the words of Bronka
Halpern, a young medical student from Warsaw who was one of the Jews
of Saint-Martin-Vésubie, it was all "too good to last."[30]

CHAPTER NINE

Crossing the Alps after September 8, 1943

THE MAIN ROAD FROM Nice to Saint-Martin-Vésubie does not end at the village. Instead, the mountains separating France from Italy, only about ten kilometers away at this point, force it to veer sharply to the west. North and east of Saint-Martin-Vésubie, two smaller paved roads twist insistently on toward the frontier, following the valleys of the mountain streams known as the Boréon and the Madone de Fenestre. These roads are postwar creations; before the war, they were mere tracks for shepherds and smugglers. The northern road ends just beyond the hamlet of Le Boréon, eight kilometers from Saint-Martin-Vésubie and 1,473 meters above sea level. Today this hamlet, a center for hikers, fishermen, horseback riders, campers, and skiers, boasts two or three small inns, an excellent restaurant, a beautiful lake, and a spectacular view. From here, the adventurous can follow a rocky footpath and climb above the tree line for another 1,070 meters, roughly, to the Col de Cerise, as the French call it, or the Colle Ciriegia, in Italian. In English it is called, less elegantly, Cherry Pass. From the top of the pass, at 2,543 meters above sea level, hikers can, if they so desire, descend undetected into Italy by another equally difficult path.

The eastern road out of Saint-Martin-Vésubie climbs for twelve kilometers through the magnificent Vallon de la Madone de Fenestre, with its dense forest of pine, larch, and oak, to a sanctuary of the same name. Set in a high mountain pasture, the sanctuary of the Madone de Fenestre, at about 1,903 meters, houses a statue of the Madonna during the summer. Pilgrims from France, Italy, and elsewhere find shelter and food in the large public buildings surrounding the chapel. In the autumn the faithful bear the statue back to the church in Saint-Martin-Vésubie. This process was not always so peaceful. During the late summer of 1938, when the French-Italian border was closer to Saint-Martin-Vésubie than it is today, a priest on the Italian side, undoubtedly inspired by Prime Minister Benito Mussolini's particular brand of nationalism, encouraged his parishioners to believe that the Madone de Fenestre was theirs. Before the regularly scheduled autumn procession, a group of young French men and women secreted her back to Saint-Martin-Vésubie, where she remained out of public view until 1945.[1]

As at Le Boréon, hikers can continue from the sanctuary of the Madone de Fenestre to another pass, the Col de Fenestre (Colle delle Finestre in Italian), at 2,471 meters above sea level. The ascent is difficult. Swinging sharply from right to left and back again in countless hairpin turns, the path consists of sharp rocks scattered between huge boulders. The footing is hazardous. Leaving all trees behind, hikers soon find themselves on a steep, desolate, wind-swept slope. Peaks up to 3,404 meters, covered most of the year with snow, tower on all sides. Grazing chamois and occasional ibex and wild sheep observe hikers with curiosity, while hawks and eagles circle overhead, tiny dots in the vastness of the landscape. The immense silence is broken by the shrill warning cries of hundreds of marmots echoing among the rocks. Only the ruins of several military bunkers tell the sorry tale of human habitation and strife. At the pass, a stone marker informs hikers that they are standing at what is today (but not during the war) the border between France and Italy. Just beyond the pass, with full command of the path descending into Italy, are the ruins of an old barracks manned by Italian Alpine troops during the Second World War. No soldiers or customs officials patrol the area today.

This haunting, wild, romantic region witnessed the exodus of the Jews of Saint-Martin-Vésubie in September 1943.

At 6:30 P.M. on September 8, 1943, U.S. General Dwight David Eisenhower announced that Prime Minister Marshal Pietro Badoglio of Italy had agreed to an armistice with the Allies. Badoglio had replaced Mussolini as head of government on July 25. At that time, fifteen days after British and American troops landed in Sicily, the Fascist Grand Council, the king, and the Italian army had withdrawn their support from the Duce. After several weeks of secret negotiations with the Allies, Badoglio's representative had signed the armistice on September 3, the same day that the Allied troops crossed the Straits of Messina to the Italian mainland. The armistice was to be made public about a week later.

Eisenhower's premature announcement caught Badoglio off guard, forcing him to repeat the information in a radio address to the Italian people an hour or two later. The Italians wildly rejoiced. In Italian-occupied France, the reaction of the French was similar. "By nightfall," one observer recalled, "Nice was one huge party. It was like the fourteenth of July [Bastille Day]. Women were kissing Italian soldiers, accordions were playing, couples were dancing in the streets."[2] But the euphoria did not last long. German troops on the borders of both Italy and Italian-occupied France were poised and ready for invasion. Badoglio had provided few details or instructions about how to deal with them.

The Italian Fourth Army occupying southeastern France had been seriously demoralized for weeks, even months, before the armistice.[3] By mid-1943, its soldiers were badly armed, badly supplied, and badly fed, especially in comparison to their German ally. They were also despised by the French as undeserving occupiers who had attacked France in June 1940 when it was being overrun by the Germans. Failing to achieve a significant victory at that time, the Italians had, in the French view, nevertheless ridden into their country in 1942 on German coattails. That German ally then treated the Italians with arrogance and contempt, denying them control of the major cities of Lyon and Marseille, adjacent to the Italian zone. French hostility and contempt were expressed through constant anti-Italian propaganda, frequent incidents, and the growing Resistance movement. The resulting demoralization increased further during the period of uncertainty between July 25 and September 8, when the Fascists were no longer in power in Italy. Italian soldiers saw themselves as fighting the unpopular Duce's war despite the fact that the Duce himself was gone. Aware that the Allies had reached Sicily, that northern Italian cities were being destroyed in British and American air raids, and that Italy was about to lose the war, they saw no reason why they should continue the struggle. They just wanted to go home.

Compounding the confusion on September 8, Axis army commanders had already agreed on August 15 that the Italians would relinquish much of their occupation zone north and west of Nice to their German partner in order to free their own troops for defense of the Italian mainland. As the withdrawal ensued on August 25, Italian officials on the scene, reluctant to leave the Jews to the mercy of the Germans, met to discuss measures to protect them. Meanwhile, an Italian-Jewish banker named Angelo Donati was working on an ambitious plan to transfer some thirty thousand Jews by ship from Italian-occupied France to Italy itself, and from there to North Africa.[4] In anticipation of this transfer, perhaps as many as two thousand foreign Jews in Megève, Saint-Gervais, and elsewhere, but not those in Saint-Martin-Vésubie, left their places of enforced residence and headed for Nice in open trucks. Some had help from the Comité Dubouchage, while others acted on their own initiative.[5] On September 8, many were still in transit.

News of the armistice hit these various plans like a thunderbolt. The German army invaded Italian-occupied France on September 9. Left without precise orders, officers of the Italian Fourth Army had no idea what to do. In his radio address, Badoglio asked soldiers to cease hostilities against the Allies but react to attacks "from any direction." As a result, an Italian unit at the railroad station in Nice resisted German disarmament attempts, without success. Further north, retreating Italian soldiers mined the tunnel at Fréjus, leading from France to Italy, and destroyed the rail lines on the Italian side. Italian Alpine troops in Albertville kept up a fusillade all night before surrendering to the Germans in the morning, while scattered battalions elsewhere also resisted briefly.[6] But many more Italian units simply surrendered without a fight. Meanwhile, every soldier who could, whether stationed on the coast or in the interior, headed for the Italian border.

Assuming that Italy was now out of the war and would be occupied by the Allies, an unknown number of Jews throughout Italian-occupied France, especially the most recent refugees, tried to follow the retreating Italian army. They could rarely keep the pace. Along the Mediterranean coast, some fled east and reached Italy by way of Ventimiglia. Others followed the soldiers north along a twisting mountain road east of Nice and entered Italy through the Col de Tende, east of the mountain passes at Saint-Martin-Vésubie. A few others managed to find a place on the last train from Nice to Cuneo, passing through the Col de Tende on September 10.[7]

Elsewhere in the Italian-occupied zone, some two hundred Jewish elderly, sick, and mothers with children who were considered too weak to travel in open trucks with the other Jews in Megève and Saint-Gervais found themselves on a train to Nice via Grenoble on September 8. When the Germans approached Grenoble, their train was diverted to Turin.[8] Still others in enforced residence in villages north of Saint-Martin-Vésubie, moving in small family units, tried to reach Switzerland or the northwestern corner of Italy known as the Val d'Aosta. German Jewish refugee Karl Elsberg, for example, with his wife and child and another adult couple, persuaded a reluctant French taxi driver to take them from Bourg-Saint-Maurice to the top of the Petit-Saint-Bernard Pass leading into Italy. From there, Karl convinced an equally reluctant Italian military truck driver to take them into the Val d'Aosta.[9] Some other refugees were similarly successful.

In Saint-Martin-Vésubie, news of Eisenhower's and Badoglio's announcements of the Italian armistice on September 8 arrived that evening. Anxious Jews congregated in the main square, trying to decide what to do. Three things were painfully clear to all: Italy was out of the war, the Italian soldiers in the village were preparing to leave for home by the shortest available route over the Alps, and the Germans would soon occupy the area. The Jews in the village had three options. They could remain where they were, on the dubious theory that the Germans would at least not bother the sick, the elderly, and the very young. They could go into hiding with local villagers and peasants whom they already knew to be friendly and with whom they could communicate in French. Or they could strike out across the formidable mountains, to arrive in a country where they knew no one, did not speak the language, and had no money, contacts, or friends, with winter coming on.

However difficult it might be, the Italian option had one apparent advantage. The Italians had signed an armistice with the Allies and were no longer at war. The Allies would be, or should be, or might be, occupying the country and helping refugees from France. Peace and security for the Jews might be waiting on the other side of the Alps. And even if the Allies had not yet arrived, the Italians had shown themselves to be sympathetic to Jews in France. They had protected them from the Germans and the Vichy French police. Was there any reason to fear that they would be less helpful in their own country?

According to many witnesses, the Italian occupation authorities in Saint-Martin-Vésubie advised the Jews to leave. Boris Carmeli, for example, recalls that shortly after the news of the armistice reached the village, the Italian commander convened all the refugees for an announcement. Until then, he told them, his official instructions had been to keep the Jews in the village and confirm their presence each day. Now things had to change. "Tomorrow or the day after," he informed his frightened audience, "the Germans will arrive. I will let you escape. I will tell my soldiers to look the other way." William Blye has the same memory, adding that the commander invited the Jews to follow the soldiers. Most did.

Still more decisive, perhaps, most Jewish leaders in the village recommended the same step. Although they had already foreseen, early in the summer of 1943, that the Germans might eventually seize Italian-occupied France, young men like Jacques Weintraub, David Blum, and Ernst Appenzeller had prepared few plans to hide Jews who might choose to remain in the area. Instead, they assumed that Italian soldiers would retreat over the Alps and defend their country until the Allies arrived. They had confidence that the Italians would succeed and would also protect the Jews. As a result, according to Blum, Weintraub instructed him upon his arrival in Saint-Martin-Vésubie to explore the mountain passes to Italy and prepare an escape route. Throughout the summer, with his brother and his friend Ernst Appenzeller, he did so. Now he did not hesitate. David Blum would himself lead the Jews over the passes.[10]

With the Germans expected in Saint-Martin-Vésubie at any time, it was hard for individual refugees and their families to resist this advice. Not all left on September 9 or 10, but most departed within the next few days. And yet many must have had doubts. Would not the Germans occupy Italy just as they were occupying southeastern France? And would the dissolving Italian army be in any condition to help Jewish refugees? As refugee Bronka Halpern later mused, "The logic inspiring this project [of crossing the Alps into Italy] has never been understood: there were no greater possibilities of survival in Italy than in France. The only logical explanation involves the impact on morale: to have the impression of doing something, of acting, of defending oneself, provided a certain courage."[11]

Lya Haberman and her father, Oscar, were among the first to leave. At first, Oscar wanted to return to Nice, where his wife, Chana, and elder daughter Hilda were living. But after learning that the Germans were already there, he realized that it would be almost impossible to reach them. "We really had no choice but to go to Italy," Lya explains. "We couldn't get to Nice. Of course, we did not anticipate that the mountains would be so big and the hike, so difficult."

Sigi Hart and his father, Hermann, brother Willy, sister Manya, and Manya's boyfriend, Ernst Breuer, also began the trek promptly, and with confidence. An enthusiastic mountaineer, Sigi had already hiked out of Saint-Martin-Vésubie, perhaps as far as the sanctuary of the Madone de

Fenestre, several times during the summer. And, he says, "When it comes to directions, I am very good." But despite those skills, Sigi recalls that most Jews tried to follow the Italian army rather than strike out on their own. They could not keep the pace for long. The army was in full retreat. Sigi remembers passing a barracks that was already mostly empty. It is not clear exactly where this was, for small Italian units were stationed at both the Col de Cerise and the Col de Fenestre, as well as at the sanctuary of the Madone de Fenestre and the lake just below the summit. The remains of several barracks are still visible today.

For all the refugees, the first part of the trip was the easiest. Whether they went the eight kilometers to Le Boréon or the twelve to the sanctuary of the Madone de Fenestre, they followed a mule track that wound along a stream and through the forest. At the end of the first day, most camped under the trees near one of those two locations. Fortunately, the weather was good, but it was cold at night. Although most refugees did not have warm clothes or blankets, the trees and the campfires offered some comfort. They ate the food they had brought with them and drank from the stream. Still more comforting were the lingering signs of civilization. Miriam Löwenwirth recalls finding a house along the way with an oven still warm and a kettle for boiling water. Her group gratefully enjoyed a tea break. Jacques Samson remembers that he and his father slept in a barn the first night. He also notes that some peasants gave them bread and polenta. Other refugees spent their first night on the trail in a former inn for religious pilgrims at the sanctuary of the Madone de Fenestre, currently being used by Italian soldiers stationed at the site, or in a carabinieri barracks. Several Italian officers and men, not yet in flight themselves, worked hard to make them comfortable.[12]

Despite the kindness of the Italian soldiers, several refugees recall strange goings-on during their first night on the trail. Sigi Hart tells of meeting soldiers who looked worried and uncertain. He and his family had camped near an Italian unit, and they received food and water from the soldiers.[13] In the middle of the night, he heard noises and scuffling. Thinking that the Germans had arrived, his group left in the dark in a panic. Sigi now believes that he heard the last of the Italians departing, fleeing the Germans just as the Jews were doing.

Charles Roman and his mother, Marianne, had an even bigger scare. Charles remembers being stopped by border guards at a checkpoint near the frontier and ordered to proceed no further. According to Second Lieutenant

Raimondo Luraghi, in charge of the sector around the Col de Fenestre and present at the sanctuary of the Madone de Fenestre on the night of September 10, this was because the guards had been ordered to prevent the refugees from continuing into Italy. That order reached Luraghi around midnight. As he recorded in his diary, "A great murmur of protest in every language of Europe issues from the immense crowd by now gathered there; some people follow me, others pull on my coat, still others put under my eyes documents of every type that I cannot even decipher." Fortunately the order was revoked the following day. Luraghi wrote, "I communicate it to [the refugees]: they leave running, shouting with joy. I breathe a sigh of relief."[14]

For most of the Jews from Saint-Martin-Vésubie, the second day on the trail, though perhaps less tense, was much more difficult. They were now above the tree line, with no visible trail through the awful boulders. Looking up, they could only see what Alfred Feldman called "a jagged wall of rocks." Alfred added, "Had I not been reassured by the sight of scattered groups of refugees progressing there, I might have been reluctant to venture onto this stretch, hewn into sheer rock, where the cliff to our right offered little to hold on to, where one didn't dare to look down, and where anyone coming from the opposite direction would have no room to pass. I had seen nothing like this with the Boy Scouts." Another refugee later wrote that it was "a miracle" that "there was no accident, no death."[15]

Lya Haberman remembers this part of the trip well. "We just followed each other like sheep," she says. "The other young people and I got to the top first. When we looked back, we saw a long straggly line. We were totally unprepared. We had wooden shoes, sandals, but we were walking on rocks and stones. There was no road at all. We followed the Italians for a while, but they soon disappeared."

Charles and Marianne Roman also found the second day more difficult than the first. They were accompanied by Franz Edelschein, the husband of Marianne's half sister, Grete, who had been arrested in Arles in August 1942 and deported the following month.[16] Franz was a former editor of the *Wiener Tagblatt*. Though only about forty-five, he had a hard time on the steepest parts of the hike and had to be helped for much of the way. Marianne, only a year younger than her brother-in-law, nevertheless had much less trouble. Charles remembers her saying to him, "Charlie, das ist wie der Auszug aus Aegypten"—"This is like the flight out of Egypt." Marianne was remarkable in another way, for she seems to have been the only person on the trek, besides her son, who had a camera. Marianne had studied photography at the ORT school in Agde and had kept her Contax camera from Vienna. Now and over the pass in Italy, she and Charles took pictures, developing the film several months later in Demonte, in the province of Cuneo. Their pictures provide a unique visual record of the flight across the Alps.[17]

"It was like a long snake," Charles says of the route above the tree line on the second day, using an image often evoked by those who were there. "You saw people in front of you and people behind. You would take a few steps up and then slide a few steps back. Some people had brought treasured possessions, like silver candlesticks, and had to throw them away." The refugees were also uncertain of the route. "On the way down into Italy," says Charles, concluding his description of the flight, "we followed a little stream, on the theory that streams went somewhere and eventually reached the ocean. And we followed each other."

The Habermans, Harts, and Romans found the trip difficult but reached their destination without excessive physical suffering, usually at the end of their second or third day on the trail. William Blye and his mother, Walter Marx and his mother, Jacques Samson and his father, and Boris Carmeli and his family all traveled with similar speed and, if not ease, at least lack of real agony. For families with young children, however, the situation was far worse. Even on the first day, Alfred Feldman writes, "I saw one [abandoned] suitcase and then another, this one half open, still fully packed. Suddenly this path felt like no other I had ever walked upon. . . . Occasionally we encountered soldiers who had joined a group of refugees, carrying their suitcases and even their children."[18] But the refugees moved too slowly, and the soldiers soon went on ahead.

Menahem Marienberg had already lost his mother, sister, and little brother in France in August 1942. Now he traveled with his father, Wolf, his brother Léon, and Aunt Eva and Uncle Isaac with their two children, one of whom, little Simone, had been born two and a half months before in Saint-Martin-Vésubie. Menahem relates that he carried the baby and went ahead of the group, in the hope of encouraging the others to keep going. They made it, but they exhausted every last ounce of their strength. They had no energy left to face the challenge of life in Italy, and, except for Menahem and Léon, they did not survive. Miriam Löwenwirth traveled with her parents and five siblings younger than herself, including a twenty-month-old baby. They too proceeded slowly, running short of food and water by the third day. Miriam and some of the other young people tried to arrange a system for sharing the food among all the walkers, according to need.

While many refugees took longer than the average three days and two nights, young men without families sometimes made the trip more quickly. Werner Isaac, for example, crossed the mountains alone, without his cousin Walter Marx and his Aunt Johanna. He explains that when the news of the armistice reached the old age home in Bertemont-les-Bains where he was working, all nonessential workers were allowed to leave.[19] The directors hoped that the patients would be safe because of their age but feared for the young. Although, like most other refugees, Werner does not remember his exact route, he thinks he made the crossing in two days and one night. Some even made it in a single day. Werner's story also indicates that not all the Jews who crossed the Col de Cerise or the Col de Fenestre to Italy were from Saint-Martin-Vésubie itself. Jews from the surrounding area poured into the French village after learning of the armistice, hoping to follow the others across the mountains. Some even came by bus or taxi from Nice.[20] Little is known of them. There are few records.

Alone or with families, however, all refugees shared the psychological burdens. Many had been fleeing from the Germans since Hitler had come to power in 1933. Others, devastated by anti-Semitism in Eastern Europe, had left parents and siblings and fled *to* Germany even before that. Men had given up professional positions and jobs not once but several times. Women had set up homes on many occasions, only to pack up and abandon them again. Their children had never known permanent homes. Now, in a desperate demonstration of courage and determination, these frightened people were on the road again. Almost no one turned back. Ahead of them lay a new country. All they knew of Italy was that its citizens had treated them well in the French village from which they were fleeing.

CHAPTER TEN

Those Who Stayed Behind

NOT ALL THE 1,100 to 1,250 Jews in Saint-Martin-Vésubie chose to flee over the mountains into Italy after the announcement of the Italian armistice with the Allies. An unknown number remained behind, trusting in the help and support of their French friends in the area and the Comité Dubouchage in Nice.[1] But, as it turned out, the Jewish committee could do little outside the city itself. Within hours, as the Italian army began its disorderly retreat behind its own frontiers, the German army marched into Nice. German police occupied bus and train terminals, blocked harbors, roads, and rail lines, and partially sealed the frontier, arresting thousands of Italian soldiers. Two days later, SS Captain Aloïs Brunner entered Nice with about fifteen highly trained SS police. A brutal indiscriminate roundup of Jews throughout the city, French and foreigners alike, began immediately.

Brunner labored under certain disadvantages in Nice. Most Jews in the city had registered in the special Jewish census called by the Vichy regime for the entire unoccupied zone in 1941, but the Italians had not kept those records updated after their arrival in November 1942. Jews throughout the Italian-occupied zone had never been required to have their documents stamped with the words "Juif" or "Juive," as happened elsewhere in France. Furthermore, both the Italian occupiers and the Comité Dubouchage with whom they worked to register and assist Jewish refugees in Nice destroyed most of their records before the Germans arrived. The SS police had no lists of Jewish names and addresses and no way to recognize Jews. But if Brunner experienced some disadvantages, so did the Jews themselves, for few had prepared hiding places and false documents. The result was chaos.

The story of the Nice roundup is best told by Russian-born, French-naturalized Léon Poliakov, who arrived in Nice at the end of August 1943 with the hope of helping Jewish refugees. Poliakov later wrote:

> Those official black Citroëns [of the police] cruised the streets
> of Nice, and passengers attentively scrutinized passers-by. At any
> moment, a pedestrian would be asked to get into a car. No use-
> less questions or identity checks. The car went to the synagogue.
> There the victim was undressed and, if he was circumcised, he
> automatically took his place in the next convoy to Drancy. . . .
>
> The official black Citroën method was not the only one. Other
> teams raided hotels, pensions, and furnished rooms, and took
> away entire Jewish families. Members of the [French] *Milice,*
> those jackals of the Gestapo, checked apartment buildings and
> made lists of names that sounded Jewish. Improvised physiog-
> nomists were posted in the stations.[2]

Once arrested, suspects were taken to the Hotel Excelsior in Nice, where they were brutally interrogated to make them reveal the locations of family members. A Jewish doctor sent to the hotel to treat victims described their condition. "Day and night, the greatest number of prisoners needed medical care: bandages for bullet wounds in the thigh, leg, buttocks; gashes in the scalp; an ear detached by a gun butt; multiple swellings and bruises all over the body; broken teeth; split lips; abrasions on the face; broken ribs; sprains; etc."[3] During the three-month period of Brunner's direct involvement in the Nice roundup, some eleven hundred Jews from Nice, another three hundred from along the coast, and about four hundred from villages in the interior of the former Italian zone underwent such treatment before being shipped to Drancy on twenty-seven separate trains. From there, they were sent on to Auschwitz on two trains in October, one in November, and two in December 1943, and others in 1944.[4] Few returned.

When Lya Haberman traveled to Saint-Martin-Vésubie to visit her father, Oscar, during her summer vacation, she left her mother, forty-four-year-old Chana, and her seventeen-year-old sister, Hilda, behind in Nice. Lya does not know how they were caught. Perhaps they were at home when German police and French militiamen combed their particular apartment building for Jews. Perhaps they were betrayed by one of the many informers in the city, paid from one hundred to one thousand francs by the Germans for every Jew identified. Shipped to Drancy, the two women were deported to Auschwitz on convoy 69 on March 7, 1944. The train carried 1,501 people, 500 more than usual. Included were 812 men and 689 women, of whom 178 were under the age of eighteen. Upon arrival, 110 men and about 80 women were selected to enter the camp for labor. The rest were immediately gassed. Thirty-four people returned after the war.[5] Chana and Hilda were not among them. Had Lya not gone to visit her father in Saint-Martin-Vésubie, she would almost certainly have shared their fate.

Perhaps not fully aware of what was happening in Nice, a number of Jews from Saint-Martin-Vésubie returned to that city during the period of maximum danger. One of these was sixteen-year-old Paulette Samson, who had traveled to Saint-Martin-Vésubie from Marseille, via Nice, with her father, Szlama, and her brother, Jacques, a few months before. After the armistice on September 8, when Szlama decided that he and Jacques would cross the Alps into Italy, he also chose to leave Paulette behind to spare her the arduous journey. After all, he did not expect to be in Italy for long. Within a week or two, he would return for her. In the meantime, why would the Germans be interested in a young girl, not strong enough for heavy labor?

Paulette relates that on September 21, ten to twelve days after most of the refugees left for Italy, German police arrived to round up Jews in Saint-Martin-Vésubie just as they had done in Nice. They ordered remaining Jews to report to the town square with their baggage, on pain of death. Some obeyed. A local informer helped the Germans identify others. Altogether, perhaps as many as a hundred, mostly elderly, Jews were caught, thrown into two waiting buses, and sent off to Nice, Drancy, and eventually Auschwitz.[6] Terrified by the initial German order, Paulette ran over to the Hôtel Stéphany where Gaston Abramovici, a young friend of Jacques and herself, was staying. Gaston was not registered as a Jew, so he was in little danger. Desperate, Paulette asked Gaston for advice. What should she do? Gaston was suave and nonchalant. Paulette obviously admired him. "Moi, à ta place, je n'irai pas," he declared succinctly, his pipe in his hand. "I, in your place, would not go." And so she didn't.

Paulette now turned to Fanny Vassallo, the owner of the Hôtel Stéphany, for help. Could she stay there with her? At first, Fanny was reluctant. Her brother was hiding from the authorities to avoid obligatory labor service in Germany, and she was afraid of endangering him. She was also responsible for two young nieces, Jeannine and Florette Boin, seventeen and thirteen years old, whom she feared might inadvertently reveal the secret. The local informer was constantly in the neighborhood, searching for Jews. And the Germans, she told Paulette, were threatening to shoot rescuers of Jews and burn their property. But finally Fanny agreed to let Paulette stay. The girl was at the hotel when the Germans came on a house-to-house search. Hovering in the dining room, she heard German voices asking her hostess if there were any Jews about. "No," the older woman replied. "See that old Jewish man crossing the square to turn himself in? He is the last of them."

The answer was apparently concrete enough that the Germans did not search the hotel. Paulette was not discovered. She later learned that Fanny was also hiding at least five other Jews: a sixteen-year-old boy, a woman whose husband was hiding in the mountains nearby, and a family of three. Fanny also collected and sometimes cooked food for other Jews in the surrounding countryside.

Despite the terrible danger, Paulette remained at the Hotel Stéphany until the end of November. Hidden in a small room on the top floor, she was not allowed to go downstairs, run water in the bathroom, or open the curtains. Fanny's niece Jeannine brought her meals on a tray. Finally, word came from Nice that a Jewish rescue organization was prepared to hide her elsewhere. Local Resistance activists, including Jeannine, supplied her and other Jews with good false papers. Fanny then accompanied Paulette in the bus to Nice, pretending that she did not know her. As they descended the bus, they spotted another informer known in Saint-Martin-Vésubie, hovering in the shadows and searching for Jews from the village who were hoping to hide in Nice. Paulette made a big show of hugging the mother of a non-Jewish friend from Saint-Martin-Vésubie whom she recognized in the crowd. The informer did not see her, and the moment passed.

Paulette then learned that the person from the Jewish committee who had promised to help her had been arrested. What should she do? Fortunately, the girl was quick-witted and had a good head for numbers. The only person she knew on the French Mediterranean coast was Simone Saïssi, a non-Jewish teenager from nearby Monaco who had spent part of the summer of 1943 vacationing with her parents and her sister Christiane in Saint-Martin-Vésubie. Paulette remembered her telephone number and called her. Simone's mother, Henriette, answered the phone. She did not hesitate. Of course Paulette should come immediately, on the bus. Buses were being thoroughly searched for Jews and other fugitives from the newly arrived Germans, but somehow Paulette made it. Henriette and her husband, Paul, had recently lost a fifteen-year-old daughter named Paule. They welcomed Paulette like a new daughter and saved her life.[7]

By a treaty of July 17, 1918, France recognized Monaco as an independent and sovereign nation so long as it respected an obligation to operate in "perfect conformity with the political, military, naval and economic interests of France."[8] During the first years of the war, including the period of the Italian occupation of southeastern France, the tiny principality enjoyed a discreet freedom of maneuver and became a haven for foreigners from all of Europe. When the Germans occupied the Italian zone, however, they began to exert pressure for the expulsion of the roughly one thousand to fifteen hundred Jews in Monaco. Local bureaucrats were unable to resist. As a result, roundups especially of foreign Jews occurred on September 17, 1943, before Paulette arrived, and again in January, February, and March 1944. About fifty-seven Jews were arrested, most of whom were sent to Drancy and from there to Auschwitz.[9]

Paulette could not stay more than a few days in Monaco. A hotel across the street from her hosts' home was full of Germans, greatly endangering her. With help from a Jewish agency—she does not recall if it was OSE or EIF—she moved to Lyon, where she hid in a different apartment each night and spent the days wandering the streets and warming herself in a local department store. She was then supplied with false papers and registered as a non-Jew at a hotel school in Poligny (Jura). When the school closed for the Christmas vacation, she was sent to a children's home in Florac (Lozère), the same town where Charles Roman had also lived for a time and where he had lost his stepfather, Wilhelm Bauer.

After the Christmas holidays, Paulette was unable to return to the hotel school. Desperate, she again phoned the Saïssi family in Monaco and was again welcomed there. But Monaco was more dangerous than ever for Jews. Paulette notes that she rarely left the house, and then only with members of the family. After a short time, therefore, she was sent to Le Chambon-sur-Lignon (Haute-Loire), the remarkable village high on a plateau in the Massif Central about forty-five kilometers east of Le Puy where some three thousand mostly Protestant townspeople and peasants hid at least five thousand Jews during the German occupation.[10] As seen, she had already lived there for a time in the spring of 1943. This time, Paulette lived at a children's home called Les Grillons and was protected by Roger Darcissac, the head of the local public school for boys. For his rescue of Jews during the war, Darcissac was honored as a Righteous Among the Nations in 1988. The local pastor, André Trocmé, and his wife, Magda, who had initiated rescue efforts in the village, had been similarly honored in 1971. André's second cousin Daniel Trocmé, supervisor of Les Grillons and the Maison des Roches, who was caught in June 1943 with some of the Jewish students he was hiding and deported to Majdanek, where he died, received the same award in 1976. Then in a highly unusual gesture in 1990, the entire population of Le Chambon was recognized as Righteous Among the Nations. Among those saved by that population is Paulette Samson, who remained there until the area was liberated in September 1944.

Still other Jews associated with Saint-Martin-Vésubie tried to hide in German-occupied Nice in September 1943. Paulette's friend Gaston Abramovici left Saint-Martin-Vésubie for the city, and survived there. Jacques Weintraub, the liaison between the Comité Dubouchage in Nice and the Jewish community of Saint-Martin-Vésubie, was not so fortunate. After sending delegates from Nice to Saint-Martin-Vésubie to advise the Jews to flee to Italy immediately after the armistice, Jacques attempted to organize help for those who could not or would not leave. He was arrested in Nice on September 23, 1943, shipped north to Drancy, and deported to Auschwitz on October 28, on convoy 61. Of the one thousand Jews on his deportation train, forty-two returned after the war.[11] Jacques was not among them.

Jacques's friend and associate Ernst Appenzeller, who, with David Blum, represented him in Saint-Martin-Vésubie, returned to Nice after most of the Jews in Saint-Martin-Vésubie left for Italy. Ernst was arrested at his home there on October 15, 1943. Sent to Drancy, this blond, "Aryan"-looking Austrian continued to protest that he was not Jewish and that his circumcision was medical in origin. He managed to convince the notorious Professor Georges Montandon, the Swiss-born, French-naturalized, self-appointed expert in the identification of Jews through their physical appearance, that he had been wrongfully arrested and was released. He then joined the Resistance and was eventually arrested again. Deported with fifty other prisoners on August 17, 1944, on the last convoy to leave Drancy, Ernst and at least fifteen others escaped from the train and survived. Most of those who were unable or too frightened to escape, especially the elderly, the sick, and the very young and their parents, were murdered at Auschwitz.[12]

Jacques and Ernst's colleague David Blum also remained in France, but he did not linger in Nice. After valiantly guiding one of the first and largest refugee groups from Saint-Martin-Vésubie to an Alpine pass leading to Italy, David joined a Zionist Resistance unit in the vicinity of Black Mountain, near Vabre (Tarn). His group merged with others to form the Organisation juive de combat (OJC) and worked closely with other local units of the general non-Communist and Communist Resistance. He and his comrades saw considerable military action against German troops. David was arrested on August 6, 1944, and deported to Buchenwald as a French partisan. He survived and ultimately returned to Belgium.[13]

Like David Blum, other Jews who stayed behind in Saint-Martin-Vésubie in September 1943 avoided Nice and hid elsewhere. No statistics exist, however, and reports are unfortunately vague. Some twenty families are known to have taken refuge in shepherds' huts or caves in the mountains, where they were helped first by shepherds and peasants and later by local French resistants and Jews from the Comité Dubouchage surviving in Nice. There may have been more. A few were caught, but the others remained in hiding until American soldiers reached Saint-Martin-Vésubie on September 2, 1944, eighteen days after the Allies landed on the French Mediterranean beaches and five days after the liberation of Nice on August 28. Other Jews from Saint-Martin-Vésubie were conducted in the autumn of 1943 to safe houses in Avignon, Marseille, Limoges, or elsewhere by friends and contacts in the French Resistance and eventually liberated there.[14]

Another group of Jews who stayed in the area of Saint-Martin-Vésubie did not do so by choice. Most of the thirty to fifty patients in the Jewish home for the elderly in Berthemont-les-Bains, where Werner Isaac worked, could never have made the hike over the Alps or sustained the rigors of hiding. One of these was Chinka Feldman, Alfred Feldman's grandmother. Alfred records that his father, before leaving with Alfred for Italy, scarcely even had time to say good-bye to the mother he had protected for years in France. Alfred thinks that his father may have simply scribbled her a hasty note. But who thought that the Nazis would be concerned with old women? Instead, when the Germans arrived in Saint-Martin-Vésubie on September 21, searching the village and consulting informers, they did not spare the home at nearby Berthemont-les-Bains. Chinka Feldman was arrested there, along with most of the other patients, probably on September 22 or 23. Sent back to Nice, thrown into a train for Drancy, and deported to Auschwitz, none of them had any chance of surviving.[15]

CHAPTER ELEVEN

The First Week in Italy, September 11–17, 1943

THE JEWS WHO CROSSED the Alps from Saint-Martin-Vésubie after September 8, 1943, entered the Italian province of Cuneo through two separate passes. Those who came through the Col de Cerise descended along a footpath or mule track into the valley of the Torrente Gesso della Valletta. No road, then or now, reaches the border at this point. Eventually picking up a road, the Jews passed through the tiny hamlets of Terme di Valdieri, Santa Anna di Valdieri, and San Lorenzo before arriving in the larger village of Valdieri, with a population of about 2,500 during the war. Residents of the isolated hamlets above Valdieri had little contact with the outside world. William Blye recalls that when his group passed through one of them, all the peasants came out to gawk. William thought it was because the Jews were speaking languages other than Italian and wearing city clothes. They did not look like mountain people. Only later was he told that the peasants were looking for horns. They thought that Jews had horns on their heads, like Moses and other Old Testament characters whose images they had seen in church.

Refugees who descended from the Col de Fenestre entered Italy slightly to the southeast of those hamlets. Their descent, again initially only a footpath, took them past tiny San Giacomo and into the valley of the Torrente Gesso di Entracque. That valley led to the village of Entracque, then about the same size as Valdieri but today a smaller but charming Alpine recreational center. At that point, the refugees had completed a descent of more than

fifteen hundred meters. A few families, the most exhausted, paused in Entracque, where they filled the inns, pensions, homes, and stables of all who
would have them. According to Bronka Halpern, the medical student from
Warsaw and refugee from Saint-Martin-Vésubie, the people of Entracque
were warm and welcoming, and the Jewish community of Cuneo sent coffee
and bread. "Our hearts filled again with hope," she recorded in her memoirs.
"The Italians were so good, everything would work out for the best."[1]

Just beyond Entracque, the two *torrenti*, or small streams, merge to form
the Gesso River and the valley that bears its name. Following the Gesso
for just a few kilometers from either Entracque or San Lorenzo, refugees
who had taken the Col de Fenestre joined those from the Col de Cerise in
Valdieri. The first arrivals from both routes were there by September 10.
Among them were Lya Haberman and her father, Oscar, who, with another
woman and her daughter, secured a room in a peasant's house. "They all
opened their houses and took people in," Lya says, "But they didn't know
how to digest us." Charles Roman with his mother and uncle also arrived
early and found a room in a farmer's house. To pay for it, Charles sold his
silver pocket watch for seventy-five lire, which he explains was a lot of money
at the time.[2] "We were well received by the local population," he recalls,
confirming the descriptions of other refugees.

Those who arrived in Valdieri a day or two later found less comfortable
lodgings. Menahem Marienberg and his family, for example, were allowed
to stay in what Menahem describes as "a big barn with fresh straw on the
floor, with many other people." But still the Jews kept coming. On September 12, Don Giuseppe Giordanengo, the parish priest of Valdieri, wrote in
his diary, "In the morning, it was Sunday, about two hundred Jews arrived
in Valdieri who had fled from France believing that Italy, having made the
armistice, would be a secure country for them, persecuted by Nazism. They
were lodged wherever possible. Twelve were sheltered in the parish house."[3]
More than seven hundred others would arrive in the days that followed.

Not all would stay. Several Jewish families believed that the crowds of
refugees in little Valdieri would attract too much attention. They continued
another ten kilometers to the northeast, still following the Gesso, to Borgo
San Dalmazzo, where they thought they could blend in better with a population nearly twice the size of Valdieri. At the eastern base of the Alps, a high
flat plateau spreads out from Borgo to the east and north. The provincial
capital of Cuneo, with a population of about forty-five thousand during the
war, sits in this plain, eight kilometers northeast of Borgo.

Among those who went on to Borgo San Dalmazzo were Walter Marx and his mother, Johanna. They must have been among the first to arrive, because they were able to book a room in the Hotel Cavallo Rosso. There they met Maddalena (Nella) Giraudo, whose father owned the hotel. About five years older than Walter, Nella was soon to play a critical role in their lives. Walter and Johanna also caught up with Walter's cousin Werner Isaac in Borgo.

Miriam Löwenwirth with her parents and five siblings also went on to Borgo San Dalmazzo, an unusual step for families with small children. Most such families were too exhausted upon arrival in Valdieri to go any further. As we shall see, that extra bit of travel probably saved their lives. But conditions were difficult in Borgo, where local civilian authorities were desperately trying to cope with the arriving refugees. As one exasperated bureaucrat explained to the prefect in Cuneo, most of the new arrivals had no money and none of the identification documents or ration cards necessary by law to stay in hotels or purchase food.[4] And in any case, the hotels and pensions were full.

Unfortunately for the refugees arriving in the province of Cuneo, all Italy was in chaos after September 8, 1943. Thousands of German soldiers waiting on the frontier in expectation of an Italian armistice with the Allies were pouring into the country; several army corps and divisions had already begun moving in mid-August. Germans already in the country as allies of Mussolini were disarming their former partners. Italian officers and their men who tried to resist were being mowed down. About 640,000 Italian soldiers eventually became prisoners of war and were shipped to German concentration camps, where about thirty thousand of them died.[5] Unknown thousands of others escaped arrest by deserting. Some of these went home, while others joined the partisans. Meanwhile, in a daring raid on September 12, German SS paratroopers rescued Mussolini from the mountain stronghold in central Italy where Marshal Badoglio had confined him. Hitler would soon set up the Duce at the town of Salò on Lago di Garda as the titular head of the new Italian Social Republic, also called the Republic of Salò. To the dismay of most, the Italians found themselves again at war on the side of the Third Reich against the Allies.

In Valdieri it was soon tragically clear that the Germans, not the Allies, would occupy the region. The result was panic, compounded by the presence in the province of Cuneo of some fifty thousand frightened deserters from the Italian Fourth Army, passing through from France at the same time that the Jews from Saint-Martin-Vésubie were arriving. On Sunday, September 12, in the same diary entry where he recorded the arrival of two hundred Jewish refugees, parish priest Don Giuseppe Giordanengo wrote, "Dissolution of the army. Invasion and looting of the barracks. The five hundred [Italian] soldiers who were based in Valdieri were only looking for civilian clothes so they could run away."[6] Of the same situation, Charles Roman says, "Everything was in chaos, and the locals were looting the abandoned military barracks in Valdieri." Charles remembers doing a little looting himself, going to the barracks to get hardtack.

Sigi Hart did the same. When Sigi's family arrived in Valdieri, his father, Hermann, immediately decided that they would not stay. Instead, he declared, they would gather supplies and settle in the mountains above the village. Observing that the people of Valdieri were helping themselves to everything they could carry from the abandoned barracks, Sigi and Ernst Breuer, his sister Manya's boyfriend, took a large sixty- or seventy-pound box of hardtack. They lived on that for several days.

On that same Sunday, September 12, the Third Battalion of the German First SS Panzer Division Leibstandarte Adolf Hitler, commanded by SS Major Joachim Peiper, occupied Cuneo, trapping Italian soldiers and Jewish refugees from Saint-Martin-Vésubie in the mountains and plateau to the west. Peiper concentrated first on the soldiers, capturing thousands. Roughly five thousand former Italian soldiers were ultimately arrested in the province of Cuneo and sent to Germany. Those who had shed their uniforms for civilian clothes were treated most harshly. At least one young soldier, Leonardo Bagni, from an Alpine unit in the Pusteria Division, was captured in civilian clothes in Borgo San Dalmazzo and shot there on Saturday, September 18.[7]

Also on Sunday afternoon, September 12, an outspoken anti-Fascist lawyer from Cuneo named Duccio Galimberti, with thirteen other young men of a similar political persuasion, settled into the sanctuary of the Madonna del Colletto, eighteen kilometers to the west. About halfway up the steep ridge separating the valley of the Gesso from the valley of the Stura to the north, the shrine overlooked Valdieri. Galimberti had acquired a reputation as an anti-Fascist on July 26, 1943, the day after Mussolini's dismissal as prime minister, when he spoke to a large crowd in Cuneo. The war would undoubtedly continue, he informed them, and it would soon be necessary to resist both the invading Germans and their die-hard Fascist supporters.

Now on September 12, he and his associates prepared to do exactly that. Three of these early partisans, the brothers Enzo and Riccardo Cavaglion, born in Cuneo in 1919 and 1922, respectively, and Ildo Vivanti, from Brescia, were Jews.[8] Calling their formation Italia Libera, the partisans immediately set about gathering recruits and arms.[9]

This dangerous mixture of German SS troops, Jewish refugees, Italian military deserters, and anti-Nazi partisans inevitably exploded. In the province of Cuneo, the trouble began in the village of Boves, about five kilometers southeast of Borgo San Dalmazzo. On a quiet Sunday morning, September 19, exactly one week after the Germans arrived in Cuneo and Galimberti appeared above Valdieri, a group of Italian partisans who had come to Boves by chance to buy bread seized and carried off two German SS soldiers passing through the piazza. Forty-five minutes later, other SS soldiers arrived and fighting broke out nearby. In the exchange of fire, one SS soldier and one partisan were killed. When SS Major Peiper arrived at Boves an hour or two later with still more troops, he charged the local parish priest, Don Giuseppe Bernardi, and a local citizen, Antonio Vassallo, with the task of recovering the two German prisoners. The two Italians obeyed, returning with their prisoners within an hour. But Peiper was determined to teach the Italians a lesson. After surrounding the village, his troops set fire to at least 350 houses and massacred at least twenty-three innocent civilians. Among the dead were Don Bernardi and Antonio Vassallo, whose bodies were thrown into the flames and charred beyond recognition. Also shot multiple times while he was attending a dying man was the twenty-three-year-old vice-curate of the town, Don Mario Ghibaudo. For the non-Jewish citizens of the province of Cuneo, the reign of terror had begun.[10]

For Jews in northern Italy, including those from Saint-Martin-Vésubie, the terror had begun even earlier. The first deportation train left Italy from Merano, near the Brenner Pass, on September 16, carrying thirty-five Jews to Reichenau in Austria, and later to Auschwitz. One person returned after the war. On September 19 in Novara, at least three other Jews were arrested and disappeared without a trace. A few days earlier, SS soldiers from the First Battalion of the German First SS Panzer Division Leibstandarte Adolf Hitler had descended upon hotels, pensions, and private homes in beautiful resort towns along Lago Maggiore, searching for Jewish families that had fled there to escape Allied air raids, especially in Milan. The men from the SS Division had recently been transferred from the Russian front to northern Italy for rest and relaxation. They had acquired a fearful reputation for violence against civilians in Russia, and now they demonstrated that capacity again. In Meina, Baveno, Arona, Stresa, Pian Nava, and Orta San Giulio, they seized fifty-four Jews, including many children and elderly grandparents. In the days that followed, they brutally murdered their prisoners. They shot some and threw their bodies into the lake. Others they beat and drowned.[11] Word of these atrocities trickled out slowly. The Jews from Saint-Martin-Vésubie knew nothing of them when their own ordeal began on September 18.

Street scene in Saint-Martin-Vésubie (Photograph by Susan Zuccotti)

Refugees from Saint-Martin-Vésubie on the path to Valdieri, September 1943
(Courtesy of Charles Roman)

The mountain path across
the Maritime Alps from Saint-
Martin-Vésubie to Valdieri
(Photograph by Susan Zuccotti)

Valdieri, in the province of Cuneo (Courtesy of Charles and Inge Roman)

The sanctuary of the Madonna del Colletto, where many refugees from Saint-Martin-Vésubie hid during and after the German SS roundup in Valdieri on September 18, 1943 (Photograph by Susan Zuccotti)

The train station in Borgo San Dalmazzo from which about 349 Jewish refugees were deported back to France on November 21, 1943, and from there to Auschwitz. Boxcars from the period of the war commemorate the tragedy. (Photograph by Susan Zuccotti)

A hut in the mountains above Demonte, in the province of Cuneo. Charles Roman and his mother hid here during the winter of 1943–44. Scores of Jewish refugees hid in similar huts, sometimes for two winters. (Courtesy of Charles Roman)

The Samsonowicz (later Samson) family at home in Rawa Mazowiecka, Poland, in 1935 or 1936. The children, from left to right, are Chana, Paulette, Jacques (standing), and Malka, with their parents, Rajzla and Szlama. Rajzla, Chana, and Malka were murdered by the Nazis in Poland. (Courtesy of Paulette Samson Grunberg)

Left: Szlama Samsonowicz in his uniform of the French Foreign Legion, 1940 (Courtesy of Paulette Samson Grunberg). *Right:* Lya Haberman in Paris in 1938 with her mother, Chana, father, Oscar, and older sister, Hilda. Chana and Hilda were arrested in Nice in September 1943. They were deported and died at Auschwitz. (Courtesy of Lya Haberman Quitt)

Lya Haberman, center, with two Italian friends in Florence in 1944, where she was hiding with a non-Jewish couple under the name Lydia Mazzola (Courtesy of Lya Haberman Quitt)

William Blye, right, in Nice in 1941 or 1942, with his mother, Maria, and his two brothers, Leo, left, and Bernhard, wearing beret. Leo, Bernhard, and their father, Chaim, were arrested in Nice by Vichy French police in August 1942. They were deported to Poland, where they died. (Courtesy of William Blye)

William Blye's father, Chaim Bleiweiss, mother, Maria, and brother, Bernhard, in Venice before the war (Courtesy of William Blye)

Left: William Blye's mother, Maria, left, in white blouse, in Nice after the war, with Sonia Futerman, whose husband, Bernardo, and sixteen-year-old son, Marcel, were murdered by Italian Fascist militiamen in Cuneo in the last days of the war (Courtesy of William Blye). *Right:* Charles Roman with his father, Leopold, in Vienna before the war. Vichy police delivered Leopold to the Germans in August 1942. He was deported to Poland, where he died. (Courtesy of Charles Roman)

Left: Charles Roman, visiting his mother, Marianne, in the town of Agde toward the end of 1942 (Courtesy of Charles Roman). *Right:* Charles Roman in his uniform as a member of the Compagnons de France, a Vichy youth organization in which he hid, with false papers, in the spring of 1943 (Courtesy of Charles Roman)

Left: Menahem Marienberg, right, in Brussels, with his sister, Mina, and his brother Léon, before the birth of their brother Maurice in 1938 (Courtesy of Menahem Marienberg). *Right:* Menahem Marienberg's father, Wolf, mother, Simone, and youngest brother, Maurice, just before or in the first year of the war. Vichy police delivered Simone, Mina, and Maurice to the Germans in August 1942. They were deported to Auschwitz, where they died. Wolf was arrested near Valdieri on September 18, 1943, and deported back to France and then to Auschwitz, where he died. (Courtesy of Menahem Marienberg)

Menahem Marienberg, middle row, third from left, with his boxing group in Saint-Martin-Vésubie, summer 1943 (Courtesy of Menahem Marienberg)

Miriam Löwenwirth, far right, with her mother, Elena, her father, Eliyahu, and all but one of her siblings, Antwerp, 1935 (Courtesy of Miriam Löwenwirth Reuveni)

Miriam Löwenwirth with her father, Eliyahu, and youngest brother, Ben Zion, in Quarante (Hérault), 1942. Eliyahu was arrested in Florence in 1944 and deported to Bergen-Belsen and then to a camp near Dachau, where he died. (Courtesy of Miriam Löwenwirth Reuveni)

Miriam Löwenwirth, second row, center, with a group of friends in Saint-Martin-Vésubie, 1943 (Courtesy of Miriam Löwenwirth Reuveni)

Sigi Hart, front left, with his father, Hermann Hartmayer, his sister, Manya, and his brother, Willy, in Berlin in 1935 (Courtesy of Sigi Hart)

Left: Sigi Hart with his mother, Adela, in Toulouse, two weeks after his liberation from Auschwitz and Bergen-Belsen. Sigi is wearing a French flag in his lapel. (Courtesy of Sigi Hart). *Right:* Walter Marx, left, with his father, Ludwig, mother, Johanna, and cousin, Werner Isaac, before the war. Ludwig was arrested by French police in February 1943. Johanna was arrested by German SS soldiers in Borgo San Dalmazzo on September 18, 1943. Both were deported to Poland, where they died. (Courtesy of Walter Marx and the Jewish Partisan Educational Foundation)

Walter Marx, far right, with Werner Isaac, center, and William Blye, left, on a visit to the Statue of Liberty, New York City, 1948 (Courtesy of William Blye)

Boris Carmeli with his mother, Rachel Wolfinger, in Germany in 1937 (Courtesy of Boris Carmeli)

Left: Boris Carmeli (then Norbert Wolfinger) with his older brother, Pinkas (later Peter Carmeli), in Germany around 1937 (Courtesy of Boris Carmeli). *Right:* Boris Carmeli in Paris just after the war. He had gained twenty-two pounds since his return from Auschwitz, but his cousin still did not recognize him. (Courtesy of Boris Carmeli)

Left: Fanny Vassallo, a French hotelkeeper, who hid Paulette Samson for two critical months after the German roundup of Jews remaining in Saint-Martin-Vésubie after the exodus of the majority in September 1943 (Courtesy of Danielle Baudot Laksine). *Above:* Giuseppe Meinardi, director of the hospital of Santa Croce in Cuneo, who saved Walter Marx and Menahem and Léon Marienberg by transferring them to his hospital when they were injured or ill, warning them when the Germans were coming for them, and, in the case of the Marienbergs, hiding them on a farm or in other medical institutions until the end of the war (Courtesy of Menahem Marienberg)

Don Raimondo Viale, the parish priest of Borgo San Dalmazzo, who enabled Miriam Löwenwirth and her large family to escape the German roundup of Jews in that town on September 18, 1943. Don Viale then organized a rescue network, staffed mostly by priests, including himself, that delivered essential Delasem funds to the Jews from Saint-Martin-Vésubie who were hiding in the surrounding mountains. He and his assistants also helped Jews escape to Switzerland or move south to Florence or Rome. (From Elena Giuliano and Gino Borgna, *Cella n. zero: Memorie di un prete giusto e resistente* [Cuneo: AGA, 1994])

CHAPTER TWELVE

The Roundup in Valdieri and Borgo San Dalmazzo, September 18, 1943

ON THE RAINY SATURDAY MORNING of September 18, 1943, SS Captain Müller, the local German commander in Borgo San Dalmazzo, printed a poster and ordered that it be put up throughout the valley of the Gesso and its tributaries. The poster announced that by 6:00 P.M. that same evening, all "foreigners" in the area must present themselves at the barracks of the Italian Alpine troops in Borgo, on pain of death for themselves and all who helped them. Müller originally used the word "Jews" rather than "foreigners" on his poster, but someone, probably an Italian official, pointed out that the local peasants had no idea what "Jews" meant.[1] They would certainly understand "foreigners."

To help persuade the Jews to surrender, Müller seems to have sent just one or two German SS soldiers to Valdieri and one to Entracque. But many Jews needed little convincing. The cold, damp autumn air already bore menacing hints of the coming winter. They had no money, no identification cards, no ration books, almost no possessions. They were exhausted and often sick. Most spoke no Italian. They knew no one. How could they find places to live when the local people were threatened with death for helping them? Roughly 350 new arrivals, especially those with elderly parents, small children, or sick relatives, either obeyed the summons or were caught.[2] The barracks in Borgo now became their prison.

Among those unable to continue was Menahem Marienberg's family in

Valdieri. Menahem's Uncle Isaac, the brother of his father, Wolf, suffered from tuberculosis. With a two and a half-month-old baby, Aunt Eva was afraid to go into hiding in the mountains. When Isaac and Eva decided to obey the summons with their baby and their six-year-old son, also named Menahem, Wolf declared that he would stay to help them. Wolf's sons Menahem and Léon had little choice. They all turned themselves in. With hundreds of other Jews from Valdieri, they were taken to the barracks in Borgo San Dalmazzo.

Also in trouble on that terrible day were Walter Marx with his mother, Johanna, and his cousin Werner Isaac. They knew that they could no longer elude the German authorities if they remained at the hotel in Borgo San Dalmazzo where they had been staying. At first they tried to hide in a barn, but the peasant owner told them to move on. Borgo was not surrounded on all sides by the mountains, as were Valdieri and Entracque. It was not easy to reach the forests to hide. With much reluctance, mother, son, and cousin went to the barracks and turned themselves in. "We had no idea what was going to happen," Walter says. "We had no money. We were tired. And the notice said we'd be shot if we didn't report." He adds that they still hoped the Allies would arrive soon and that they would be held by the Germans for only a few weeks, as a security measure.

Each of our other seven families had a close brush with disaster in or around Valdieri on September 18, but each was ultimately more fortunate than the Marienbergs and the Marxes. Fourteen-year-old Lya Haberman was alone in Valdieri that day, in the home of the peasant woman where she and her father, Oscar, had found lodgings. Early on that morning Oscar had taken a bus from Valdieri to Borgo San Dalmazzo, probably, Lya says, to sell something and get some money. Lya recalls the arrival of two Germans, one on a white horse and another on a motorcycle. The Germans put up the infamous poster and announced that all Jews in Valdieri were to go to the piazza, on pain of death for disobedience. Even without her father, Lya bravely prepared to disobey. When she came out of her house and turned toward the nearby mountains, however, the Germans were there. She was sent to the piazza.

What happened next is amazing only if one does not understand Lya's character. It was raining hard. In the piazza, Lya still saw only the same two Germans. She said to one of them, about seventeen or eighteen years old, she thinks, "What you do to the Jews, the Russians will do to you." "How did I have the nerve?" she wonders today. Then she asked him if she could go back to her house to get a blanket. He agreed, and when she reached the house, she kept right on going. The woman who owned the house saw her climbing the ridge on the north side of the village. It was dark and thundering. "Every time there was lightning," Lya shudders, "I thought it was a German in the bushes with a flashlight. To this day, I am still scared of thunder and lightning." But she was no longer alone. She met several groups of Jews doing the same thing, going up into the mountains.

Lya ultimately reached the sanctuary of the Madonna del Colletto, where Duccio Galimberti and other young men from the area had announced their defiance of the Germans and established their tiny band of partisans less than a week before. Consisting of a chapel and a small adjoining building, the sanctuary offered some shelter but nothing to eat. Someone had to go back down to the village to buy food. "I did not look very Jewish," says Lya, "whatever that means. I had fair hair with braids." She was chosen, among others. The German with the horse was still in Valdieri, making rounds. She waited until he was out of sight and then went to the house on the edge of town where she had been staying. The woman gave her some polenta. "To this day, I love polenta," Lya says gratefully. The woman told her that her father was looking for her, so she told the woman where she was hiding. From the Madonna del Colletto, the Jews could look down on the village. Finally they saw Oscar coming up the ridge with the woman's little boy as a guide.

Oscar told the group his story. He had finished his business and was sitting in a café in Borgo San Dalmazzo, waiting for a bus to return to Valdieri. Other Jews who knew him and were aware of the roundup told him not to go back there. They informed him that all the Jews in Valdieri had been caught and that his daughter had been seen in the piazza. She had undoubtedly been taken with the others to the barracks in Borgo, where he was. Sitting there smoking and trying to decide what to do, Oscar saw an Italian woman who had been a guard at Sospel pass by. Like so many Italian military personnel, she had retreated to the province of Cuneo. The woman immediately recognized him; Lya explains that he was a handsome man, charming and well-spoken. When Oscar informed her that his daughter had been caught, she assured him she would do what she could to help. She went to the barracks in Borgo and learned that Lya was not there. She then located the woman in Valdieri in whose home Lya and her father had been staying and discovered that the girl was in the mountains. Oscar was reunited with his daughter.

◇ ◇ ◇

Charles Roman, with his mother, Marianne, and her brother-in-law, Franz Edelschein, was also among the Jews at the Madonna del Colletto, although they arrived there a little later than Lya. When the poster went up in Valdieri, the three went out the back door of the farmhouse where they were staying and kept going. At first, they went only part way up the mountain ridge on the north side of the town, from where they could look down on the road leading from Valdieri to Borgo. Charles recalls, "From where we were, we could see people being herded like sheep in the rain, under guard, along the road to Borgo San Dalmazzo." It must be an image difficult to forget.

The mountains around Valdieri were heavily terraced for agriculture. Charles and the two adults found a little niche used by the farmers for shelter from the rain. They spent two nights there, but it was so small that their feet stuck out. They had nothing to eat until the second morning, when a woman from the house where they had been staying brought her cow up to them and milked her right there, giving them the milk. But the woman advised them not to return to the village, which was under German scrutiny and very dangerous. So the three fugitives went further up the steep mountain until they found a cave where they rested for a few hours until a downpour filled it with water. Ascending further, they finally reached the sanctuary of the Madonna del Colletto.

Charles estimates that there were fifty to seventy-five other Jews from Saint-Martin-Vésubie hiding at the sanctuary. They came and went, so their number tended to change, but such a large group was dangerous. Some of the partisans were also still in the immediate area. The Jewish partisans Enzo and Riccardo Cavaglion, from Cuneo, who are today Charles's good friends, were especially attentive to the refugees, putting down straw for them to sleep on. Sixteen-year-old Charles met Lya Haberman for the first time at the Madonna del Colletto. Lya, two years younger, does not remember him. Sixty years later, she asked him what she was like then. "You were cute," Charles replied, without missing a beat.

Both Lya and Charles note that food at the sanctuary was a problem, for there were only chestnuts and a few potatoes in the surrounding fields. Charles met Leopold (Poldi) Neumann, a boy about his own age, also from Saint-Martin-Vésubie, and together they went back to Valdieri several times in search of food.[3] The trip was difficult as well as hazardous. Charles notes that there was no road from the Madonna del Colletto down the southern slope of the ridge to Valdieri, as there is today. There was only a steep and rocky footpath. The only road on the ridge led down the northern side, to the village of Festiona and the valley of the Stura.

One day at the end of September or early October, as Charles and Poldi approached Valdieri in search of food, they were spotted and chased by a group of Fascist militiamen. Poldi managed to escape, but Charles was caught and taken to the local barracks for interrogation. Still in his uniform as a French Compagnon de France (he had little else to wear), Charles claimed that he was lost and hungry. Not unkind, the men took his money and bought him a sandwich. They then turned him over to other Fascists with instructions to take him by bus to the barracks in Borgo San Dalmazzo—the same place where the Jews arrested on September 18 were being detained. Charles's new guards were equally friendly and had no idea what to do with him. When they reached Borgo, they dropped him off in front of the barracks, told him to go inside, and drove off. Charles saluted the German sentinel at the door but kept on going down the street. Again, as at the roll call with his father at Rivesaltes and the roundup with his mother in Valdieri, he had escaped death by a hair.

Charles admits that he was terrified as he walked the ten kilometers through the valley of the Gesso back to Valdieri, all alone. "I had a small leather pack strapped to my belt," he recalls. "It kept clicking, sounding like an approaching car. In those times, only German or Fascist officials had cars. I would dive over to the side of the road, only to realize that the noise was from my pack. In Valdieri, everyone was asleep and it was very quiet. I had old army shoes with heavy soles that made a lot of noise. I can still remember vividly trying to tiptoe through Valdieri without making any noise." He returned to the Madonna del Colletto to find his mother, who had already lost two husbands and a half sister, in tears. She thought her son was gone forever, like the others.

Jacques Samson and his father, Szlama, also found their way to the sanctuary of the Madonna del Colletto on September 18. While there, they met a mother with her two children and a niece, also Jews from Saint-Martin-Vésubie, who would remain their friends for life. Serena Szabo was born in 1911 in Vylok, Galicia, in a region that became part of Czechoslovakia after the First World War. She immigrated to Antwerp in the 1920s, married a diamond cutter named Leopold Gerhard, and had two children, Régine in 1933 and Jacky in 1935. When the Germans invaded Belgium in May 1940, the Gerhards fled to France, where Leopold joined a military unit of foreign volunteers, associated with the French Foreign Legion, for the duration of hostilities. Despite his military record, he was arrested in February 1943 in the same reprisal roundup of foreign Jewish men that claimed Walter Marx's father, Ludwig, and Charles Roman's stepfather, Wilhelm Bauer. Like Bauer, Leopold Gerhard was deported from Drancy on March 4, 1943, in convoy 50.[4] He did not return.

With her children and her five-year-old niece, Rosa Eller, whose parents were too ill to care for her while at Agde and were eventually deported, Serena made her way to Nice, Saint-Martin-Vésubie, and Italy. In Valdieri, she found a room with an elderly peasant woman named Signora Orselina, who lived at the edge of town. On September 18, 1943, Signora Orselina hid the refugees in a barn for a time and brought them food and blankets. She saved their lives. After a German antipartisan raid a few weeks later, Serena, Régine, and Rosa fled up the mountain to the sanctuary, leaving eight-year-old Jacky in the care of the kindly local baker. A few weeks after that, the baker sent Jacky up the mountain too. The Germans were again searching the town, and he feared for his own family. After wandering for hours in the snow, Jacky ran into Jacques Samson, who took him to his mother.[5]

Two of our families seem to have found shelter not at the Madonna del Colletto but in the surrounding area. With the small stock of food he had obtained at the barracks in Valdieri, Hermann Hartmayer had settled his children, Sigi, Manya, and Willy, up on the mountain ridge north of town. From where they were hiding on September 18, 1943, they could see the Germans putting up the poster and watch the Jews from Saint-Martin-Vésubie being arrested. As they went up higher, they were joined by two Italian men claiming to be deserters or partisans who seemed to be as afraid as they were. Because they had heard about bandits in the area, this made them very nervous. Manya's friend Ernst Breuer, who was also with them, had taken a bayonet from the barracks in Valdieri. He quietly announced that he would bring up the rear as they all moved around the mountain, to watch the two men. Eventually, to everyone's relief, the men left.

Sigi and his family were in the mountains for three weeks. They survived on the hardtack they had taken from the local barracks, along with the ubiquitous chestnuts and some bread from the peasants. Finally, Sigi says, Manya and Ernst, who were very much in love, pointed out that smaller groups had a better chance to escape notice and survive. They asked permission to leave the family and strike out on their own for the Allied lines in the south. It is a sign of the difficulty of the times that Hermann finally agreed and gave them his blessing. They left, survived, and were later married. Sigi, Willy, and Hermann left soon after.

Boris Carmeli, with his father, Hermann, mother, Rachel, and brother, Peter, hid in the cemetery in Valdieri on September 18. From there, they could see the older people, the sick, and the women with babies, gathering in the town square. "Nobody really knew what to expect," Boris says. His family spent that cold, wet night in the open. The next day, they knocked on the door of a peasant they knew only as Pietro. The man was tall, Boris recalls, with a huge moustache. As he describes him sixty years later, Boris Carmeli, who experienced the horrors of Auschwitz and Bergen-Belsen, breaks down and weeps for the only time during our interview.

Pietro immediately responded, "Come in! Come in!" He took the family to his barn. Pointing to the loft, he instructed them, "Stay there. Don't come down, and keep quiet. I will feed you, but our little children mustn't know you are here. Children talk." Pietro was very poor, but when Boris's father offered him one of the pieces of jewelry he was still carrying, he refused it. "You are going to need it yourselves," he explained quietly.

Boris and his family stayed in Pietro's barn for about two weeks. Then one day, Pietro came to tell them that their presence was known and people were talking. They had to move. Pietro returned at 4:00 the next morning to escort them to a mountain hut used by shepherds in the summer. There was snow on the ground, so he told the family to walk exactly in his footprints, to disguise their numbers. "Don't go out in the daytime," he instructed. "I will bring you food." And he did. Others also helped. One day an eighty-year-old man appeared with a sack of potatoes on his back. "The Italian people have their faults like any other people," says Boris, who lives today in Rome and knows them well. "And I don't know what this younger generation today is like. But I will never let anyone say anything against the Italians. When you needed them, they were there."

After another ten days or so, Pietro reported that people were again beginning to talk about refugees in his hut. "I'll take you to the partisans," he told them. "We went further up into the mountains, and there we stayed," says Boris. Every few evenings, he went down into the nearest village to beg for food. He does not know exactly where they were. He was, after all, still only fifteen years old, and he was not to be there long.

◇ ◇ ◇

When the German SS poster went up on Saturday, September 18, order-ing "foreigners" to turn themselves in, the large Löwenwirth family was in Borgo San Dalmazzo. Miriam's parents, Elena and Eliyahu, were inclined to obey. How could they survive in hiding and feed their six children, including a twenty-month-old baby, throughout the coming winter? But seventeen-year-old Miriam refused to submit. "My father wanted us to report to the headquarters, but something inside me told me that we should not do so," she says. "I told my father that I would not give myself up voluntarily to the Germans, even if they threatened to kill me. This was the first time in my life that I had defied my father."

The question then became, what else could they do? Miriam heard church bells ring. Why not ask for advice from a priest? He might not be willing to help them, but he certainly would not turn them in. And he might speak French. With her mother, Miriam rang the doorbell of the lo-cal church. Thus it was her immense good fortune to meet Don Raimondo Viale, the remarkable parish priest of Borgo San Dalmazzo whom we shall meet again because of his later assistance to William Blye, Walter Marx, Charles Roman, and Lya Haberman.

Don Viale did not hesitate. "He told us to bring the rest of the family to the church and not report to the Germans," Miriam recalls. At 4:00 that afternoon, the Löwenwirths, divided into pairs, were scattered among the mourners in a Catholic funeral procession. Just before the cemetery out-side the village, Don Viale led them off the main path and pointed them in the direction of the forest. After reluctantly leaving baby Ben-Zion with a parishioner on the edge of the village, Miriam's family headed for the mountains.

PART III

Deportation from and Survival in Italy,
September 1943 to the Liberation

CHAPTER THIRTEEN

Deportation from Borgo San Dalmazzo

The Marx and Marienberg Families and Boris Carmeli

Walter Marx

When Walter Marx, his mother, Johanna, and his cousin Werner Isaac turned themselves in to the German SS in Borgo San Dalmazzo on September 18, 1943, they must have been terrified about the future. They had seen Walter's father arrested in Lamalou-les-Bains seven months before. They knew he had been interned at Gurs before being sent north to Drancy. They were aware that thousands of other Jews, especially foreigners, had been arrested throughout France, sent to Drancy, and deported somewhere "to the East." While in Saint-Martin-Vésubie, as seen, they had also heard rumors of the murder of deported Jews. If the Germans really were deporting and murdering Jews from occupied France, there was no reason to think it would be any different in occupied Italy.

In the meantime, however, Walter, Johanna, and Werner had to cope with life in the barracks in Borgo. Walter recalls that there were one or two large rooms in the structure, which Italian soldiers had abandoned only ten days before. Families remained together and were given pallets of straw for sleeping. Werner also remembers the dirty straw, as well as the rats and the terrible insipid soup. According to Walter, there was one Italian carabiniere outside, but the commander and most of the guards were Germans. At one point, a group of Italian Jews arrested in and around Cuneo arrived, but they were kept separate and eventually released.[1] Of his time in the barracks, Walter says, "I don't remember that we were hungry or mistreated. . . . But the SS ordered all adult males to work, which consisted of loading all material found in the barracks, such as weapons, ammunition, food, clothing, etc., on trucks for transportation to railroad cars waiting on a siding near the railroad station." Clearly the Germans were helping themselves to Italian war matériel. But both Walter and Werner recall that the work was not hard and the guards were not brutal.

Late on the evening of October 16, the truck carrying supplies to the nearby railroad station ran out of gas. The German SS guards ordered Walter and seven or eight other young men to roll the truck down the slight incline to the nearest railroad car. "It was pitch dark," as Walter describes it, "and there were no lights, and neither I, being the first one on the left side of the truck, nor my companions saw the tank on the left side of the road until I felt an impact. My right leg went numb. I screamed and fainted. My fellow prisoners had pushed the truck into the tank and I got caught between the two vehicles." Walter was taken first to the small hospital in Borgo, and then to the larger hospital of Santa Croce in Cuneo. He had broken a vertebra in his back and had to lie on a board in a hospital bed for nearly four months.

As frequently happened with foreign Jews interned in southern France and Italy, Walter's mother, Johanna, was allowed to visit him in the hospital in Cuneo. From his arrival there in the middle of October until just before November 21, she did so, three times a week, always accompanied by an Italian policeman working for the Germans. After that, she did not come again.

Walter also received visits in the hospital from Nella Giraudo, the daughter of the owner of the hotel in Borgo San Dalmazzo where he and Johanna had stayed for a few days. Nella also took extra food to Johanna in the barracks. From Nella, who witnessed the whole tragedy, Walter eventually learned why his mother stopped coming. On November 21, in full public view, approximately 349 Jews then in the barracks of Borgo San Dalmazzo were forced to march a short distance to the local train station, where they were crowded into four or five waiting cattle cars. Among the prisoners were Johanna Marx and her nephew Werner Isaac.[2] The train left Borgo about 2:00 P.M., passed through Savona and Ventimiglia on the Mediterranean coast, and arrived in Nice that evening.

In Nice, the prisoners were taken to the Hotel Excelsior, where SS

Captain Aloïs Brunner, charged with rounding up the Jews in the former Italian-occupied zone, had his headquarters. Nearly all of them were sent on to Drancy within the next two or three days. From Drancy, 309 were among the one thousand Jews transported to Auschwitz on convoy 64, on December 7, 1943. Johanna Marx was on that train. During the journey to Auschwitz, four prisoners escaped. At the final destination, 267 men and 72 women were selected to enter the camp. The remaining 657 were gassed upon arrival. Of those selected to enter the camp, forty-eight men and two women returned after the war. About eleven of these survivors were from the group of about 349 who had been deported from Borgo San Dalmazzo to Drancy on November 21. Johanna Marx was not among them.[3]

Menahem Marienberg

When Menahem Marienberg's father, Wolf, decided on September 18, 1943, to stay with his brother and his brother's young family, his own sons had little choice but to turn themselves in as well. Like Walter Marx and Werner Isaac, Menahem records that many of the men in the barracks in Borgo San Dalmazzo had to perform hard labor, moving war matériel from one place to another. But unlike Walter, he remembers that the German SS guards were vicious. They tormented the Jewish workers for fun, he says. One guard amused himself by shooting between their legs. Another made sixteen-year-old Menahem ride behind him on his motorcycle while carrying heavy tools and then tried to make him fall off. A third put a pole between his legs to make him fall and then beat him while he was down. One time when the beating was particularly painful, Menahem stayed down for a few moments to catch his breath, although he knew he would be hit again. Then he saw his father coming past the guards to help him. He got up right away, to save his father from getting into trouble. But his arm had been broken, and he was in bad shape. One German soldier was then kind to him, telling him to sit next to him and giving him some make-work so that he could rest. At the sudden unexpected kindness, the boy burst into tears.

Menahem relates that on an average day, there were some one hundred men working outside the barracks, with only a few guards. Looking back, he often wonders why the prisoners did not run away. But he answers his own question, because he knows that most of the Jews were unwilling to leave their families. An unknown number of young men did escape—records are meager, for that was not information that the SS wanted to share. But family men did not leave. Their families, if they were lucky enough to have them still, were all they had left in the world. They may sometimes have encouraged their older children to venture out, but they themselves stayed with the younger ones if they could.

At night in the barracks, Menahem tried to comfort the younger children, telling them stories about their traditions and culture and teaching them Jewish songs. These were the things that had given him courage in the EIF children's home in Lautrec, and he was trying to pass that courage on to those younger than himself. His father told him to be careful, but from the look in his eyes, Menahem could tell that he was proud. It is a memory that has stayed with him for more than sixty years.

Three days before Menahem broke his arm, his ten-year-old brother, Léon, had been taken to the hospital in Borgo with what Menahem remembers as appendicitis. Because Menahem's arm was badly broken, his father begged the guards to send him to the hospital too. Menahem believes that while the guards at the workplace were Germans, some of those in the barracks itself were Italians. That fact, he thinks, facilitated his move. In any case, he arrived at the local hospital, where he encountered Giuseppe Meinardi, the director of the much larger hospital of Santa Croce in Cuneo.

During an earlier visit to the Borgo hospital, Meinardi had arranged for Léon to be transferred to the Cuneo facility. When he met Léon's brother, he immediately had him transferred as well. Menahem arrived at the hospital in Cuneo on October 7, 1943. For some reason, his hospital affidavit gives the official diagnosis as "rheumatism" rather than a broken arm.[4] Menahem believes that although Meinardi did not know what was about to happen to the Jewish refugees confined in the barracks at Borgo San Dalmazzo, he understood that they were in danger. Léon and Menahem were the youngest patients from the barracks in the little hospital in Borgo. When Meinardi met them there, he picked them out as youngsters whom he could help. He had them transferred to the hospital in Cuneo and kept them there. He saved their lives.

Like Johanna Marx, who was able to visit Walter when he was flat on his back in the same hospital at the same time, Menahem's father and uncle came to see Léon and him once, with an Italian guard. The boys were able to give them some hospital food, a great improvement over what they were receiving in the barracks. Wolf seems to have had no illusions about his future. He asked his eldest son always to take care of Léon. They never saw each other again.

The list of Jews from Saint-Martin-Vésubie who were marched from the barracks to the train station of Borgo San Dalmazzo on November 21 for expulsion to Nice and Drancy includes Menahem Marienberg's Uncle Isaac, Aunt Eva, and cousins Menahem and baby Simone. Strangely enough, the list also includes Marco and Leone Michel, the names on the false papers of Menahem and Léon. Menahem is at a loss to explain this. Perhaps his father, Wolf, tried to convince the guard who made the list at the last minute that his sons were present so that the Germans would not search for them in the hospital. Equally puzzling is the fact that Wolf's name is not on the list. But the correct names with accurate dates and places of birth of all of the five Marienbergs deported from Drancy to Auschwitz are among the one thousand prisoners listed on the manifest for convoy 64 on December 7, 1943. Wolf and his brother, Isaac, then forty-two and thirty-seven years old, respectively, may have been among the 267 men selected for labor, although Isaac, with his tuberculosis, probably did not live long. Thirty-four-year-old Eva was undoubtedly not among the seventy-two women admitted to the camp, because of her two children. Mothers accompanied by small children were invariably sent directly to the gas chambers with them. None of the Marienbergs was among the fifty survivors of convoy 64.[5]

Boris Carmeli

Boris Carmeli, his parents, Rachel and Hermann, and his brother, Peter, had not been captured in the roundup on September 18 but had hidden in the mountains above Valdieri. As the weather turned cold, however, Boris developed a painful earache. After telling his parents that he had to have some medicine, he descended to the town in daylight. Two Italian Fascist militiamen, seeing him enter the pharmacy, arrested him as he came out. They delivered him to the Germans, who sent him to join the other Jews from Saint-Martin-Vésubie interned in the barracks at Borgo San Dalmazzo.

Most of the prisoners were with their families, but fifteen-year-old Boris was alone. The guards were mostly Italians, he recalls, although the Germans came in from time to time. Like Walter Marx and Menahem Marienberg, Boris had to work. He describes being taken to a German building with a big courtyard where he and the others had to carry heavy loads of hay. They had to run while carrying them and were beaten by the Germans as they passed by. The prisoners could receive visitors, packages, and mail, although of course no Jews could safely come and go. Rachel and

Hermann learned where their son was and sent him a message, instructing him to walk out with the peasant who brought it. They must have bribed a guard or made some other arrangements. But the Germans had told the prisoners that if anyone escaped, they would shoot ten people from their group. To his parents' request, Boris wrote, "Dear Father, I will not leave here. I don't want to have the deaths of ten people on my conscience." His father kept the note, in the handwriting of a child. His sentiments he kept to himself.

Boris Carmeli was among the approximately 349 Jews marched from the barracks to the train station of Borgo San Dalmazzo on November 21.[6] Someone saw him in the group and informed his parents. Their feelings can only be imagined. Of his trip back to France, Boris says, "The train from Borgo San Dalmazzo to Nice consisted of cattle wagons that were crowded. The Excelsior in Nice was a good hotel and we stayed there only one night. We were aware that it was a pre-station for Drancy." Sure enough, the next morning most of the refugees were sent north. Boris spent about a week at Drancy. The boy who had attended the Conservatoire in Nice while in enforced residence in Saint-Martin-Vésubie survived to become a prominent opera singer, but the memory of Drancy never left him. "Since [the war] I have sung many times in Paris," he confides, "at the Opéra and in other theaters. Each time I go there, entering Paris from Charles de Gaulle Airport, I pass a sign that says 'Drancy.' Each time, I get cold shivers. The horror does not go away."

With Johanna Marx, the Marienbergs, and most of the other prisoners from Borgo San Dalmazzo, Boris joined the one thousand Jews on convoy 64 from Drancy to Auschwitz on December 7, 1943. He was among those admitted to the camp and among the fifty survivors.[7]

Werner Isaac

Most of the prisoners from Borgo who were not deported to Auschwitz on December 7 were sent there on subsequent trains. But not all. Walter Marx's cousin Werner Isaac remained at Drancy until the liberation of Paris and survived. His story is indeed remarkable. While still at the barracks in Borgo San Dalmazzo, the young man was selected to be a translator for the Germans. He proved so useful that, when he was deported with the other Jews back to France, he traveled in a separate compartment, still translating. In Nice, he went with the others to the Hotel Excelsior but did not accompany them to Drancy. Instead, he was held in Nice for a couple of weeks. By the time he arrived in Drancy, most of the Jews from Borgo San Dalmazzo had been deported to Auschwitz. His aunt Johanna Marx was among them. Werner never saw her again.

At Drancy, Werner was again given a job. This time, in the unfinished housing project's beehive of raw concrete rooms accessed by separate stairways, the young man was expected to see that the soup went to the right place. Not much of a job, perhaps, but it kept him in the camp. Werner was not selected for deportation until mid-August 1944. As the Allies approached Paris, he says, he and other prisoners were sent by bus to the railroad station at Bobigny, from where the trains left for Auschwitz. It looked as if their final moments in France had finally come. After a few hours, however, the bus turned around and returned to Drancy. Werner does not know the reason. He says, "I only remember that the train was either not available or was being disabled by the Resistance." Astonished and traumatized, the prisoners back in Drancy gathered up their meager possessions and waited until the Red Cross liberated them the following day. Werner's memory after that is blank. He was alone in a newly liberated city, stunned and amazed to be alive.

Werner's memory of a round-trip bus trip from Drancy to Bobigny is difficult to confirm with other sources. It is clear, however, that as the Allies approached Paris in August 1944, SS Captain Aloïs Brunner, the camp director since July 1943 as well as the hunter of Jews in Nice that September, tried desperately to deport the roughly fifteen hundred Jews still at Drancy. In the end, he was able to requisition only three railroad cars attached to a larger military transport. He filled two of the cars with his retreating Gestapo and German police, including himself. The other he used to deport fifty-one prominent Jewish prisoners and their families, including, as we have seen, Ernst Appenzeller. It is possible that Brunner transported many more Jews, including Werner, to the station in the hope of finding space on the train but was then forced to leave them. This last convoy from Drancy departed on August 17, 1944. At least fifteen of the fifty-one prisoners managed to escape, but most of the remainder died at Auschwitz or in other German camps.

CHAPTER FOURTEEN

Hiding in the Province of Cuneo

William Blye, Charles Roman, Walter Marx, and Menahem Marienberg

AT BORGO SAN DALMAZZO, travelers going west toward the mountains and the French frontier can fork to the left and enter the valley of the Gesso, where they will soon arrive in Valdieri. They can also fork to the right and enter the valley of the Stura, formed by a river known as the Stura di Demonte.[1] A steep mountain ridge separates the two valleys, with Valdieri at its southern base and Demonte, the principal town of the Stura valley, on the north. Wider and flatter than the Gesso, the valley of the Stura contains a major highway that follows the river all the way to France. Because that highway constituted the only motorized route from the province of Cuneo to France during the war, the valley had enormous strategic importance. It was the scene of continuous confrontations between the Germans and their Italian Fascist allies, on one hand, and Italian partisans on the other. In addition, the valley of the Stura provided shelter for many of the roughly six hundred Jewish refugees from Saint-Martin-Vésubie who escaped the German roundups in Valdieri, Entracque, and Borgo San Dalmazzo on September 18, 1943.

William Blye

William Blye and his mother, Maria, it will be recalled, had lived in Leipzig, Milan, and Nice. William's father and two brothers had been arrested in

Nice in August 1942 and deported without return. William and Maria had fled over the mountains from Saint-Martin-Vésubie to Italy on or about September 9, 1943, and escaped the roundup on September 18, but William has blotted these events from his memory. He vividly recalls the struggle for survival afterward, however, as these two city people moved through a succession of huts and stables to escape arrest. Stables were preferable in winter because the livestock provided heat. Nevertheless, William remembers that he was always cold and his hands were often blue. Everyone in his group had lice. "Do you know how to kill a louse?" asks this gracious Old World gentleman. "You crack it between two fingernails. It isn't easy to kill a louse." The stables had an overpowering smell, and rats climbed constantly on the beams overhead. Once a rat fell off a beam and landed on William. Not surprisingly, it was a great relief to leave the mountains for a short period and hide in Demonte, a town of about 3,500 people at the time. William and his mother stayed in the home of a retired Italian general and his unmarried daughters. One of the daughters taught William some Italian, and he taught her the limited English that he had learned in school.

By this time, William had false papers identifying him as André Matisse from Abbeville (Somme), northwest of Amiens and not far from the English Channel. That northern origin, it was hoped, would help explain his slight accent when speaking French. False papers provided little security, however, for they were usually of poor quality and fooled no one. In this partisan-infested area, any young man of military age was regarded with suspicion and had to maintain a low profile. Like most survivors in their late teens during the war, William does not know who provided the papers. Probably, he never knew. It was safer that way. His elders undoubtedly had the contacts and made the arrangements. The fascinating story of rescuers is thus difficult to unravel.

Nor does William remember who provided the money essential to survival. The peasants in the mountains would sell almost anything to anyone with money, he notes. Young people from every Jewish group in hiding bought supplies from them as well as from shopkeepers in Valdieri or Demonte. But money was in short supply. William does not mention receiving money from priests, but he says, "I do recall a priest who helped us and several other Jews in [Demonte] with some clothing and food." When asked more about him, William says sadly, "I don't even remember his name. He was one of the few people to whom I owe a lot. I don't even remember how I found this priest." He then continues, "The help we received was from many individuals. There was one peasant I always went to. He always gave me some loaves of bread that he had baked. I thanked him and also said that the peasants are always so helpful and he said, 'We are not peasants [*contadini*], we are farmers [*agricoltori*]!'"

In fact, whether William knew it or not, he and his mother did receive money from priests. The remarkable story of cooperation between Italian Catholics and foreign Jews from which William and hundreds of refugees like him benefited began in Genoa a few weeks after the armistice and the German occupation of Italy. Realizing that the national Jewish assistance organization Delasem could no longer function safely to distribute subsidies to refugees and other needy Jews, its national president, Lelio Vittorio Valobra, a lawyer in Genoa, paid a visit to the archbishop in his city, Cardinal Pietro Boetto. Could the cardinal, he asked, take over the job? In the words of Boetto's secretary, Don Francesco Repetto, who was present at the meeting, "The cardinal paused for a moment, but he did not think about it for long; he said: 'They [the Jews] are innocent; they are in grave danger; we must help them regardless of all our other problems.'"[2]

Valobra turned over his organization's funds and lists of clients to the cardinal, who assigned to Don Repetto the dangerous job of distribution. Repetto, in turn, recruited priests and other Catholics in the archdiocese of Genoa to help. He also contacted other prelates, especially Cardinal Maurilio Fossati in Turin, asking for and receiving their cooperation. In other dioceses, such as the archdiocese of Florence, local Delasem leaders and other prominent Jews themselves went to the resident bishop or archbishop for help. It is not clear whether anyone specifically asked Bishop Giacomo Rosso of Cuneo to help Jewish refugees; wartime documents in the archives of the diocese of Cuneo are not yet available to scholars. But, almost certainly with the consent if not the encouragement of that bishop, Cardinal Fossati of Turin contacted the parish priest of Borgo San Dalmazzo, Don Raimondo Viale.[3]

Don Viale was an exceptional man and a dedicated anti-Fascist. Alberto Cavaglion, the son and nephew of Jewish partisans from Cuneo and a respected historian of the Jews from Saint-Martin-Vésubie, calls him "a stubborn, non-conformist, and rebellious curate."[4] The description is meant to be complimentary. Born in Limone Piemonte in 1907, Don Viale was ordained in 1930 and became the parish priest in Borgo San Dalmazzo in 1936. Throughout the 1930s, he was in trouble with the Fascist authorities because of his public criticism of the regime's authoritarian and militaristic rhetoric and its interference with Catholic youth organizations. A severe beating at the hands of the Fascists in March 1939 did not discourage him from making a discreet antiwar speech on June 2, 1940, when the Germans were overrunning France and Mussolini was about to intervene at Hitler's side and get in on the spoils. For this Don Viale was arrested and sentenced to four years in *confino*, or exile, in a mountain village in the Abruzzi, in southern Italy. The sentence was reduced when Pope Pius XII intervened on his behalf. This "meddlesome priest" from Borgo San Dalmazzo returned to his parish in October 1941, unsubdued and as anti-Fascist as ever.[5]

When he recruited Don Viale in late September or early October 1943, Cardinal Fossati certainly knew what he was doing. According to the young priest, "by the beginning of 1944 my contacts with the archdiocese of Genoa intensified, and the contribution of [Delasem] money that I received [from Repetto] became regular and consistent." Those "contacts" and "regular" contributions entailed dangerous journeys to Genoa, which Don Viale made on several occasions and which his carefully chosen couriers did on others.[6] Upon receipt of the money, Don Viale, a passionate mountaineer in the best of times, climbed mountains, fought snowstorms, and dodged German and Fascist patrols to distribute subsidies to indigent Jewish refugees in hiding. He also sheltered Jews and partisans in his home, helped them move north to Switzerland or south toward the Allied lines, and prepared false documents for them. In early November 1944, he was forced to go into hiding, but his network of faithful priests continued his rescue efforts until Liberation in May 1945. Without the money they brought, the refugees could not have remained where they were. Accountable to Delasem for the use of the funds, Don Viale and his assistants also kept careful distribution lists. Some of those lists have survived, and on them appear the names of Maria Blaiwaiz (Bleiweiss) and her son, Wolf (William Blye), described as "Poles taking refuge in Demonte."[7]

Charles Roman

After escaping up into the mountains above Valdieri on September 18, Charles Roman, his mother, Marianne, and Marianne's brother-in-law, Franz Edelschein, settled in at the sanctuary of the Madonna del Colletto for several weeks. By mid-November, however, it was too cold to stay where they were. Some refugees sought shelter in scattered hamlets and isolated shepherds' huts on the other side of the ridge, on a slope facing north toward

Demonte. Charles, Marianne, and Franz, however, with many others, descended the northern side of that ridge, reaching the valley of the Stura. Then they crossed the Stura River and went up into the mountains on the other side of that valley. Now they were on south-facing slopes where it was slightly warmer but where the snows would reach a great depth. Charles's group of about fourteen refugees settled into a crude hut that farmers and shepherds used for temporary shelter and storage in the summer, about six to eight kilometers from the nearest village. The owner of the hut knew they were there, as did the peasants in the village, but no one ever reported them. One day Charles even saw an American flier who had been shot down pass by. He never learned what happened to that man, but he believes that another flier was stuck in a tree and caught.[8]

And so, toward the end of November, Charles and Marianne and those with them, including the family of Poldi Neumann, settled down to a winter routine. Charles and Poldi continued to do the essential shopping, now in Demonte rather than Valdieri. As the snows deepened, they learned to ski. Sometimes the local peasants took pity on the boys and invited them to share a simple meal. Charles especially remembers a woman in one tiny village whom they fondly called "la donna degli undici bambini," "the woman with eleven children." Despite her own burdens, she gave Poldi and him hot soup every time they passed by. But still they were always hungry. After the war, Marianne used to tell anyone who would listen, "Were we ever hungry!" She also constantly reminded her son, "You see, Charlie! I promised you that we would eat bananas again!"

For money, the boys went regularly to Rialpo, a village between Borgo San Dalmazzo and Demonte, north of the Stura River. A priest there had been giving them regular distributions since October. Although Charles laments that he never knew his name, the priest was almost certainly part of Don Raimondo Viale's network. Don Viale's fragmentary list of those to whom he distributed a monthly subsidy from Delasem does not include Charles and his mother, who left for Rome in March 1944, but it does mention Hans Neumann with his wife, his son, Leopold, and his daughter, Margheritte, known to Charles as Margit.[9] If Charles went with Poldi for the distributions at an earlier time, he probably received money from the same source. "We assumed the money was from the Vatican," says Charles, but in fact it was from a Jewish charitable organization.

Dealing with the cold was equally difficult. The refugees had left France without warm winter clothes. Marianne somehow acquired an old army blanket and made Charles a pair of warm pants. Because it was a capital offense to have military equipment, she tinted the fabric blue. The problem was that when the pants got wet, they left a telltale pool of blue water wherever he went. Blankets were equally scarce. Charles recalls that he and Poldi used to go down to a small hamlet in the valley east of Demonte every night to borrow the blankets that the peasants used for their cows when they were out during the day. The refugees used the blankets at night and returned them to the peasants in the morning.

The Germans and their Fascist allies knew that people were living in the mountains on either side of the valley of the Stura because they could see chimney smoke in areas where there were no villages. Because of the snow, they could not easily get there, but they sometimes fired what Charles describes as a cannon from the road toward the smoke. Johanna Greve, the mother of Ludwig (Lutz), Charles's friend from Montintin and Saint-Martin-Vésubie, who was hiding in the same general area as Charles and his mother, was seriously wounded in this way in January 1944.[10]

Walter Marx

When Johanna Marx was deported from Borgo San Dalmazzo to Drancy and then Auschwitz, her seventeen-year-old son, Walter, was left alone in a strange land, without money, flat on his back in a hospital in Cuneo, and unable to speak Italian. He set about solving the last problem as quickly as possible. He also had to learn to walk again. This he also accomplished, with some help from Menahem and Léon Marienberg, who were patients in the same hospital. Toward the end of January 1944, German SS police came to the hospital to ask the director, Giuseppe Meinardi, if Walter had recovered enough to be moved. Meinardi replied vaguely that the young man might be ready in a week and immediately advised Walter of the inquiry. Meanwhile, Meinardi asked a representative of Bishop Giacomo Rosso to visit Walter. That delegate told the young man that the bishop had arranged for Cardinal Pietro Boetto of Genoa to hide him. Walter was to travel to Boetto's residence and ask for a priest named Don Francesco Repetto. The next day, January 30, 1944, the young man walked out of the hospital on crutches to a waiting taxi that took him to the train station.[11] Two other young Jewish hospital patients from Saint-Martin-Vésubie, Hertzek Gerszt and Isidor Grunfeld, went with him. What Meinardi told the SS agents when they came for the young men is not clear. Meinardi had saved their lives.

Or at least, he saved them temporarily. Walter could not have known it at the time, but the instructions he had received were excellent. As seen, twenty-eight-year-old Don Repetto, the secretary of Cardinal Boetto, was charged with the immense job of distributing Delasem subsidies to Jewish refugees and some Italian Jews, finding hiding places for them, relaying them to safer regions, escorting them to Switzerland, and contacting priests and prelates in other dioceses to help. Repetto dedicated himself totally to the assignment and saved hundreds.

With Walter Marx, however, things somehow went terribly wrong. Walter recounts, "Upon arrival in [Genoa], we went to the cardinal's residence. . . . Don Repetto came out to greet us. We had assumed that he had been advised of our impending visit. Great was our surprise when he denied any knowledge and stated that there was nothing he could do. When we exited the cardinal's residence we went to a nearby restaurant to contemplate our next move. While sitting at the table, a man passed us several times, mumbling what sounded to us like 'Shalom.' Was it a trap? Was it a test? Or was it our imagination? We played it safe and did not respond. We felt betrayed by Don Repetto, the cardinal, and the bishop of Cuneo."

Years later, Walter Marx learned that Don Repetto had been honored at Yad Vashem. At that point, he reconsidered this wartime incident and understood that the young priest had been afraid of him and his companions. The request for help from the bishop of Cuneo had somehow failed to reach Cardinal Boetto in Genoa, and without it, Don Repetto could not be certain that Walter was not an informer. After their encounter, Don Repetto probably sent another man to the restaurant to try to find out whether Walter and the other two were really Jews. "If we had responded to his 'Shalom,'" says Walter, "we would have saved ourselves a lot of trouble!" But there was good reason for both parties to be afraid. Walter knew that there were spies and informers ready to betray Jews and sell them to the Germans, and Don Repetto knew that he himself was vulnerable. In fact, a few months later, on July 3, 1944, that courageous young priest narrowly escaped arrest. He was forced to hide for the remainder of the war while the priests he had recruited continued his work.

Walter Marx, however, was now desperate. The only person he could think of who might help was Nella Giraudo back in Borgo San Dalmazzo, who had visited him in the hospital in Cuneo. He had another narrow escape on his way to find her, when the Germans searched his train at Savona. Perhaps because he was still on crutches, they did not stop him. In Borgo,

Nella put him up in the hotel for a few days, but with Germans going in and out, it was too dangerous for her to shelter him there. She suggested that Walter join the partisans, and he agreed.

Menahem Marienberg

A week or two before he helped Walter Marx get out of the hospital in Cuneo, Giuseppe Meinardi was confronted with the problem of what to do with Menahem and Léon Marienberg, who were no longer able to pass as sick patients. On January 12, 1944, this exceptional man, with a wife and two sons of his own, placed the boys on a farm he owned outside the city.[12] There they were disguised as farmworkers assisting the tenant. Menahem recalls that when the tenants paid them the first time, Meinardi was amazed that they bought shoes with the money rather than candy. But they were no longer children, Menahem explained to him. They were fighting for their lives and obliged to act like adults.

The boys stayed at the farm for several months, but eventually Italian Fascist militia raided it, looking for escaped soldiers and partisans. Ten-year-old Léon was too young to be suspicious, but Menahem, sixteen, was arrested and sent to a makeshift jail in the basement of a school in Cuneo. Most of the Italian guards were unpleasant. At one point, Menahem recalls, they informed him, "If there is no train for Germany in a few days, we are going to shoot you." He knew he had to get out. He found one decent Italian guard who took a message to Meinardi.

Meinardi was in hiding by this time because of his anti-Fascist sympathies. He received the message, however, and immediately arranged for Menahem to be visited in jail by an Italian countess. The woman made a big show of hugging him and saying, "Marco, what are you doing here? How are you?" She then left, but through her political influence, she was able to obtain Menahem's release. The guards were not pleased, and one of them warned the boy not to get into trouble again. He would not get a second chance. The decent Italian guard took him back to the Cuneo hospital, where the staff remembered him and admitted him on August 3, 1944, with "bronchitis." Eventually, the staff bandaged his eyes and sent him to a special eye hospital outside Cuneo. He remained there for the rest of the war, helping the nuns. Léon, who was also at the Cuneo hospital again between February and June 1944, was able to visit him occasionally.[13] And so the two boys survived the war.

CHAPTER FIFTEEN

Resistance

Walter Marx and William Blye

Walter Marx

For obvious security reasons, it was not possible for unknown strangers, especially with German accents, to join the Italian Resistance without a personal introduction. In Walter Marx's case, that introduction was provided by Nella Giraudo, whose father owned the hotel in Borgo San Dalmazzo where he and his mother had stayed when they arrived in Italy. When Walter returned from his disastrous trip to Genoa in search of help from Don Repetto, Nella accompanied him to nearby Demonte, in the valley of the Stura on the critical military highway leading to France. There she introduced him to a group of partisans whom she knew personally. Walter was accepted. His new documents identified him as Giuseppe Barale, born in a city in France near the German border to explain his accent. His career in the Resistance had begun. Asked why he joined the partisans, Walter replies, "I felt I had to do something, and once you started you couldn't just leave."

Walter's particular unit was one of four bands that had grown out of Duccio Galimberti's Italia Libera by February or March 1944. All were associated with Giustizia e Libertà, a non-Marxist anti-Fascist movement founded in 1929 by Carlo Rosselli.[1] Although the bands officially had a secular and mildly Socialist orientation, the politics of the individuals involved varied greatly. Walter was a relatively early participant. Between September 12,

1943, and March 10, 1944, 220 men are believed to have joined up. Many more local lads volunteered after German sweeps of the area in the spring and summer of 1944, when it became clear that young men of military age living at home were not safe from arrest or conscription. By early August 1944, partisans in the Stura valley numbered at least six hundred, with thirty officers and twenty-five junior officers. There may have been as many as six thousand in the entire province.[2]

Walter explains that during much of the summer of 1944, the partisans controlled part or all of the highway that ran through the valley of the Stura from Borgo San Dalmazzo to the French border. At the time, however, he knew little about other partisan units or about the total numbers involved. He was familiar only with fighters in his own unit, who usually numbered about twenty. Most of these men wore civilian clothes, but a few had tattered Italian military uniforms. Many were former soldiers from southern Italy, unable to get home, unwilling to fight for the Germans, and anxious to escape arrest and deportation to the Third Reich as prisoners of war. Walter knew only one other Jew in his unit, Harry Burger, known as "Biancastella," a Viennese refugee who had also crossed the Maritime Alps from Saint-Martin-Vésubie.[3] But Walter never experienced any anti-Semitism in the Resistance. He says, "I'm not sure that the Italian partisans with me even knew what Jews were."

Because he was still on crutches, Walter was initially assigned to an "office job" in Demonte. The word "office," of course, is too grand a description of his assignment to a barn with no electricity and a single typewriter. His first job was to issue his fellow partisans passes for twenty-four-hour leave and requisition papers for food from the local peasants. Most peasants were reasonably supportive, he says, but they did not like to have their food taken.[4] They gave up cheese, eggs, chickens, and bread because they were intimidated by the partisans' demands. Walter left receipts with them that said, "Paga Mussolini"—"Mussolini will pay"—but that, he says, was really a joke.[5] He believes that the partisans were also supplied by British and American air drops, but he did not personally see this and does not know the details. He adds, "I don't recall ever being hungry when I was with the partisans. . . . Within a three-mile area, we probably had twenty to thirty farms."

While they may not have starved, the partisans in Walter's band did have to contend with the cold. During the particularly snowy winter of 1943–1944, they had some wood to burn, but they often slept in barns with the animals, especially the cows, to keep warm. Like the Jews in hiding, however, they felt safer in the winter, because the Germans and their Fascist collaborators only rarely came up through the snow to look for them. When asked if they feared the Fascists as much as the Germans, Walter replies, "In the beginning, we had no experience with the Fascists . . . we knew the Italians had been good to the Jews . . . we were afraid of the Germans . . . but later we learned of Fascist brutalities." Occasionally Walter and Harry Burger went to visit Harry's mother, Theresia, who was hiding in Moiola, in the valley of the Stura about halfway between Demonte and Borgo San Dalmazzo. Like William Blye and his mother, Maria, Theresia was kept alive by the monthly stipends from Delasem distributed by priests in Don Raimondo Viale's network.[6]

As his injured back improved, Walter received some military training. He practiced using a rifle and, like the other partisans, was given a revolver. His, he says proudly, was a Beretta. He also learned to handle an 81-millimeter mortar but did not actually fire it. His luck held for a few months. As the snows melted in the spring of 1944, the Germans and Fascists made several forays into the Stura valley to drive out the partisans. Partisan units usually just disbanded for a while, but occasionally there were skirmishes. Toward the end of May, however, Walter's luck turned for the worse. While walking through a market in Demonte, he and a small group of partisans were arrested by Italian Fascists. The only man in the group carrying a gun was shot on the spot. The others were taken to a prison in Cuneo. After a few days there, Walter, while walking to an interrogation session, was approached by a man whom he recognized from his activities with the partisans. The man, a double agent, was clearly trusted by the Germans. He quietly told Walter that they could help each other if Walter would agree to be placed as an interpreter with the Germans. Walter would then report every night about what he learned. When Walter asked what might happen if he refused the offer, the man told him, "You can take your chances. Maybe they will send you to Germany to work, or maybe it will be even worse." Walter agreed to the assignment. The man took him to a German SS office, where he was accepted as Giuseppe Barale.

Walter was now ensconced in the enemy's lair. His worst moment came on the day a German SS agent brought in a Hungarian Jew he recognized from Saint-Martin-Vésubie. Walter gave the prisoner a signal, and he did not acknowledge him. Since the prisoner spoke German, Walter was not needed for the interrogation and was able to leave the room. Increasingly nervous, he continued to report to the double agent every evening for two or three weeks. One evening, Walter had important news. The Germans were planning a raid in the Stura valley. A young Italian woman named Maria, who was living with and spying for the Germans, was scheduled to take a train to Demonte the next morning to gather information about the locations of partisans and Jews in advance of the attack. Walter offered to point out the woman, as long as the double agent then allowed him to leave the Germans and return to his partisan unit. He did not want to have to return to the Germans after it became known that the spy had been discovered. The agent agreed. The two men traveled through the night by bicycle from Cuneo to Demonte, where they met the spy as she got off the 8:00 A.M. train. Walter says, "The raid never materialized, probably because the spy did not return from her mission and because of my disappearance." Justifiably proud, he adds, "Because of what I did, I certainly saved a lot of partisans in the area, and I also saved a lot of Jews."

Walter's unit encountered the enemy on several occasions. Four men, for example, were killed in a firefight with German troops near Vinadio in July 1944. As Walter explains, "There was shooting going on all the time." He does not even remember the time or circumstances in which he was wounded. In addition to these skirmishes, Walter participated in one longer battle. After the Allies landed in southern France on August 15, 1944, the Stura valley with its highway leading across the Alps acquired great strategic importance. The Germans immediately realized that to keep open the possibility of helping their troops in France and to prevent the entry of Allied forces into Italy, they would have to control it. As German troops from Cuneo began to move west in force on both sides of the Stura River on August 17, the partisans tried to slow them down as much as possible by blowing up bridges and mining the roads. On August 18, Allied air attacks supported the partisan effort, but two days later, the Germans reached Vinadio, about halfway between Borgo San Dalmazzo and the frontier. The principal confrontation involving Walter Marx occurred on August 20 at Pianche, west of Vinadio, where the valley narrows. Walter remembers, "Maybe we delayed them [at Pianche] for a day or two, but they ultimately went through. We were up on the mountain and we shot down on them. We killed a driver with a mortar, and he fell on the horn. It made a terrible noise that lasted a long time."[7]

After the battle of Pianche, Walter's unit almost totally disbanded. Many of the partisans crossed the mountains into France, where they joined

French fighters and, ultimately, the Allies. Walter and his friend Harry Burger considered doing the same, but found themselves separated from the group and confused about the correct route to France. Harry adds that they were concerned about leaving Harry's mother. Consequently, they returned to the valley of the Stura, where they continued to divide their time between the partisans and various Jewish families in hiding. Probably at this point, Walter Marx also received a stipend from the Delasem funds distributed by Don Viale's network. The Germans now controlled the valley, posing a greater danger than ever for those hiding in the mountains. In March and April 1945, eight partisans from Walter's unit were killed—six in combat, one captured and executed, and one from wounds incurred in action.[8]

When asked what the Resistance accomplished, Walter replies that just by being there, the partisans prevented the Germans in Italy from reinforcing their troops in southern France for a crucial week. Also, the very existence of the partisans forced the Germans to keep troops in the province of Cuneo that might have been useful elsewhere. Walter adds, "I believe that the Italian partisans did a lot to reestablish the good name of the Italian people by wiping out some of the bad things the Fascists did; by putting themselves on the side of the Allies, [the Italian partisans] negated the role that the Italians had played in being part of the Fascist Axis comprising Germany, Italy, and Japan."

William Blye

It was impossible to hide in the mountains near a major road to France without encountering partisans. William Blye's group of seven Jews, including his mother, occasionally shared hiding places with a small partisan unit of about sixteen men. William identifies the group's leader as Almo Renato and has a note from him, certifying that he, William, belonged to his unit for a short time. This same Renato was identified with the unit in which Walter Marx served for well over a year. Walter remembers the partisans as active and confrontational, but to William, a more sporadic observer, they seemed less militant. William describes most of them as young men of conscription age or deserters from the Italian army who did not want to fight for Mussolini or the Germans but just wanted to survive the war. That was fine with William, who says, "I didn't care about politics. I also just wanted to survive." But he adds, "Only four of the seven Jews in our group survived."

The Germans knew that there were partisans and Jews in the mountains and occasionally came up after them. For William, the worst incident occurred on April 20, 1944, after the snows had melted, when, he says, the Germans came "with a vengeance, guns blazing, shooting at anybody who was a male, whether young or old." It was not difficult to see them coming, so the partisans and Jews simply ran into the woods and hid. With their lack of numbers and arms, there was little else they could do. In frustration, the Germans then turned against the local population. During the raid of April 20, 1944, and others later, they searched and burned entire villages, destroyed crops, stole household items and livestock, desecrated churches, rampaged through hospitals, raped and murdered a local teacher, Maria Isoardo, and shot prisoners and hostages.[9] One particularly horrifying incident involved the execution of thirteen partisan prisoners in the cemetery of Borgo San Dalmazzo on May 2, 1944. Prepared to be shot at 2:00 in the afternoon, the prisoners were forced to wait until 6:00 before the execution squad showed up. Through all that time, Don Viale remained with them as their confessor and only solace.[10]

William's most terrible memory of his time in Italy, however, does not involve the Resistance. It concerns, instead, the end of the war and his young friend Marcel Futerman. Marcel had been in Saint-Martin-Vésubie and had shared William's ordeal in the Italian mountains for two winters. Apart from the occasional terror and constant tension of hiding in the mountains, it was also, according to nearly all reports, dreadfully boring, especially in the winter and especially for young people yearning for a more lively social life.[11] William recalls that in April 1945, Marcel decided to go to Demonte to visit two young women he knew there—two hairdressers, known for consorting with the Germans. The retreating Germans were preoccupied and in disarray, so everyone thought that Demonte would be safe. Marcel wanted William to go with him, but William's mother, when she heard of it, wept and begged her son not to leave her alone. William was annoyed, but he did as she wished. Marcel went and was caught by a group of Italian Fascists. A week or two later, at the moment of liberation, William saw his friend's body lying in a dry riverbed in Cuneo. He was still holding a blanket and a loaf of bread. He had been shot in the chin, and the bullet had traveled through his skull. He was sixteen years old.

The complete story of this incident, as revealed by Cuneo prison records from the period, is, if possible, even more terrible than William relates. Marcel was arrested on April 12 in Cornaletto, a small village at the base of the mountains just a few kilometers north of Demonte. Also arrested on that day in the same village, probably with Marcel, were Marcel's father, Bernardo Futerman, born in Warsaw in 1903 and also a refugee from Saint-Martin-Vésubie; Armando Epolbon (or Appelbaum, or Apelbaum) from Warsaw, age fifty-two, Bernardo's brother-in-law; and Georges Joseph from Luxembourg, age twenty. The four men were thrown into a prison at Cuneo where two other Jewish refugees, also from Saint-Martin-Vésubie, had been languishing since their arrests on March 19. These two had been caught in Cervasca, also at the edge of the mountains some ten kilometers west of Cuneo. They were fifty-year-old Hugo Korbel and forty-two-year-old Siegfried Schwarz, both from Vienna. All six men had been fleeing from the Nazis for years and hiding under desperate conditions in the Italian Alps for a year and a half. Their journeys ended on the evening of April 25, 1945, when a group of embittered Fascist militiamen, fleeing to Germany just ahead of the partisans and the Allied troops, paused in Cuneo long enough to seize them from prison. In a senseless act of vengeance, the Fascists drove their Jewish prisoners by truck to a spot under the principal bridge of the city and murdered them all.[12]

William does not believe that the two women Marcel had wanted to visit betrayed him. Most local people hated the women, however, because they were friendly with the enemy, and after the war they exacted retribution. William relates, "I knew these two girls. When they were marched with their shaven heads and cowbells hanging around their necks through the streets, they saw me and screamed, 'Andrea, guarda ciò che mi hanno fatto'—'Andrea, look what they have done to me!' I kept quiet."

CHAPTER SIXTEEN

Traveling to and Hiding in Florence, September and October 1943

Miriam Löwenwirth, Sigi Hart, and Lya Haberman

ALL REFUGEES FROM Saint-Martin-Vésubie who escaped arrest on September 18, 1943, or later eventually had to make an agonizing choice. Should they stay in the mountains of the province of Cuneo, among the thousands of Jews, partisans, deserters, and even bandits who were attracting so much German attention, or should they attempt the dangerous journey south, to seek anonymity and await the Allies in Genoa, Florence, or Rome? Despite the horrendous shelter, terrible cold, and danger of detection in the northern mountains, it became apparent to many after the first few weeks that Don Raimondo Viale's network of priests would bring them the Delasem subsidies necessary for survival. Who would help them in the south, if they were fortunate enough to get there?

Among our witnesses, Boris Carmeli had no choice. He was arrested and deported from Borgo San Dalmazzo in November. William Blye, Walter Marx, and Menahem Marienberg remained in the province of Cuneo until the end of the war, while the other five moved out. Two of the five—Jacques Samson and Charles Roman—hid in the mountains around Valdieri until January and March, respectively, before setting out for Rome. Their story will be told in Chapter 18. But three others—Miriam Löwenwirth, Sigi Hart, and Lya Haberman—left almost immediately, directed to Florence by an increasingly coordinated group of Italian Jewish and Catholic rescuers. Once in Florence, they were helped by that same group, hidden in convents and monasteries throughout the city and supplied by Delasem. The dramatic story of Jewish rescue in Florence has never been told in all its details. Indeed, many of those details may be lost forever. But the testimony of Miriam, Sigi, and Lya is invaluable in any attempt to reconstruct events.

Miriam Löwenwirth was the first of our witnesses to leave for the south. She relates that two days after the roundup of September 18, 1943, Don Viale came to see her family in their hiding place outside Borgo San Dalmazzo. The young parish priest had helped the Löwenwirths evade the Germans on September 18. Now he told them that he wanted to send a woman from his parish to Turin to inform the Jewish community there about this desperate Jewish family with six children. For credibility, he asked that a couple of the children go with her. After much hesitation, Miriam's parents decided to send Zehava and Shlomo, the next oldest after Miriam. The children left with the woman, returning two days later with someone Miriam describes as "a bearded man about forty years old."

The stranger from Turin escorted the entire Löwenwirth family, including baby Ben-Zion, first to Turin, then to Genoa, and finally to Florence. "We traveled with him on the train and did not speak to him or make any sign that we knew him, during the entire journey," Miriam says. She never discovered who he was. There is probably no way to learn his identity. If Miriam's chronology is correct, he could hardly have been sent by the Jewish community of Florence in such a short time. He may have been a social worker or representative of the Jewish community in Turin, but Miriam is not even certain that he was Jewish. Whoever he was, he was a brave man. The country was in chaos in the first weeks after the armistice, travelers were not yet carefully watched, and Italian Jews were, for the most part, not yet being arrested. He was, nonetheless, protecting foreign Jews who had been ordered to report to the German authorities, on pain of death for them and anyone who helped them. The man took the Löwenwirths to the synagogue in Florence and then disappeared.

Sigi Hart with his father, Hermann, and brother, Willy, remained on the mountain slope north of Valdieri for at least two weeks after the September 18 roundup. As the weather turned cold and the Allies did not arrive, Hermann decided that they should also move south. They had a little money left from the sale of a ring and some gold from a tooth. Without a guide, they took what Sigi calls a little *trenino* down the valley—he does not remember the exact route—to Savona on the coast and then to Genoa. In Genoa, they went straight to the nearest church. Sigi explains that they did not think it was smart to go to a synagogue. They calculated that if the Italian people were helping Jews, as they seemed to be doing around Valdieri, certainly their priests would be doing the same. They were correct in that assumption. The priest they contacted by chance took them to another who was specifically involved in helping Jews. When asked if the second priest was Don Francesco Repetto, charged by Cardinal Boetto of Genoa with helping Jews, Sigi replies that unfortunately he does not know. Whoever he was, the second priest bought them train tickets to Florence, gave them directions to the synagogue there, and instructed them to go to a particular church. They followed his advice and arrived in Florence a few days later, probably during the first week of October.

Lya Haberman and her father, Oscar, lived in huts and barns in the mountains around the Madonna del Colletto a little longer. Lya knows that they were still there on October 9, because she remembers her father saying, "Look where we are for Yom Kippur." The weather was cold, however, and Lya and Oscar were wondering what to do next. Their first contact with the outside world was a young priest who, about a week or ten days earlier, had come to tell them that he would notify the Jewish community in Florence that Jews were hiding in the mountains of the province of Cuneo. This was probably Don Francesco Brondello, vice-curate of Valdieri at the time, who, on his own initiative, collected contributions of clothing and food from his parishioners and distributed them to the Jews in hiding during their first weeks at the Madonna del Colletto.[1]

Around Yom Kippur, Lya says, she and her father received a second visitor. This time it was a Jewish man who spoke only Italian, probably sent by the Jewish community of Florence. The stranger informed them that the Allies were still only in the boot of Italy, well south of Rome, and that the refugees from Saint-Martin-Vésubie could not stay where they were. They would never make it through the winter. Explaining that leaders of the Florence community advised them to go there, the man gave them tickets for the train.[2]

Other survivors share this memory of an unidentified Florentine Jew who visited them in the mountains around the time of Yom Kippur.[3] The man was probably Guido De Angeli, a Delasem representative who met with Don Viale in his home in Borgo San Dalmazzo on October 8. Don Viale described the visit in his diary, although he was not sure who the man was. The two men discussed the best routes and methods for getting refugees out of the mountains and moving them south. At this early date, Don Viale was not yet distributing subsidies to Jews in hiding in any systematic fashion, but he was sheltering some individuals and knew the whereabouts of many others. The visitor therefore asked the priest to do him the great favor of reminding the dispersed Jews that the following day was Yom Kippur. Then the visitor left, evidently to visit Lya and other Jews in the area around the Madonna del Colletto. Don Brondello confirms Don Viale's account, for he relates that on October 8, "a dignified Italian Jew from Florence" came to him in Valdieri and said, "Don Viale has sent me. Please distribute this money to Jews you know about, and please remind them that it is Yom Kippur." Don Brondello adds, "I didn't know what Yom Kippur was, but I did as he asked."[4]

Thus, not long after Yom Kippur in October 1943, Lya and her father boarded a train, presumably without identity papers. "We were a large group," Lya explains, "but we traveled in small groups. We passed through Savona, Genoa, Viareggio." Everywhere they were treated by men and women of the Catholic Church. Lya did not sit on the train with her father, who told her, "In case I am taken, stay put." She comments, "You know, if all this were not confirmed by other people, sometimes I would think it was all a bad dream." She and her father reached Florence safely.

Even before the first Jews from Saint-Martin-Vésubie began to trickle into Florence, small numbers of Jewish refugees from elsewhere in the former Italian-occupied zone of France had begun to arrive. These men, women, and children desperately needed shelter, food, documents, and subsidies. To provide these essential services, a group of Florentine Jews set up what they called the Comitato di Assistenza Profughi—the Refugee Assistance Committee. Among the founders of the group were Chief Rabbi Nathan Cassuto, Raffaele Cantoni, Matilde Cassin, and Giuliano Treves. Cassuto was already a leader of Delasem in Florence, while Cantoni was a national coordinator. Cassin, Cantoni's secretary, was also involved with Delasem locally. The new committee was actually an extension of Delasem itself, and its operating funds came from Delasem as well as from the Florentine Jewish community and private Jewish donors.[5]

Exactly as was happening in Genoa at about the same time, however, the founders of the Refugee Assistance Committee soon realized that they could not deliver services without outside help. The situation for all Jews in Florence was becoming increasingly dangerous. As early as September 13, leaders of the Jewish community heard rumors from friendly local politicians and police that the Germans had requested lists of all Florentine Jews and of specific individuals who would make useful hostages.[6] As a result, the community offices were closed, and many of the employees who operated Jewish schools and social services fled. Fearing arrests of its personnel and confiscation of its assets, Delasem was forced underground.

In a similar situation around the same time, as seen, national Delasem president Lelio Vittorio Valobra went for help to Cardinal Boetto, who agreed and appointed his secretary Don Repetto to distribute subsidies and hide refugees. Now in Florence also, someone from the local Jewish rescue committee went to Cardinal Elia Dalla Costa, the local archbishop. The cardinal agreed to help around September 20 and called upon his secretary, Monsignor Giacomo Meneghello, to serve as a liaison with the Jewish committee. He also contacted Father Cipriano Ricotti, a Dominican priest at the Convento di San Marco, famous for its early-fifteenth-century frescos by Fra Angelico. Father Ricotti later recorded that he began working with Matilde Cassin to find lodgings for Jewish children as early as September 25.[7] About a month later, the number of refugees had risen to such an extent that Cardinal Dalla Costa asked Don Leto Casini, a parish priest from Varlungo, outside Florence, to join the effort to hide Jews and distribute subsidies.[8]

Miriam Löwenwirth with her parents and five brothers and sisters probably reached Florence during the last week of September. With the Refugee Assistance Committee in its infancy, relationships with local priests were still being worked out. Thus, Miriam says that for a time after their arrival in Florence, she and her family slept on the floors of various rooms in or around the synagogue, surely not the safest place to be. Other refugees were lodged temporarily in schools and other properties owned by the Jewish community.

By the time Sigi Hart reached Florence a week or two later, the situation had changed. Services for Rosh Hashanah on October 1 and 2 were held at the synagogue, but by Yom Kippur on October 9 and 10, they were held elsewhere. Like the Löwenwirths, Sigi and his father, Hermann, and brother, Willy, went first to the synagogue, but they found the people there uneasy. Hermann was told that the synagogue was being watched and that it was not safe to stay there. With at least twenty refugees, Sigi, Willy, and Hermann were sent to a Catholic school at La Pietra, in a suburb of Florence. While there, they were delighted to be joined by eighteen-year-old Louis (Ludi) Goldman, with his father, Pinkus, his mother, Maniush, and his brother, Harry, age twelve. Hermann had been a friend of Pinkus Goldman in Berlin before the war. The boys had gotten to know each other in Agde and Saint-Martin-Vésubie. Years later, Ludi wrote a memoir of his experiences, which confirms much of what Sigi has to say.[9] Of La Pietra, he remembered the immense pleasure of the clean beds and the hot meals.

Lya Haberman, who arrived in Florence after Yom Kippur, never went to Jewish properties at all. Her group was sent directly to the archbishop's palace opposite the magnificent cathedral of Santa Maria dei Fiori, Giotto's campanile, and Lorenzo Ghiberti's bronze doors at the Baptistery. There they were met by Matilde Cassin of the newly established Refugee Assistance Committee. They were also introduced to the tall, white-haired Monsignor Giacomo Meneghello, whom Lya soon came to adore. For greater security, the kindly Meneghello broke up Lya's group, sending individuals to separate convents, seminaries, and other Church institutions. Lya's father, Oscar, went to the private home of a priest, not far from the Pitti Palace. Lya was sent to a Catholic boarding school run by the Suore Serve di Maria Addolorata in the via Faentina, which accepted twelve girls. Lya recalls that she and the other Jewish boarders were kept separate from the Catholic students. The archbishop's office paid their expenses from Delasem funds.[10]

Around the time that Lya and her father were settling into Catholic institutions, Miriam Löwenwirth and her family were being moved, sometimes to the same places. Miriam's father found himself at La Pietra with Sigi Hart and Ludi Goldman's families for a few nights before he was placed in the attic of a house at 3, via Vignia Vecchia, a narrow, old street in the city center. The owner of the house was Leonilda (Ilda) Pancani, who had three young children and a husband in the army. Miriam's two sisters, Dalia and Zehava, were sent to the same Catholic boarding school run by the Suore Serve di Maria Addolorata in the via Faentina where Lya Haberman was hiding. Miriam confirms that the twelve Jewish girls lived apart from the other boarders, in part so that their Jewishness would not become public knowledge.[11]

Miriam's two oldest brothers, Shlomo and Aryeh, were placed in the Collegio di Santa Marta, a boarding school and orphanage for boys in Settignano, on the outskirts of Florence. There, they and some fifteen other young Jews blended in with about two hundred non-Jewish students. Everyone treated them with great kindness, but only two of the nuns knew that they were Jews.[12] In all these various hiding places, the Löwenwirths were supported by subsidies from Delasem, distributed by Monsignor Meneghello and Don Casini.

Miriam, her mother, Elena, and her baby brother, Ben-Zion, were sent in early October to the convent of the Suore Francescane Missionarie di Maria in the Piazza Carmine in Florence. Ever defiant, Miriam informed her father that she "would not go to any missionary place where they would try to convert me to their faith. However, my father decided that I was to remain with Mother and there was no further discussion." Miriam later admitted that the nuns made no conversion attempts. She records that forty to fifty women and children were sheltered in a large hall at the convent, with a stage and curtain at one end.[13] They did not live in the cloistered sections of the buildings. "The main entrance to the monastery [sic] was in the Piazza del Carmine," Miriam says, "and the hall where we were hidden was on the other side of the monastery, behind a large garden. [She later identified the entrance to the hall as being at 9, via Leone.] There was also a boarding school in a different section of the monastery. . . . there were many people coming and going. It was a very dangerous situation."

With the closing of the synagogue after Yom Kippur and the arrival of news of the roundup of 1,259 Jews in Rome on October 16 and the deportation of more than a thousand two days later, tension within the Jewish community of Florence greatly increased. Nevertheless, Jewish young people in the city, if not their elders, were determined to enjoy life a bit. Along with Ludi and Harry Goldman, Sigi and Willy were overwhelmingly bored by their enforced leisure at La Pietra. Deprived of an urban environment for more than three years, they were now expected to be quiet and immobile in one of the most beautiful cities in the world. It was impossible. To the utter despair of their parents, they made several hair-raising trips into Florence, walking an hour each way without legal documents and spending what little money they had at the movies and on snacks.

In his memoirs, Ludi left a vivid description of Sigi and Willy at that time:

> Sigi was seventeen, jet black hair and matching eyes, serious-minded but always ready for a practical joke. He projected absolute loyalty in friendship and also a magnificent set of pearly-white teeth. . . . Willy was fifteen, a thin and sickly-looking fellow, with blond hair and blue eyes. Running down the side of the neck behind his right ear was a large scar from a glandular operation some years back. . . . The one outstanding trait about Willy was his stupendous talent for making people laugh.

A great mimic, he could be funny under any circumstances, look innocent in the most compromising squeezes, or keep an absolutely straight face while everybody else was doubling-up laughing. A truly remarkable and welcome companion to have at your side in those gloomy times. . . . The odd thing about these two brothers was that although both had been exposed to the same linguistic environment, Sigi spoke only in Berlinese slang whereas Willy, who could improvise a Hitler speech in faultless German, actually preferred Yiddish.[14]

But the teenagers from Saint-Martin-Vésubie were not to enjoy life in Florence for long. As Ludi explained, "Dr. Nathan Cassuto, the thirty-four-year-old chief rabbi of Florence and a prominent optometrist [and a leader of the Refugee Assistance Committee], arrived one day to tell us that raids against Jews were imminent, and that we would have to go into hiding immediately." Apparently the school at La Pietra was not secure. Thus, Maniush, Ludi's mother, was sent with some other women to the Convento del Spirito Santo in Varlungo, in Don Casini's parish. At this convent, according to Ludi, about sixty nuns lived under strict rules of cloister. They could receive outsiders only from one particular room, where they spoke through a screen in a wall to visitors in an adjoining area. Also according to Ludi, even the priest during Holy Communion passed the sacred Host to the nuns through a hole in another screen in the chapel. The Jewish women at this convent slept in rooms on the first floor that were not part of the cloistered quarters. They remained isolated from all the nuns except the abbess and about four others who knew they were Jews.[15]

Meanwhile, Sigi, Willy, and Hermann, along with Ludi, Harry, and Pinkus Goldman, were among about forty Jewish men and boys sent to temporary quarters in a large, abandoned movie house. As Sigi describes it, there was a big stage at one end of the auditorium. The seats on the ground floor had been removed and about fifty or sixty cots set up. Ludi wrote the same, adding that his family settled in at the base of the stairs leading to the balcony, where the folded chairs were stored. This detail is crucial to the story to come. The men and boys in the movie house had access to the courtyard for food, conversation, and exercise, in full view of the neighbors who were supposed to believe that they were Italian refugees. Sigi says, "It was madness to be there, in a quiet neighborhood, with so many people going in and out."

CHAPTER SEVENTEEN

Arrests and Narrow Escapes in Florence, November 1943

Sigi Hart, Miriam Löwenwirth, and Lya Haberman

THE RAID THAT Rabbi Nathan Cassuto warned of was not long in coming. At dawn on Saturday, November 6, German SS agents aided by Fascist collaborators launched their first major anti-Jewish raid in Florence, arresting scores of people at the Jewish community's school in via Farini and the Jewish orphanage in via Bolognese, both of which had been vacated to house refugees. Apparently the large numbers involved, mostly from Saint-Martin-Vésubie and the province of Cuneo, exceeded the ability of the Refugee Assistance Committee to place them in safer quarters. A nearby garage housing fugitives was another target. Then at about 5:00 A.M. on the drizzly, foggy morning of either November 7 or 8, the police reached the movie theater where Sigi Hart and his father and brother were hiding.[1] Within a few minutes, some forty sleepy men and boys who had been evading the Nazis for years had scrambled into their clothes, grabbed a few belongings, and been shoved into waiting trucks. The few who tried to hide under cots or luggage were discovered, beaten, and pushed along with the others. But not quite all of them. Sigi's fifteen-year-old brother, Willy, had run up to the balcony and hidden under the chairs. For some reason, the Germans did not check the balcony, and Willy escaped.

Along with the Goldmans and the other men from the movie house, Sigi and his father were taken to an Italian military camp near the Arno River. The installation consisted of several barracks surrounded by a twenty-foot concrete wall surmounted by strands of loosely coiled barbed wire. After being searched and relieved of their valuables, the arriving prisoners were assigned to a miserable stable once used for horses. As more and more prisoners arrested elsewhere in Florence arrived throughout the day, Sigi and Ludi looked around for a way out. Toward evening, twelve-year-old Harry Goldman, Ludi's clever little brother, beat them to it. After telling Ludi that he was going to try to escape, the boy found a tin can and converted it into a soccer ball. Kicking it ever closer to the entrance of a large courtyard, he managed to reach an area of the camp where there were few people and security was low. Once inside the courtyard, he kicked his "ball" to the wall, which had iron reinforcing bars protruding from it at regular intervals. Scaling the wall in a matter of seconds, he was then afraid to jump the twenty feet to the ground on the other side.

As Ludi described it from Harry's later explanation, "He called out to a cyclist passing by. The man, puzzled, looked up, got off his bicycle and leaned it against the wall. Then, when he was standing directly under him, Harry said, 'Catch me,' and jumped. Instinctively the man opened his arms and braced Harry's fall." Annoyed at first by what he took to be a childish prank, the cyclist changed his mind when Harry explained that he had just escaped from the Germans. He drove the boy away from the wall as quickly as he could and, if Harry had been willing to give him the address of his mother in the convent in Varlungo, would gladly have taken him there. But Harry kept the address to himself and, as Ludi wrote proudly of his little brother, "took the tramway to the Varlungo convent, paying his fare with a ten-lire note he had kept from the Germans."[2]

Around 8:00 that night, after Harry had escaped, a German guard came into the stable to distribute bread rolls. Each prisoner was told to take four, two for the evening and two for the next morning. When asked why, the guard, according to Ludi, answered, "the transport leaves early for Auschwitz and there won't be time for distributing bread then."[3] Because survivors of deportations rarely mention that they knew where they were going, this statement must be treated with caution. Also, even if they were told the destination, it is doubtful that they understood what it entailed. But whatever they knew, Ludi and Sigi certainly realized that they were to be deported the next day. They redoubled their efforts to escape. During the day, they had noticed that the toilets were located about seventy feet from the stable, near the outside wall. Prisoners went to the toilets in groups, accompanied by a guard. Ludi and Sigi had also noticed that this part of the wall had metal reinforcing bars sticking out at various intervals. They did not know then what Harry had done, but they too had the idea of climbing it.

Ludi's father, recovering from emergency hernia surgery performed in Demonte when he was hiding there, could scarcely walk. He certainly could not scale a twenty-foot wall and jump down the other side. Ludi said good-bye to him, promising to beseech the priests they both knew in Florence to intervene on his behalf. With Sigi and Sigi's father, Hermann, he then joined a group to go to the toilet. Sigi explains that the guard at the toilet was pacing along a fixed route. When he faced a different direction, it was possible to get to the wall. Ludi went first and was over in a minute. Hermann took longer. On the second bar, he slipped and fell, making a loud noise. To escape the notice of the guard, father and son returned to the toilet. On the second attempt, Sigi gave his father a boost, and he made it. Then it was Sigi's turn, but the guard had turned back toward him. Sigi returned to the toilet, but the guard had noticed him and was suspicious. Sigi tried to stay in the toilet until the guard left, to no avail. Finally the guard hauled him out, sent him back to the stable, and locked the prisoners in. There was no more possibility of escape.

Sigi Hart and Pinkus Goldman were deported to Auschwitz the following morning.[4] With them were perhaps as many as four hundred other Jews, many of them newly arrived, unregistered refugees whose names remain largely unknown. Passenger lists for this particular convoy apparently do not exist. Only Sigi and perhaps one other person returned.[5] Pinkus Goldman did not survive. In a prime example of the value of survivor testimony, Sigi's account, complemented by that of Ludi Goldman regarding the raid itself, is all that is known of these events.

For the Jews still in Florence after the German raids of November 6, 7, and 8, the terror was only beginning. On Friday night, November 26, as a result of an informer, German police and their Italian collaborators raided "a meeting of the Refugee Assistance Committee at 2, via dei Pucci, near the cathedral and the archbishop's palace. Don Leto Casini was arrested there, along with Rabbi Nathan Cassuto and four other Jews. Don Casini was later released, but Rabbi Cassuto and the other Jews were deported to Auschwitz on January 30, 1944, in a convoy carrying at least 605 prisoners. Twenty-two of the deportees returned, including two of the four arrested with Rabbi Cassuto. The rabbi himself did not return.[6]

Later that same night, November 26–27, German SS police and some

Fascists launched three other raids. Little is known of two of them, involving the San Giuseppe recreation center in the via Domenico Cirillo and the Convento delle Suore di San Giuseppe dell'Apparizione in the via Gioberti. The recreation center was sheltering twenty Jewish men, the convent an unknown number of Jewish women and children. These victims were arrested and deported, but the details are not recorded. The third raid, however, is better known. In this case, the target was the convent of the Suore Francescane Missionarie di Maria, attached to the church of Santa Maria del Carmine in a quiet residential neighborhood across the Arno River from the center of Florence. Today, tourists visiting the renowned Masaccio frescoes in the church's Brancacci Chapel have no idea of the brutality and horror that occurred there more than sixty years ago. Some forty to fifty Jewish women and children were being hidden in the convent at the time of the raid. Among them was Miriam Löwenwirth.

About thirty German police and Fascist collaborators arrived at the convent at 3:00 A.M. on Saturday, November 27. "We woke up to the sounds of breaking glass," says Miriam. "There was total chaos all around. I think that [the Germans] did not know how many women were there." According to a report by Mother Superior Sandra written for Cardinal Dalla Costa soon after the raid, the Germans gathered all the terrified Jews in the main hall and left them under guard, informing them that they would return. Not until 6:00 P.M. on Sunday did they finally get down to the business of registering their prisoners along with their possessions. At that point, wrote Mother Sandra, "The [German] commander took a dear young woman named Lea, who was among our protected ones and who knew some German, to be an interpreter of the two languages spoken by the Jewish women: French and Italian. . . . This young woman understood her position so well that she succeeded in getting a few of the women freed, along with herself." When the interrogations were over, according to Mother Sandra, about thirty women and children remained in detention. Since she placed the original number of Jews at the convent at fifty, her implication is that about twenty had been released.[7]

The "dear young woman named Lea" was Miriam Löwenwirth, whose second name was Léa or Leah. She generally used that second name during the war. Miriam confirms Mother Sandra's report. She explains that she volunteered to act as an interpreter, adding, "There were rumors that the Germans and the Hungarians were cooperating with each other and I intuitively had an idea that perhaps if we posed as Hungarians, we might be released." Hungary was indeed allied with the Third Reich at this point, and as a result, Hungarian Jews both inside and outside that country were not usually being deported. Miriam's family came from a Slovakian village not far from the Hungarian border. "I did not know a word in Hungarian," Miriam admits, "but my mother could speak the language." She and her mother, Elena, hid their documents under their mattresses and Miriam told the German who interrogated her that they had been lost. "How do you expect me to believe you?" asked the German. As usual, Miriam was undaunted. "At that moment," she says, "I thought that I have nothing to lose and told him to speak to me in Hungarian. He looked at me and simply said that I can go but I had better make sure that I obtain some documents."

Miriam quickly realized that others might pass as Hungarians as well. She and her mother advised the women they knew from Slovakia to do what they had done, and it worked. Including her mother and Ben-Zion, Miriam saved about nine people. Three of these were Edith Silberstein, from Vienna, with her two daughters, Elena and Suzanne. Edith's husband, Walter, was hiding with Miriam's father. According to Miriam, the two girls were released and immediately placed in other convents. Elena, age four, went to the same Collegio di Santa Marta where Miriam's brothers were. The school took only boys, but since no one could find a place for Elena, it made an exception for her. Despite the devoted care of nuns there, however, Elena soon died in a hospital in Florence, Miriam says, "pining for her mother." Miriam adds that after the war, she kept in touch with the school's mother superior, Benedetta Vespignani, who "was unable to talk about the tragedy of Elena, it was too difficult for her."

One-year-old Suzanne Silberstein was more fortunate, surviving the war in another convent near the Piazza Michelangelo. Tragically, Suzanne's mother, Edith, and her father, Walter, who had left the house where he had been hiding with Eliyahu Löwenwirth, were arrested in Florence on January 20, 1944, and sent to the Italian internment camp of Fossoli, five kilometers from Carpi in the province of Modena. Until July 1944, when the approaching Allies threatened the camp and forced it to transfer operations to Bolzano, Fossoli was the assembly point for most Jews arrested in Italy and awaiting deportation to Auschwitz. Edith and Walter Silberstein's son Richard was born at Fossoli on March 29. All three were deported to Auschwitz on May 16, and all three died there. Walter may have been admitted to the camp and died from deprivation and hard labor. With a tiny baby, Edith would not have been admitted. She and Richard were almost certainly gassed.[8]

Miriam also saved Lottie Brender, whose husband was also hiding with Miriam's father, as well as Lottie's twenty-three-month-old daughter, Eliza, and two other women whose names she never knew. Lottie and Eliza moved to Israel after the war. Still another woman, a Madame Rathaus, whose husband was also hiding with Eliyahu Löwenwirth, survived the raid on the convent because she had been taken to the hospital just before it occurred. Her son Yitzchak Rathaus, age three in 1943, was saved by the nuns and lives in Israel today.

On Monday or Tuesday night, November 29 or 30, German SS guards took away the thirty or so women and children who had not been released at the convent. The nuns supplied them with bread from their own meager rations. Miriam said her painful good-byes and watched them leave. The victims were shipped to Verona. From there, on December 6, 1943, they were included in convoy 5 from Milan and Verona to Auschwitz. Also deported at that time were the victims of the other two raids in Florence on November 26, at the San Giuseppe recreation center and the Convento delle Suore di San Giuseppe dell'Apparizione. Two hundred forty-six of the deportees on the train have been identified, but the total number is not known. Five people are known to have survived.[9]

After the raid in the Piazza del Carmine, Miriam, her mother, and Ben-Zion stayed on at the convent for a time. Miriam visited her father often in the house in the via Vignia Vecchia where he was hiding, but early in 1944, she arrived to learn that he had been arrested by Italian police on January 5 along with his two friends, Hermann Brender and Enrico (Henri) Rathaus. About a month earlier, on December 1, 1943, Mussolini's puppet regime had ordered that all Jews in Italy, with a few exceptions, were to be arrested and interned in camps within the country.[10] After that decree, regular Italian police and carabinieri joined the Germans in the hunt for Jews. Better able to recognize and find them, they often did the job more effectively. Miriam believes that, in the case of her father, the police were tipped off by an informer. Ilda Pancani, the woman who was hiding him, was also arrested and subjected to harsh interrogation, but Miriam later learned that she was released with a warning after about two weeks.[11] The three Jewish men were interned in a prison in Florence.

Miriam and her mother, Elena, now realized that they were not safe at the convent in the Piazza del Carmine because the police might learn from Eliyahu that they were not Hungarians and therefore not exempt from arrest. Elena therefore placed her baby at the same school of Santa Marta where her other two sons were living. She then collected her two younger daughters from the convent of the Suore Serve di Maria Addolorata and embarked on a hazardous train trip to Rome. Before she left, a Dominican priest named Father Taddei, in the same convent as Father Cipriano Ricotti, gave her the name and address of Father Maria Benedetto. This Capuchin priest was doing in Rome what Monsignor Meneghello, Father Ricotti, and Don Casini were doing in Florence, Don Viale and his priests in and around Borgo San Dalmazzo, and Don Repetto in Genoa. All were hiding Jews and distributing Delasem money to support them. Father Benedetto provided Elena Löwenwirth and her daughters with an apartment, which she shared with another Jewish family. He also gave her false documents and a monthly financial subsidy on which to live.

Despite the dangers, Miriam insisted on remaining at the convent in the Piazza del Carmine in Florence in order to help her father. In desperation, she went to the Hungarian consulate for assistance. There she received false documents verifying her Hungarian citizenship and that of her father, but she was not able to obtain his release from prison. Every Wednesday for about six weeks, she took food packages to him, but she was never able to see him. She was not even sure he received the packages, yet she never gave up.

At one point in the middle of February, Miriam received a request from her mother. Elena wanted her eldest daughter to bring her three younger brothers from Florence to Rome, where they could hide with their mother and sisters. Miriam thought it a reasonable request. To her, Rome seemed safer and better organized for Jewish rescue than Florence. With her sister Zehava and another girl her age, Elisheva Drezner, both of whom were sent up from Rome to help her, Miriam went to the school of Santa Marta to collect her three brothers and Elisheva's three brothers as well. The nine youngsters then embarked on yet another incredible odyssey. The trip took five days. As Miriam writes, "We rode on whatever came by, horse and cart and any other available form of transport. . . . It was snowing all around." At Perugia, two families took them in, fed them, and gave them beds for the night. A German soldier put them in the back of his jeep and drove them to Arezzo, where they again found shelter with a kind family. They divided into two groups for the remainder of the trip, but somehow they all made it.

Miriam was anxious to return to Florence to be near her father, but she wanted to meet and thank Father Benedetto before she left Rome. Her account of their meeting is invaluable, for there is little survivor testimony about this remarkable priest. "Padre Benedetto was a very special person," Miriam writes, "and when I spoke to him I felt most comfortable. It was as though I was speaking to a rabbi and not a priest of the Catholic faith. He listened to me as I spoke to him of Zionism, my plans for going to Eretz Yisrael after the war." After a discussion of ways to help the Jews hiding in Florence, Miriam volunteered to carry money from Father Benedetto's Delasem group to the Refugee Assistance Committee there.[12] She also offered to take fifteen false documents to Jews in the area around Borgo San Dalmazzo where she had hidden and which she knew quite well. Her only condition was that Father Benedetto not tell her mother. Then at the end of the meeting, she says, "When I left Padre Benedetto, he made a gesture that I have never forgotten. He accompanied me to the door and said that he would bless me as is customary in Judaism. He placed his two hands on my head and made a blessing. . . . When we parted he said to me: 'Continue to be a good Jewess!' That was the first time I had ever had a conversation with a priest and I said to myself: 'He is a good priest.'"

On her way to Borgo San Dalmazzo from Rome, Miriam stopped in Florence on February 26, 1944, to make her weekly visit to the prison where her father was being held. There she learned that Eliyahu and his two companions had been transferred to Fossoli the day before. At that point, she realized that the prison guard to whom she had been delivering packages for her father had known all along that she was Jewish. He had never reported her to the police.

Although Miriam was devastated by the news of her father's transfer to Fossoli, she resumed her journey toward Borgo San Dalmazzo the following day. She met her two contacts in Demonte, where, she recalls, the surrounding mountains were covered with snow. The documents and money that she delivered enabled several Jewish refugees hiding in the area to travel to Florence or Rome. As we shall see in the next chapter, Charles and Marianne Roman, who were in hiding around Demonte and left for Rome in March 1944, may have been two of them. Thus, those refugees were liberated in Rome in June or in Florence in August 1944, rather than in the province of Cuneo in April 1945, and were spared the cold and deprivation of yet another winter in the mountains.

In the snowy mountains of northern Italy, however, Miriam's heart was with her father. She returned to Florence the same day that she delivered the documents, to see if she could help him. Of course, there was nothing she could do. She returned to the convent in the Piazza del Carmine, where she remained until the liberation of the city in August.

Father and daughter were able to exchange letters until May 16, when Eliyahu was deported from Fossoli to Bergen-Belsen.[13] Eliyahu's letters to Miriam were addressed to the convent, but to a false name. The nuns understood. In a last letter to his daughter, Eliyahu wrote, "We are being taken to an unknown destination. God willing we will meet again and tell each other everything. I am feeling well in view of the situation. Thank you for all your help and for the pictures of mother and the children. Now you will understand why I hinted to you not to come to visit me in the camp. I hope that you are well and that you have some news of the family. Take care of yourself and also of Mother and the children. A thousand kisses, Father."

In fact, two trains departed from Fossoli on May 16, 1944. One carried about 580 prisoners to Auschwitz, of whom sixty returned after the war. The second train took 166 mostly Libyan Jews with British citizenship to Bergen-Belsen, which was not technically an extermination camp.[14] The second convoy also included some Turkish, Swiss, and Hungarian Jews. Perhaps because of the Hungarian identification papers that Miriam had secured for her father, Eliyahu was part of this group. Because Turkey and Switzerland were neutral, the Germans treated Jews from these nations differently from those in the countries they occupied. Hungary was a former ally of the Third Reich, and its Jews were also treated differently for a time. Nevertheless, special consideration for Hungarian Jews as late as May 1944 is puzzling. The Germans had occupied Hungary in March 1944 and initiated mass deportations of Jews on April 27. By the end of June, more than 380,000 Hungarian Jews had been deported to Auschwitz, and a large majority of them were dead. Yet Hungarian Jews in Italy in May were not being deported to Auschwitz.

After about six months at Bergen-Belsen, most prisoners in Eliyahu's group were transferred to Biberach, where most survived. Eliyahu, however, did not survive. Miriam has evidence that her father was transferred to Sachsenhausen in November 1944 and from there to one of the eleven camps in the Kaufering system, near Dachau.[15] There he performed hard labor until he died, Miriam believes in a typhus epidemic, on February 11, 1945.

Lya Haberman was not petrified with fear after the German SS roundups of Jews in Florence in November 1943. "We had no idea where the concentration camps were, or what was happening there," she says. "We were scared, but when you are young, you are not so scared." Her father was clearly more concerned. When Oscar heard that some convents in Florence had been raided on November 26, his first thought was for his daughter. Learning that she was safe, he decided to take no more chances with large institutions. After taking Lya from the Catholic boarding school of the Suore Serve di Maria Addolorata, he stopped in the Piazza Dalmatia to buy cigarettes, chat with the owner, and make some sort of plan. Oscar, whose hair had turned white even though he was only about forty years old, told the man that his "granddaughter" needed to find a family to live with. The man referred them to a French woman and an Italian man who had no children. Oscar told the couple that Lya was French, to explain her accent. They accepted her, and she paid them for her room and board. Lya took the name Lydia Mazzola, although she does not remember if she had false papers. To maintain her disguise as a non-Jew, she went to church regularly. Meanwhile the Allies were bombing the factories and the railroad stations. She does not remember being particularly frightened.

Lya has particularly clear and fond memories of Monsignor Meneghello. "He was a saint," she declares, noting also that he and her father became great friends. Each month, Lya went to the archbishop's palace, which housed the offices of the archdiocese, to pick up the Delasem subsidy that enabled her to pay her rent. "Meneghello was always wonderful," she says, "and always greeted me with a 'Ciao, piccola!'" On her father's suggestion, Lya sought additional help at the Swiss consulate, where she met a man whom she believes was a vice-consul. She explained to him that she and her father were Jews. "He was very humane," she says. "I told him that we had some money in America [which was true], and that after the war we would pay back anything he could give us now. So he gave us some money too." She was even able to save a bit, for the uncertain future.

Lya's father was eventually moved to a Catholic nursing home, where Lya visited him once a week. Because clandestine life was boring, she also sought the company of other teenagers. Occasionally she met with Willy Hartmayer, Sigi's younger brother, and Ludi Goldman, refugees her own age from Saint-Martin-Vésubie. The three young people met in a movie house, where they sat in the back row and talked. Food was a major topic of conversation, since they were always hungry. Finally, Lya recalls, Willy figured out how to falsify bread coupons, using the edging of maps to make an official-looking border. She was never sure whether the baker who accepted the coupons knew they were false and was just being nice or if he was really fooled.

Sigi and Willy's father, Hermann Hartmayer, was also sheltered in the nursing home with Oscar. After all they had been through, they looked much older than their years. Because they sometimes worked in the fields for the nursing home, the other patients marveled that "old people" could do such work. Eventually Oscar brought Lya there also. When she contracted typhoid fever, she says, the nuns in the nursing home took good care of her. A week or two later, Florence was liberated.

CHAPTER EIGHTEEN

Traveling to and Hiding in Rome,
January–June 1944

Charles Roman and Jacques Samson

Charles Roman

When Miriam Löwenwirth, Sigi Hart, and Lya Haberman set out for Florence in September and October 1943, Charles Roman and his mother, Marianne, chose to remain in the mountains of the province of Cuneo. Don Viale's subsidies would keep them alive through the winter, they reasoned, and perhaps the Allies would arrive in the spring. They spent the winter of 1943–1944 in a rough and freezing hut on the northern slopes of the valley of the Stura. Spring brought an easing of the physical discomfort, but it did not bring the British and American troops, still stalled south of Rome. The melting snows also encouraged partisan and German activities. All too aware of that danger, Charles and Marianne eventually decided to try to move south. Marianne's brother-in-law, Franz Edelschein, had already left, heading for the Swiss border alone in February. He was never heard from again.

In March 1944, Marianne obtained false documents on official legation paper, identifying seventeen-year-old Charles as a Hungarian national who had to go to the Hungarian consulate in Rome to be inducted into the army. Charles and his mother may not have known it at the time, but these documents were probably supplied by Delasem in Rome, which was receiving help from the Hungarian consul Viktor Szasz there.[1] The documents may have been conveyed to Genoa and then relayed to Don Viale's priests in the province of Cuneo by the same network that relayed Delasem funds. Or they may have been carried directly to Don Viale by couriers from Rome, one of whom was eighteen-year-old Miriam Löwenwirth. In any case, Don Viale's priests made the final distributions. Letters to Don Viale after the war thanking him for the monthly stipends that his priests distributed make it clear that he was also dealing in documents.[2]

With their new false documents, Charles and Marianne set out on a hazardous journey. In March 1944, they took a train first to Cuneo, then to Turin, and then to Bologna. In Bologna, the tracks had been destroyed by bombs, so they walked for two kilometers until they could get on a train to Florence. There again the tracks had been bombed. Forced to wait until the next day but afraid to stay at the station, where passengers were constantly subjected to police inspections, they walked around Florence and rested in churches until the curfew forced them back. Predictably, the station was locked at 10:00 P.M. and a German officer with an Italian translator began a document check. Charles and Marianne were sleeping on the floor. When the officer reached them, someone called him out of the room. When he returned, he had forgotten where he left off. He started again with the people on the other side of Charles and Marianne, passing them over. When asked why, since he had false documents, he was so worried, Charles replies that the papers were not particularly convincing and any German would soon have discovered that he did not speak Hungarian. Yet again, Charles had the narrowest possible escape.

The following morning Charles and his mother took a train to Orvieto and had another close call. The tracks outside the city had been bombed, so they walked to the station. They heard a loud siren, but since it was noon, they thought that it was sounding to tell the time. A passing motorist cried out, "Andate via, andate via!" They still did not understand until the bombing began. In a panic, they jumped onto a passing truck, rode up to the oldest part of the city on the top of a hill, and gaped at planes almost at eye level. Bombs hit the station they had just come from, blowing up an ammunition train. The explosions and fire went on for hours. Then Marianne began to cry. "Why?" asked her son. "You are safe." "Yes," she replied, "but we left all our luggage down there." She had even lost a shoe.

In the chaos following the bombing, an Austrian *Feldpolizei* was directing traffic. Charles recognized his Viennese dialect and, in his own best version of the same and with what he calls his "most authoritative Germanic pose," informed the man that he had to report to Rome. The Austrian stopped a flatbed ammunition truck on which three Italian girls and three German soldiers returning to the front were riding. There was no special relationship between the women and the soldiers. Charles, it was decided as he and his mother clambered aboard, would be the interpreter. "For the Germans, I was the Italian who spoke German. For the Italians, I was the German who spoke Italian," Charles recalls gleefully. After about forty kilometers, the eight passengers hitched another ride, this time in a normal truck. All along the road there were signs reading "Caution, low-flying planes." This time Charles's job was to stand on the tailgate and kick the canvas-covered back of the truck when he saw planes coming. The passengers in the back of the truck would bang on the cab and the driver would find some shelter, preferably a group of trees, in which to hide the truck. At the roadblocks, Charles spoke perfect German and looked the part. When asked if everyone else in the truck was German, he replied, "Jah, natürlich."

A few weeks before Charles arrived, the Germans had accepted the proposal of Pope Pius XII and the Badoglio government that Rome be declared an open city. According to Charles, military trucks within the city limits were therefore subject to tight control. As a result, the eight people in Charles's group had to leave their truck at the Ponte Milvio, which crosses the Tiber well to the north of the city center. All eight had to walk the long distance to the girls' home, but it was after curfew. When the first Italian patrol stopped them, there was no problem. The three soldiers in the group simply said, "We're Germans, and we're escorting these Italian girls home." The second Italian patrol was more difficult. An Italian officer who spoke German threatened to arrest them all. The three soldiers with Charles became indignant, and Charles joined them. One of the three then pulled a gun on the Italian officer and declared that the group was going on despite his objections. It did, but the officer threatened to return with a German patrol. Given Rome's open city status, Charles believes, even German soldiers had to have permits to be wandering freely through the city after curfew, and those in his group did not have them. The young people reached the girls' house safely, however, and once there, the German soldiers shared their food with the others, and they all fell asleep. Charles shared a field cot with one of the soldiers. The next morning, the soldiers went on to join their unit at Monte Cassino.

When Charles and his mother arrived in Rome in late March or early April 1944, the city was a dangerous place for Jews. On Saturday, October 16,

1943, just six weeks after the armistice and the German occupation of Italy, German security police had launched their first major Jewish roundup. The victims were 1,259 Jews living in the former Roman ghetto and throughout the city. Of the 1,259 arrested, at least 1,023 were deported directly from Rome to Auschwitz two days later.[3] Most Jews in the city went into hiding after that roundup, but the manhunts continued with undiminished ferocity until the liberation of Rome on June 4, 1944. German police continued to make most of the arrests for another six weeks, but after Mussolini ordered his own police and carabinieri to arrest and intern all Jews throughout the country on December 1, 1943, Italian agents took over with a vengeance.

At least another 671 Jewish men, women, and children were arrested in Rome after the October 16 roundup until June 4, 1944. Most were held for a time in filthy cells in Rome's Regina Coeli Prison, on the banks of the Tiber just a kilometer or two from the Vatican. Toward the end of February 1944, many were sent to the central Italian internment camp of Fossoli. Others, arrested later, followed them. They were included among the 2,461 Jews deported from Fossoli in six different convoys between February 19 and June 26, 1944. Still other Jews arrested in Rome were on seven other deportation trains that originated in Milan, Mantua, Verona, Bologna, or Florence; three from Bolzano; and many from Trieste. From October 1943 to June 1944, Rome was a city of terror.[4]

When they left their northern hiding place, Charles and his mother were instructed to report to the Jewish committee in the Albergo Salus, in the Piazza Indipendenza near the Stazione Termini in Rome. They had no idea how to get there, so one of the girls accompanied them on the long trip across the city. She even paid the streetcar fare and, somewhat to their embarrassment, went into the hotel with them. She did not seem to want to leave. The situation became tricky when other Jews from Saint-Martin-Vésubie in the hotel began to recognize them. Finally, however, the girl left. Charles never told her who he was or what he was doing, and she never found out.

The fact that Charles and Marianne were directed to the Albergo Salus is another indication that they had been receiving help in the province of Cuneo from Don Viale and Delasem. Don Viale distributed Delasem subsidies, documents, and information in the north, while the Albergo Salus was a Delasem shelter for Jewish refugees from France in Rome. The Jewish committee that Charles and his mother were instructed to contact in

Rome was certainly a Delasem affiliate. Without knowing it, Charles had become indirectly involved with two remarkable men, Settimio Sorani, the Jewish director of Delasem in Rome, and a French Capuchin priest named Father Marie Benoît or, in Italian, Maria Benedetto—the same priest who had so impressed Miriam Löwenwirth.

When the Germans occupied Rome after the Italian armistice with the Allies, Sorani, like his colleague Lelio Vittorio Valobra in Genoa, realized that he could no longer operate legally to help the rapidly increasing number of Jewish refugees in Italy. Sometime in mid- or late September 1943, Sorani turned to Father Benedetto, who had already been involved in Jewish rescue in Marseille and Nice before his order called him to Rome in late June. When Benedetto agreed to help, Sorani transferred Delasem's operations from its offices at 2, Lungotevere Sanzio to the priest's monastery at 159, via Sicilia. There, the French priest and the Roman Jew, with Giuseppe Levi from Yugoslavia, Stefan Schwamm, a non-Jewish lawyer from Vienna, and Aron Kastersztein, a Polish Jewish refugee from France, set up a truly international rescue committee. Until the liberation of Rome, the committee, with help from an unknown number of Jewish and Catholic volunteers, contacted, hid, and supported more than two thousand, and perhaps as many as four thousand, Jews in Rome. Of these, between one thousand and fifteen hundred were Jewish refugees, especially from France and Yugoslavia, while the remainder were Italians.[5] Most were provided with false documents and hidden in *pensioni* and private homes and apartments.

While Sorani and Benedetto's successes were impressive, Charles and Marianne stumbled into those rescuers' only major disaster. The Albergo Salus was full when the mother and son arrived. The Jewish committee there referred them to the Pensione Heslin, 28, via Palestro, not far from the main railroad station. A short time after they had settled in, probably around May 1, the Albergo Salus was raided. Aron Kastersztein, charged by Sorani and Benedetto with sheltering refugees from France, had been betrayed by two French spies. Now he and an unknown number of other Jews at the Salus were arrested. Sorani and his aides, terrified that the Germans would return for the Jews remaining at the hotel, immediately and successfully moved them into other lodgings. Thus, according to Sorani, many of them survived. According to Charles, however, the nearby Pensione Heslin was also raided a few days later. Charles and his mother were staying in a maid's room behind the kitchen. The Italian police (Charles thinks that there were no Germans present) searched the pensione, looked into the kitchen, but never went back to the maid's room. Another narrow escape. They were certainly lucky. At least twenty, and perhaps as many as sixty-two, refugees like themselves had been caught.[6]

After the raids on the Albergo Salus and the Pensione Heslin, Charles and Marianne had to move again. This time Charles went to a conventional real estate agency to rent a furnished apartment. There he met Carmen, a young agent whom he befriended, he says, after a little flirting. Within a few days, Carmen found Charles and Marianne an apartment at 21, via Santa Maria Ausiliatrice in the Tuscolana section of Rome. When the landlord, who worked for the Ministry of Finance, demanded references, Carmen told him that they came from the German High Command and she would guarantee them. Her recommendation was all the more credible because she had worked for the German military command for a time and spoke a little German. The private apartment must have seemed like pure luxury to a mother and son who had recently spent several winter months with about twelve other people in a tiny cabin in the mountains without heat or water. On the eighth floor, their new quarters included a separate bedroom, kitchen, and terrace. The fact that the elevator had been shut down because there was not enough electricity and because it was too expensive to operate was a minor inconvenience. Charles and Marianne were still receiving money from Delasem to pay for their room and board.

During his period of enforced leisure in via Santa Maria Ausiliatrice, Charles became friendly with the landlord's son. Together the two young men listened to the BBC, or Radio Londra, as it was called. On June 3, 1944, the Germans set up a defense post at the base of their building, which made them nervous, but the following day, Charles and his friend had the immense pleasure of sitting on their terrace and watching them leave. That night, says Charles, "it was an unbelievable sight—an unending line of equipment coming into Rome with the American army. If the Germans had had that much, they would certainly have conquered the world."

Jacques Samson

Jacques Samson and his father, Szlama, left for Rome in January 1944, about two months earlier than Charles and Marianne Roman. Until then, they had hidden with their new friend Serena Gerhard and her children and niece in a succession of mountain huts above Valdieri until the freezing weather and lack of supplies forced them back to the town. There they hid with Signora Orselina, the elderly peasant woman who had sheltered the Gerhards for a time in September 1943. The Germans launched another raid on Valdieri on January 7, 1944, however, and three young men were killed. One of the victims, Abraham Goldemberg, was a Jewish refugee from Saint-Martin-Vésubie.[7] The raid convinced Jacques's group that they had to leave. For safety, they decided, the Gerhards would leave first. Jacques and Szlama would follow.

Jacques remembers the trip well. Sometimes he and his father hitched rides with German soldiers who, he says, were always very pleasant. Szlama must have been in touch with Delasem while hiding in Valdieri because, like Charles and Marianne Roman, he and his son had instructions to go to the Albergo Salus in Rome. Fortunately, however, they did not stay there long. Szlama developed pneumonia and was sent to a hospital, where he remained until the liberation of Rome. Jacques was supplied with false papers and sent to the Pontificio Seminario Francese, in the heart of the old city. He speaks warmly of a Father Meunier, who taught Italian to anyone who wanted to learn. The young man worked hard at the task. Nevertheless, he must have been desperately bored because he could not leave the building. He was not, however, the only outsider in the seminary. He remembers that there were also some American and British soldiers hiding there, along with many other Jewish men and boys. After the war, another source confirmed that priests at the Seminario Francese had hidden fifty Jews.[8]

The Gerhards survived with false papers. Because Serena's birthplace was on the Hungarian border, and because she spoke Hungarian, she was able to obtain documents from sympathetic Hungarian diplomats in Rome, identifying her and her children and niece as Hungarian non-Jews. She also almost certainly received food coupons and financial subsidies from Father Benedetto's and Settimio Sorani's rescue network. Like Charles and Marianne Roman, she was among the thousands of Jewish refugees in Rome who were sustained by those two brave men and their many assistants.

CHAPTER NINETEEN

Auschwitz

Sigi Hart and Boris Carmeli

WHEN THEY WERE CRAMMED into boxcars for the trip to Auschwitz, Sigi Hart and Boris Carmeli were both without their families. Seventeen-year-old Sigi traveled with Pinkus Goldman, the father of his friend Ludi, who was also alone.[1] Sigi would turn eighteen on November 15, 1943, the day after his arrival at the camp. Of the trip, Sigi says, "When I was in the train, I realized that I was no more a child. It came to me like you take away a curtain, that this is the real thing, that something is going to happen." The train stopped at the Brenner Pass leading from Italy into Austria, and the German guards began checking all the names. "They wanted to know how many people were coming into the Third Reich," Sigi explains. "They were very methodical." When the Germans asked Sigi where his father was, he said he did not know but that he must be somewhere in another car. They told him that if they did not find his father, they would shoot him. Sigi insisted that his father was on the train, and apparently the Germans never learned otherwise.

Fifteen-year-old Boris Carmeli was also without his family on the train that carried him from Drancy to Auschwitz on December 7, 1943.[2] Unlike Sigi, however, he knew many of the roughly one thousand passengers, for a large portion of the approximately 350 Jews from Saint-Martin-Vésubie arrested in the area of Valdieri and Borgo San Dalmazzo on September 18 and held in the barracks in Borgo until November 21 were on the same train. Of the trip, Boris recalls, "It was terrible! The cattle wagons were overcrowded and we had to stand up and were squeezed together. There was no toilet and we had to do our needs where we stood. I cannot remember how many days that trip lasted."

When Sigi's train arrived, he recalls, "I saw a round gate, a platform, the Germans were shouting." He also witnessed the selection process. First the men and women were separated and then a German with a whip tapped a few of the younger and stronger people on the shoulder and sent them into yet another line. Ludi's father was selected that way, and so was Sigi. Men not selected by the guard with the whip were then sent to join the women and children. Then a German guard asked the group of selected men if they all felt well enough to walk and work. Pinkus Goldman said no, he had just had surgery. He was also sent to join the women, children, and older men.

Records preserved at Auschwitz indicate that thirteen men and ninety-four women from Sigi's convoy were selected to enter the camp. Those not selected, perhaps nearly three hundred, were sent directly to the gas chambers.[3] When the selected prisoners were being shaved, tattooed, and disinfected, Sigi says, a guard pointed to the chimneys of the crematoria and said, "You see, this is where your people will be coming out." He did not believe it at first.

Boris's account of his arrival at Auschwitz is not dissimilar from Sigi's. He says, "I immediately realized the existence of gas chambers. When we arrived, we saw the inscription above the entrance: 'Arbeit macht frei.' A German SS man told us, 'Here you entered,' and, indicating the chimneys of the crematorium, 'There you will come out.'" The unbelievable became all too real.

Boris is reticent about the selection process for his convoy, in which he and 266 other men and seventy-two women were admitted to the camp—chosen, that is, to live a little longer. The other 657 people, many of whom he knew, were immediately gassed. These memories are painful beyond words. But if Boris finds it difficult to evoke the details, another survivor from the same train was determined to preserve a record of her experience. She was Elena Rudnitzky, born in Warsaw in 1920, a refugee in France who was sent by the Italians to Saint-Martin-Vésubie and later crossed the Alps to the province of Cuneo. Like Boris Carmeli, Elena was deported from Borgo San Dalmazzo to Drancy with her mother, father, sister, and brother. On December 7, 1943, the family was deported to Auschwitz. She was the only survivor. On June 12, 1945, Elena returned to Borgo to tell the mayor what had happened to the Jews imprisoned in his town. The horrified mayor recorded her report:

> As soon as they arrived [at Auschwitz] they were divided into two groups: on one side all the women with children along with the sick and the old; on the other side, the young and physically able.
>
> Rudnitzki [sic] found herself separated from her parents and from a sister, and begged the German soldiers to leave her with her family; she was told that she was young and able to walk the roughly four kilometers to the baths where everyone had to be washed and disinfected. . . .
>
> Vehicles in fact arrived to take the women with children, the old and the sick; but the young people, instead of setting out toward the baths, entered the camp, where prisoners already there soon informed them . . . that the baths to which the German soldiers referred were no more than the poison gas works and crematoria that could be seen not far away!
>
> The new arrivals remained incredulous and terrorized; they later realized that it was true!
>
> Women, children, old people were all killed with gas and their bodies were cremated. . . .
>
> The young women and men were held in the camp and given various types of work: on roads, on railroads, and in industrial plants.
>
> Every day, however, a certain number of prisoners were seized and taken to their deaths.
>
> Every day the smoke from the crematoria could be seen, and the prisoners lived in continual anxiety about tomorrow.[4]

Sigi Hart was admitted to Birkenau (Auschwitz II), a vast, newer section of the camp with barracks for thousands of workers but also with four gas chambers for the "special treatment" of those not selected for labor. He remained in quarantine for the first four weeks, working only inside the camp. After another five or six months of hard labor at Birkenau, he was transferred to nearby Monowitz (Auschwitz III), the industrial sector of the camp, also called Buna for the artificial rubber that was produced there. Sigi labored at Buna until January 1945. He says, "I lived in the shadow of the crematoria. . . . I saw the flames shooting up into the sky every day. I saw the trains arrive with men, women and children destined to die there. And there were selections from among the workers every two weeks, sometimes every week. Those no longer fit for work were sent to the gas chambers."

When Sigi speaks of those working at Auschwitz, he especially recalls the deliberate, demeaning daily cruelty. He says, "No one ever called your name. You were just a number. If you didn't learn your number in Polish, you didn't get your soup." Prisoners' numbers were tattooed on their arms. Sigi's tattoo is still visible, more than sixty years later. For him, with a mother actually born in Oświęcim (the Polish name for Auschwitz), learning the number in Polish was easy, but for others it was more difficult. Sigi also remembers that the Germans did everything possible to make the work even harder than it had to be. When the exhausted prisoners marched back to camp, for example, they all had to carry bricks. The extra weight was hard to manage. But the Germans were constructing a new building in the camp, and rather than waste gasoline by driving a truck out to get the bricks, they made the prisoners carry them. The prisoners also carried loads of dirt from place to place in a box, with one man on each side. They were not even provided with wheelbarrows. They were often brutally beaten. Sigi once received five lashes because he dozed off when he was on latrine duty inside his barracks, charged with watching the pail to determine when it had to be carried outside to be emptied.

How did Sigi endure conditions that killed a majority of the prisoners at Auschwitz? He explains, "I survived in part because I was young and very strong. . . . I said to myself, I am not going to die where my mother was born." Knowing the languages of his captors and guards, both German and Polish, was also a great advantage. Sigi also believes that he survived in part because he made some friends from Berlin. "We helped each other," he says. "I survived by washing socks and pants for the kapo [a prisoner in charge of a barracks] . . . and I got some extra bread for that." He also had a job washing dishes, and sometimes he was able to scrape a little extra food off the sides of the bowls. On other occasions, British and French prisoners of war working in the area left a little extra soup for the Jews. Both groups had to hide the soup, since it was forbidden for them to speak to each other. Sigi's youth, strength, personal background, and determination all helped him survive. Also essential to the mix was good luck. Sigi was lucky that he did not run afoul of a sadist, live in a barracks where someone contracted a contagious disease (the entire barracks could have been exterminated), injure himself at work, or encounter any of the other deadly pitfalls of existence at Auschwitz.

Boris Carmeli does not like to dwell on his experiences at Auschwitz. For a while, he explains, he worked transporting iron pipes; then he labored at the IG Farben factory in Monowitz (Auschwitz III). Of Auschwitz in general he says simply, "My wife and I today often visit a composer friend in Kraków for New Year's Eve. Sometimes, when we drive from the airport, we see the sign 'Oświęcim,' and the cold shivers come again." Poland is haunted with memories.

But for both young men, the worst was yet to come. On or shortly after January 18, 1945, with the Russians about to arrive, Sigi and Boris were among the roughly fourteen thousand prisoners still able to work who were marched out of Auschwitz and its satellite camps and forced to walk to the railroad junction of Gleiwitz (Gliwice), northwest of Katowice.[5] The men, still in what Sigi calls their "pajama-like prison garb," took three to four days to cover a distance of about seventy-two kilometers (forty-three miles). When asked if that was not a long time for the distance, Sigi observes quietly, "When you are wearing wooden clogs, it takes a long time." Without warm clothes or proper shoes, and weakened by disease and starvation, thousands of prisoners were shot because they could not keep up.

At Gleiwitz, Sigi, Boris, and the other survivors were forced into open cattle cars, with sides five feet high and no roof. "I had a friend," Boris says, "who wanted to go to the end of the long line of prisoners waiting to get on the train. Maybe a miracle would happen. Maybe the Russians would arrive before the train was loaded. Maybe, maybe. . . . But I was beyond caring. I told him I would go where my destiny dictated." A sign on the outside of his wagon said, "Forty people, or ten horses." Nearly one hundred men were forced to stand in that car, with their arms folded across their chests to make room for the others. For three days and three freezing winter nights, the train switched back and forth across the damaged rail lines of Czechoslovakia. The prisoners were reduced to eating the snow. "People died standing up," Boris says, the horror still in his eyes. "There was no room to fall down." At one point in Czechoslovakia, the train passed under a bridge where peasants were standing, looking down from above. The prisoners could hear the shocked peasants murmuring, "Holy Jesus!"

The train finally stopped near Nordhausen (Thüringen), in the southern Harz Mountains of Germany. Outside Nordhausen was the concentration camp of Dora-Mittelbau, with its infamous underground installations. Toward the end of the war, thirty-five thousand Jews and other slave laborers were working there on various industrial and military projects, especially the

V1 and V2 rockets expected to produce a German victory. Of the sixty thousand prisoners sent to Dora during the war, some twenty thousand died.[6] Sigi recalls that his train went right into the camp. He and Boris worked at the underground rocket factory for about two and a half months.

At the end of March 1945, Sigi, Boris, and many other prisoners were moved again, this time to Bergen-Belsen, at Celle, near Hannover, in northwestern Germany. Again the men traveled in open railroad cars, this time for about a week. Sigi remembers that when the train was attacked by planes, the prisoners cheered because they knew that the Allies were striking the Third Reich. They reached Bergen-Belsen in early April, at a time when, according to the testimony of camp commander Josef Kramer, twenty-eight thousand starving prisoners arrived in a single week.[7] The camp had originally been built for just a few thousand. Because camp administration had broken down, there was no distribution of food or shelter, no disease control, and no burial of the thousands of dead. There was also no labor. Prisoners just sat around on the ground and waited. Boris states flatly, "In another couple of days, I would have died."

But then, says Sigi, "One morning we heard a funny noise, like hundreds of chains rattling. The guards were gone. It was the British army." The date was April 15, 1945. Some sixty-one thousand half-dead prisoners greeted the startled soldiers. But for many of those prisoners, it was too late. Many were too sick or malnourished to survive. Others died from the rapid transition. "They gave us too much to eat, too soon," Boris remembers. "We were so starved that we drank the oil they gave us, straight from the bottle. And they gave us jams and jellies." Of the sixty-one thousand prisoners, eleven thousand died within a few days.[8]

PART IV

Aftermath

CHAPTER TWENTY

After the War

Jacques and Paulette Samson, Charles Roman, Lya Haberman,
and Miriam Löwenwirth

Jacques and Paulette Samson

As the Allies worked their slow and painful way up the Italian peninsula, liberation came first to cities in the south. For Jacques Samson and Charles Roman in Rome, the date was June 4, 1944, nearly eleven months before the liberators reached the province of Cuneo. Young Jacques knew exactly what he wanted to do with his newly acquired freedom. "To be scared without having done anything wrong—that was terrible," he says. "That is why I wanted to join the French army after liberation—for revenge." The day Rome was liberated, Jacques left the Pontificio Seminario Francese in Rome, where he had been hiding, and went to see his father in his hospital refuge. "Papa, I have to join the army," he declared. "If you don't let me, I'll die." Szlama did not want his son to go. As far as he knew with certainty, Jacques was his only remaining child. He had received little news from his daughter Paulette, left behind in Saint-Martin-Vésubie, and none at all from his wife and two younger daughters in Poland.

Szlama could not hold back a nineteen-year-old son who was now a man, had suffered, and had enjoyed no semblance of normal life for years. Jacques joined the army, serving as an interpreter until the end of the war. But he did not seek revenge. On one occasion, he was translating during the interrogation of a German prisoner. The German began to talk about his family in Germany. Jacques, thinking of his own shattered family, began to cry. "I had received no news from my mother [in Poland]," he explains. "I was grieving for her, I felt sorry for my own situation, and I felt sorry for the German too. My friends said I was stupid. *Le retour des choses, c'est terrible.*"

One day soon after liberation, Jacques, still in the Rome area, "requisitioned" an army jeep, filled it with food from the U.S. Army Post Exchange, and took it to the Seminario Francese. A Polish non-Jew who had also been sheltered there had recently stolen supplies from his benefactors. Jacques's protector Father Meunier, disillusioned by that experience, was overjoyed to receive the food from Jacques. To the young man he said, "I always knew you were different." Jacques was grateful that he could help the man who had been so good to him. But his faith in God and humanity was gone. He had prayed throughout the war that his mother and sisters would survive. When he realized that they were dead, he lost his faith and became an atheist. "How could such things happen?" he asks without hope of an answer. "How could people do such things?"

With his sister, Paulette, liberated in Le Chambon in September 1944, Jacques never hesitated in choosing Paris as his place of residence after the war. Jacques went into the fashion business and was very successful. In 1952, he married Nadine Tabachnik, who despite her name was from a family that had been French for five generations. The couple had three daughters, Patricia, Natalie, and Katia, and five grandchildren, a boy and four girls. Nadine died in 1994. Also in 1952, Paulette married Georges Mabe. A few years later, when she was pregnant with their first child, Georges died at the age of twenty-seven of acute leukemia. The child, a daughter, was named Georgia in honor of her father. Paulette later married Fred Grunberg, with whom she had a second daughter, Laurence. Fred died in 2002. Paulette has six grandchildren.

Jacques and Paulette's father, Szlama, also had the courage to begin a new life after the war. In 1953, he married Serena Szabo Gerhard. Like him, Serena was a widow of the death camps; he had met her at the sanctuary of the Madonna del Colletto above Valdieri in September 1943 and had later seen her again in Rome. To this day, Jacques and Paulette regard Serena's children by her first marriage, Jacky and Régine, as their brother and sister and see them often. Szlama died in 1973, Serena in 2001.

Charles Roman

Charles Roman found several different jobs in Rome after liberation. He worked first for the Hebrew newspaper of the Jewish Brigade, then in a map depot, and then as a handyman at the Jewish Soldiers' Club of the American and British armies. Finally he was hired by the American Jewish Joint Distribution Committee as a warehouse man, truck driver, and assistant purchaser. He also went to Paris as soon as possible to seek news of his father, whom he had last seen in August 1942 in Rivesaltes, boarding a train to Drancy. In Paris he learned that Leopold Roman had been deported to Poland and would not be coming back. Charles then focused on getting to the United States, where he and his mother, Marianne, had relatives. They had no trouble getting personal affidavits of support, but Charles was blocked by a doctor at the American consulate in Naples who insisted that he had trachoma. As a result, Charles lost his visa and Marianne was obliged to leave for the United States without him. Only after a long and persistent struggle with several doctors was Charles finally able to join a refugee transport out of quota and sail on the SS *Marine Jumper,* a U.S. Navy troop transport, on November 10, 1949. He arrived in New York eleven days later. Those are dates he remembers well.

After eleven months in the United States, Charles was drafted into the army. There he became a specialist in pole line construction in the Signal Corps. When his unit was sent to Germany, however, he was removed because he was Austrian-born and not an American citizen. He served for a time as an ammunition handler but then joined a military intelligence unit as an interpreter. That unit, he recalls sadly, was full of White Russians who hated Jews. Next, after going to army radio school, he was sent to Korea to maintain radio teletype equipment. He was finally discharged in 1953. Eight months later, he received his American citizenship. The next year, he opened his own appliance business, selling and servicing televisions, radios, and air conditioners.

On December 25, 1955, Charles married Inge Rose, who was born in Frankenau, Germany, and came to the United States with her mother and grandfather on January 29, 1941. Inge's father and brother had come earlier, to prepare the way. Charles and Inge live in Teaneck, New Jersey, and have one daughter, Carol, and two grandchildren. Charles's formidable mother, Marianne, who braved the mountain crossing from France to Italy, took, with her son, the only known photographs of the event, and endured a winter snowbound in a cabin in the Italian Alps without losing her good spirits, died in 1984 at the age of eighty-four.

In a taped interview for the Museum of Jewish Heritage in New York in November 1991, Charles was asked how his wartime experience affected his life. He first replied, "I have put it behind me. I don't speak of it." That statement is probably only half true. He may not speak of it much, but the experience is always there, inescapable and decisive. As if to confirm that suspicion, he then observed, "I still don't trust people in uniform, whether it is the post man, the bus driver, or a railroad worker." The scars remain. Charles then expressed a more positive, life-affirming sentiment. "The Italian people were wonderful in helping us," he said. "They did not care about 'race.' . . . They shared what they had." And finally, Charles Roman declared, his wartime experience "taught me not to worry too much about tomorrow . . . to take it one day at a time."

Lya Haberman

It took the Allies exactly two months to advance from Rome to Florence, liberated on August 4. Lya Haberman and her father, Oscar, then traveled by truck with the British army to Rome, where Lya enjoyed her first taste of freedom without fear of arrest in almost six years. She had a kilogram of salt, she says, that was like gold. She and her father went to the synagogue in Rome, talked openly to whomever they wished, in whatever language they wished, and secured a room with a nice owner. There was also a house where all the Jews could gather together. The Americans were in Rome, as was the Jewish Brigade. At last she had company.

Lya did not return to Nice after the war to look for her mother and sister. While in Rome, she received a card from the sister of Chief Rabbi Chaim Herzog in Palestine, with whom her mother's family was related by marriage. The woman had learned, perhaps from the International Red Cross, that Chana and Hilda had been arrested in Nice in September 1943, after the Germans occupied the former Italian zone, and deported to Auschwitz. They would not return. Lya was now ready to leave Europe. Applying for permission to go to Palestine, she said she was the niece of Chief Rabbi Herzog, which was almost but not quite true, and got on a list. In Palestine, she finished high school and met her future husband. Born in Bratislava, Eugene Quitt had been among the last Jews to leave freely, in 1941. Lya and Eugene were married in Israel in 1948.

Lya's father, Oscar, who had never been a Zionist, returned in 1945 to the Paris where he had so wanted to live in 1933. When Lya's husband in Israel became sick and suffered terribly from the heat, Oscar advised his daughter to go to the United States. Lya was reluctant, feeling that it was wrong to leave Israel. She refused to go to the American consulate, but her great friend Sigi Hart, who had also settled in Israel, went for her. To her surprise, she found that the American visas her parents had secured just before the war and never been able to use were still valid. She and Eugene and their daughter, Anna, settled in Forest Hills, in New York City, in 1958. A second daughter, Daniella, was born in New York, as was their grand-daughter. Eugene Quitt died there in May 2005. Anna also died in New York in March 2006.

"Mine is a story like all the others," says Lya. But the story has taken its toll. "I am a friendly and sociable person, but deep down I am a loner. I think that is because of what happened to me. I am the kind of person who closes the book, who just goes on. But it isn't easy." After her experiences in Italy, Lya also has a special fondness for the Italian people. "I often met Italians during my work in New York," she says. "And I always gave them special consideration. I can never forget what they did for me during the war."

Miriam Löwenwirth

The months between her father's deportation from Fossoli to Bergen-Belsen on May 16, 1944, and the liberation of Florence, where she was hiding, were difficult for Miriam Löwenwirth. The only Jewish guest at the convent in the Piazza Carmine, she slept in the same hall where the raid had occurred in November 1943. She had no cause or purpose to channel her considerable energies, and time on her hands. Desperately lonely, she began, as she puts it, to read and think about Jesus. On the eve of the liberation, she converted to Catholicism. Not long afterward, she went to see her mother and siblings in Rome and visited Father Benedetto. He did not approve of her conversion under conditions of great emotional distress. As Miriam puts it, "He indicated that he would have prevented this step." She was not deterred, however. When her entire remaining family moved to Israel, Miriam stayed in Rome to study nursing.

In time, Miriam joined the Carmelites, an order of nuns who live under strict rules of cloister. After four years in a Carmelite convent in Rome, her superiors, believing that her place was with her people, as Miriam puts it, sent her to a convent in Nazareth, Israel. There she continued her life of cloister and seclusion, although she was permitted to write to and occasionally see her mother. Gradually she began to have doubts. Eventually, she asked her superiors for permission to leave the convent to reflect and reconsider. She then worked as a nurse and, after about a year, asked to be relieved of her vows.

In 1970, at the age of forty-four, Miriam married Zvi Reuveni, who had lost most of his family in Poland during the Holocaust. The marriage was happy, lasting until Zvi's death in 1994. There were no children. Miriam's mother died five years after her daughter's marriage, leaving fourteen grandchildren and fifteen great-grandchildren.

After her mother's death, Miriam explained in her memoirs:

> I have always thought that when one opens the Bible, to the
> Book of Genesis, the key to everything that ever happened in
> the world is to be found there. No religion is mentioned nor are
> there any borders; only God and Man. I feel complete identifica-
> tion with that universal approach, with all humanity wherever
> it may be. Each nation has its own traditions and God is known
> by different names, but there is only one God. The basis of every-
> thing is the connection between Man and God. . . . In my life,
> both Judaism and Christianity have provided me with answers
> during difficult times and they forced me to challenge myself
> and my abilities.[1]

Miriam's attitudes and opinions were influenced by many individuals —her traditional Jewish parents, the French officer who released her father from detention in 1942, the Italian authorities who sent her from Nice to Saint-Martin-Vésubie and treated her well there, her Zionist friend David Blum, Don Raimondo Viale in Borgo San Dalmazzo, many priests and nuns in Florence, Father Maria Benedetto in Rome, and the many other religious Jews and Christians she met after the war. She has had the wisdom to draw on what is best in all of them. Her life of service, nursing and caring for others is a testament to both Judaism and Christianity, but Miriam is now irrevocably committed to Judaism and the nation of Israel.

CHAPTER TWENTY-ONE

After the War

William Blye, Walter Marx, Menahem Marienberg,
Sigi Hart, and Boris Carmeli

William Blye

When he was liberated in the province of Cuneo after two winters in the mountains, William Blye immediately returned to Nice to search for his father and brothers. He knew that they had been arrested by French police in Nice, in the unoccupied zone, in August 1942, and delivered to the Germans in the north. When he found no more information in Nice, William went on to Germany, where he had been born. To no avail. "Nobody from my large, extended family had made it. My father and brothers were gone. Of all my uncles, aunts, cousins, and nieces, none survived. My mother and I were alone." A recruiter from Palestine then tried to convince him to go there, telling him, "We need young people." William had just agreed to go when he received an affidavit for immigration from an uncle in the United States. He changed his mind. "I suppose that if I had gone to Palestine, I would have been killed in the 1948 War of Independence," he muses. William had had enough of war.

In the United States, William worked as a translator for the United Nations at Lake Success, New Jersey, for a while. "I found it horribly boring," he says, "Italian to French, French to Italian, official documents, reports, bureaucracy. But I earned $20 a week, plus my food. My apartment in Washington Heights was $10 a week. So I had plenty of money left." Eventually he left and worked as a furrier for a while, like his father, but then he went to night school to become a technical draftsman and engineer. It was hard to find a job as Wolf Bleiweiss, so when he became an American citizen on March 31, 1952, he changed his name to William Blye. Once he did that, he says, he found a job right away. He adds, "I hadn't realized how much anti-Semitism there was in the United States, 'the Land of the Free.'"

Until 1950, William shared an apartment with three other young Jewish men who had been refugees in France during the war. Two of these were Walter Marx and Walter's cousin Werner Isaac from Saint-Martin-Vésubie. The third was Jacques Ulrich, who had hidden in Nice throughout the German occupation. In 1950, William married Lottie Landau, who was Polish like his parents and had also lived in Leipzig before the war. Lottie had attended the same Jewish school as William, but they had not known each other then. Lottie was twelve years old when her parents put her on a *Kindertransport* to England in 1939. She never saw them again. Lottie and William live in Great Neck, Long Island, today. They have three children, Jeffrey, Sandra, and Bernice, and five grandchildren.

William Blye has an immense sense of gratitude to the Italian people. He says, "I love that country. If I hadn't come to the United States, I think I would have gone there. The people are so warm." In a brief written account of his wartime experiences, he writes, "Thinking back on those years, I realize that if it were not for the Italian people, who put their lives on the line to save so many of us, I would not be alive today. I will never forget them."

Walter Marx

Walter Marx was on a farm in Demonte on May 8, 1945, when he learned that the war was over.[1] For about a week, he helped interrogate German soldiers still straggling through the valley of the Stura from France. "They were as arrogant as ever," he recalls. "Told they were to be shot, they said they would 'die for the Führer.' I don't know if they were shot." Then on May 16, Walter received his release papers from the Resistance. Four days later, with about twenty other Jews from the area, he was on a truck to Nice. There he contacted a Jewish assistance committee in the avenue de la Victoire. The committee found him a place to stay and, more important, helped him with his search for his parents. Walter's father, Ludwig, it will be recalled, had been arrested in Lamalou-les-Bains on February 20, 1943, and deported from Drancy to Poland. His mother, Johanna, had been sent from Borgo San Dalmazzo back to France in November 1943, and from there to Auschwitz. Walter had no brothers or sisters.

Every day the headquarters of the Jewish committee in Nice were full of anxious survivors searching for their families. Every day the committee published the names of people who had returned from deportation, and every day Walter was there to study the lists. During the war, he explains, "I didn't know or want to know what had happened to my parents," but now he had to find out. But a message never came. Only several months after the end of the war in Europe did he receive official notice of his parents' deportations and deaths.

During his stay in Nice, Walter also visited Saint-Martin-Vésubie to try to find the few possessions he had left behind when he fled over the Alps. The owners of the building where he and his mother had stayed told him that they had nothing. "The Germans," they informed Walter, "took everything." Walter does not know who took his things but suspects that the Germans did not take everything.

In September 1945, the Jewish committee in Nice sent Walter to Paris, where he enrolled in a training program in dentistry operated by OSE. After an uncle in the United States signed an affidavit of support for him, the young man went to New York in October 1946. There, as seen, he shared an apartment for a few years with his cousin Werner Isaac, William Blye, and another survivor from France. In 1950, he married Ellen Appel, whom he met at a French-speaking club in New York.

Ellen's parents had been born in Germany but moved to Belgium before the war. In May 1940, her father, Josef, born in 1888, was arrested as a German enemy alien in Belgium and expelled to France. He passed through several camps in unoccupied France, including Saint-Cyprien, Récébédou, Noé, and Gurs, before the Vichy police delivered him to the Germans in the occupied zone in early August 1942. He was deported to Kosel or Auschwitz on convoy 25 on August 28, 1942, and did not return.[2] Ellen survived by hiding at the Pensionnat des Jeunes Filles Saint Charles, operated by nuns from a convent in Herseaux, Belgium. Her mother, Leni, was hidden by the head of the Brussels Stock Exchange.

Ellen and Walter Marx have three sons, David, Ronald, and Gary, and five grandchildren. Walter has retired from the air freight company in which he was a partner and lives with Ellen in East Hills, near Roslyn, New York.

Of his experiences during the Second World War, Walter Marx reflects,

"Being a survivor of the Holocaust, you have dual feelings. Of course you are happy and proud to have survived, but you also have a certain guilt feeling, because you ask why is it me—why did I survive, and not some of my friends, not my father and mother, not my uncles and grandfather. On the other hand, having been a partisan, I have the feeling that I am proud of it and it gives me a certain satisfaction that I fought the evil that caused the death of my family and friends. That sort of offsets the negative feeling of being a survivor." He adds firmly, "People should be aware of the fact that Jews also resisted."

Menahem Marienberg

Menahem's first move after liberation was to bicycle from the eye hospital where he had been hiding to Cuneo to find out if Giuseppe Meinardi, the man who had protected him throughout the German occupation of Italy, was safe. He was. Meinardi then asked the young man if he and his younger brother, Léon, would consider living as Catholics, now that their family was gone. A fervent Catholic himself, Meinardi had had the boys baptized during the war, thinking that such a step would protect them. Menahem explained gently that he and his brother were irrevocably committed to Judaism. Meinardi then asked if the pair would remain with him, as Jews but as part of his own family. Again Menahem declined, explaining that they were determined to go to Palestine. But he was deeply touched by the offer, and grateful.

Next, Menahem set about trying to trace his family. He learned from a man who had been at Auschwitz with his father that Wolf, deported there from Borgo San Dalmazzo via Drancy, was dead. He then went to Toulouse to get news of his mother, sister, and youngest brother, arrested in the unoccupied zone in August 1942. He found nothing. Finally he traveled to Brussels, where he found his paternal grandmother, Sara Marienberg, and two cousins still alive. Menahem describes Sara as a veritable dynamo, strong and independent. After losing her husband in Poland during the First World War, she continued to run his business until she left for Belgium. She survived the war in Belgium because the Germans put her in an old age home, said they would come back, and apparently forgot her. Menahem later brought her to Israel, where she lived to the age of 105, was never sick, and never needed glasses.

Menahem explains that he was committed to going to Palestine to help create a country for the Jewish people. He also wanted to build his own future there because he had lost his family and his past. It was not easy to get to Palestine after the war, but he and Léon were lucky. They traveled to the port of Marseille, where hundreds of Jews were boarding a ship. As a sympathetic guard took the entry papers for Palestine from the people qualified to leave, he passed them out again to be reused. The boys boarded with papers that were not theirs. They have spent their lives in Israel.

After arriving in Palestine in 1945, Menahem joined the Haganah and participated in the struggle for a Jewish state. After Israel became a nation in 1948, he served in both the army and the navy. Trained as a mechanic, he continues working to this day. In 1949, he married Miriam Benbenishti, who also fought with the Haganah. Miriam died in 2003. Menahem and Miriam had three children, Sima, Zeev, and Amir Moshe, and seven grandchildren. The fourth generation began on August 19, 2004, when Menahem's granddaughter Rakefet gave birth to twins, Noam and Lior.

After finishing high school in Israel, Léon also did his military service. He then went to the university to prepare for a career in the aeronautic industry. He married Mira Kanyevski and had two children, Orit-Malka and Eran, and five grandchildren.

Menahem and Léon said good-bye to Giuseppe Meinardi at the train station in Cuneo in 1945 as they left to search for their family in France. Menahem remembers the farewell as a difficult moment, for Meinardi had been like a father to the boys for a year and a half. They never saw him again. They exchanged letters for years, with pictures of their growing families. Menahem remembers that he used to send Meinardi photographs and gifts from the "Holy Land" during the Christian holidays. Then in the 1960s, Meinardi's son Eugenio traveled to Israel and met both Menahem and Léon. Years later, Eugenio wrote with the news that Giuseppe Meinardi had died in 1979, at the age of eighty-seven. Thanks to the testimony of Menahem and Léon Marienberg, Giuseppe Meinardi was honored as a Righteous Among the Nations by Yad Vashem in 1998.

Sigi Hart

After liberation, Sigi remained at Bergen-Belsen for about a week. He was desperate to get out of Germany, however, because he was always afraid that the Nazis would return. "For months afterward," he says, "I always looked behind me when I walked anywhere." So he took immediate steps to leave the country. He explains that every formerly occupied country had a commission at Bergen-Belsen, and the French and Belgian commissions took their citizens out right away. Because he spoke French well, he went to the French commission to claim that he was a French national. His slight accent, he informed the commission, derived from his origins in Alsace. His claim was accepted. After he received official permission to go to France, the British took him to Brussels. There he marched in a victory parade in his pajama-like camp pants, a German military coat he had taken from a dead German at Bergen-Belsen, and a French soldier's cap. He then took a train to Paris, where he was put up at the Hotel Lutétia and given money and a good bath.

Sigi had no intention of remaining in Paris, but was determined to go to Nice to find out what had happened to his family. When the French government gave him a card to travel anywhere in the country without charge, he left the next day. The trains were full of soldiers, survivors of deportation, and ordinary French citizens, all trying to get home. At every station, his train stopped and local bands played "La Marseillaise," the French national anthem. And at every station, more and more passengers left the train. By the time Sigi reached Nice, his train was nearly empty. A Jewish committee was meeting survivors at the station, however, and Sigi ran into a young girl he had known from activities at the synagogue in Nice in 1943. She was able to assure him that his mother, father, and siblings were alive. His mother was in Toulouse, his father in Rome, and Willy in Israel. Manya, now married, had immigrated to the United States, believing that her entire family was dead.

Sigi's parents and siblings all had different experiences. After Sigi was deported, his father, Hermann, and brother, Willy, remained in Florence. Hermann was sheltered in the same Catholic nursing home as Lya Haberman's father, where they were liberated when the Allies reached the city in August 1944. Willy, along with Louis Goldman, was hidden by a number of dedicated priests in and outside Florence.[3] Sigi's mother, Adela, in contrast, deathly sick in Gurs and unable to travel when her husband and children fled to Nice, had been left by the Germans to die in the camp. She was never deported because the German and French police were afraid of her contagious disease. Believing that she would die anyway, they paid her little attention. Somehow she recovered, received false papers, and was befriended by an elderly Jewish refugee couple named Friedberg whom she had known earlier in Bagnères-de-Luchon. She and they lived in a village near Toulouse, helped by the local people, and survived. Sigi does not know the details. Adela was liberated about the same time as her husband and younger son in Italy, after the Allied landings in the south of France in August 1944.

Sigi's sister, Manya, on the other hand, had a diverse set of adventures. After she and her future husband, Ernst Breuer, left Sigi, Willy, and Hermann in the mountains of the province of Cuneo, they made their way to Rome with Ernst's sister, Lisa. In Rome, Manya and Lisa went from convent to convent, explaining that they were Jews who had converted to Catholicism. The claim was untrue, but in their desperation, they felt that it might help convince the nuns to accept them. They were finally accepted at the convent of Notre Dame de Sion, on the Janiculum Hill across the Tiber from the central synagogue and the former ghetto of Rome. A Catholic boarding school for girls before the war, the convent in 1943 was primarily a study center for about twenty-four novices. Jews fleeing the roundup in Rome on October 16, 1943, had found shelter there—about forty by one estimate and as many as one hundred by another.[4] These fugitives were not converts, nor were most of the Jews accepted later. The Order of Notre Dame de Sion had been founded in France in 1843 for the purpose of establishing dialogue with and ultimately converting the Jews, but during the Second World War that objective was secondary to the effort to assist and rescue them. Those sheltered at the convent of the order in Rome do not report attempts to convert them.

After Rome was liberated on June 4, 1944, Manya, Ernst, and Lisa were among the 982 refugees, including 165 children, from eighteen countries who were chosen by delegates of the War Refugee Board to be sent to the United States. Within the group, 874 were Jews, seventy-three were Roman Catholics, twenty-eight were Greek Orthodox, and seven were Protestants. The criteria for selection were flexible, but those who had been in concentration and forced labor camps were favored, along with family groups and those with the greatest need. After arriving in New York on August 3, the refugees traveled by train to Oswego, New York, about forty miles north of Syracuse, where they lived in what was called an Emergency Refugee Shelter in Fort Ontario. The former army camp, the only wartime center in the United States for refugees from the Holocaust, was surrounded by a wire-mesh fence surmounted by barbed wire. Refugees were technically in internment. They were not free to come and go without permission or even visit relatives already in the country. They lived comfortably, however, and soon established schools, clubs, and theater groups.[5] Manya, a talented singer, was active in theater. Manya and Ernst were married at the camp on August 17 by the local rabbi of Oswego. Their daughter Diane was born there the following year. In December 1945, they and the other refugees were permitted to leave the camp and enter the United States through normal immigration channels. Manya settled in California, where she lives today. She and Ernst had two other children, Marsha and Gregory.

After her liberation in France in August 1944, Adela contacted Hermann in Italy and asked him about the children. Hermann did not tell her that Sigi had been deported. Because he wrote only about Manya and Willy, she became suspicious. When she asked specifically about Sigi, Hermann said he was fine. When she asked for photographs, he sent some taken before the deportation. Adela had more or less guessed the truth, but nevertheless, when she heard in the synagogue in Toulouse that Sigi had been deported, she fainted. Then in May 1945, when she heard that Sigi had come back, she fainted again.

From Nice, Sigi went to Toulouse to stay with his mother. For a while, he hid his bread under his pillow. After a few months, the French government sent him to a rest facility in Lourdes for four weeks of rehabilitation, to gain weight and get his strength back. Sigi then decided that he wanted to go to Palestine. At the British consulate in Paris, he explained that he had been liberated by the British, that his family was in Palestine (his grandmother had immigrated there before the war, and Willy moved there in 1945), and that the authorities must allow him to go there. He was able to obtain a certificate and get on a troop transport that took about 250 young men and boys, all former deportees, from Marseille to Haifa. On the way, the ship stopped in Naples. When Hermann learned that his son was on the ship, he took a taxi from Rome to Naples to try to stop him, to convince him to stay in Europe. As he reached Naples, the transport was just pulling out. It was too late.

In Haifa, the British put Sigi in another camp, this time for quarantine for two or three weeks. The confinement was hard to bear, and at one point the inmates revolted. Once released, Sigi lived with Willy and his grandmother until Hermann and Adela joined them. Like Menahem Marienberg, Sigi enlisted in the Haganah and fought in the 1948 war. After that, he had trouble settling down and finding work. His life finally changed for the better in August 1953, when he met a French tourist in Israel named Vera Vogel. It was love at first sight.

Vera's parents, Golda Stein and Salomon Vogel, had immigrated to France from Poland before the war. Vera, born in France in 1931, had five brothers and sisters. All of them were at home in Poitiers, in the German-occupied zone, at about 8:30 one evening in the first or second week of October 1942 when a French policeman knocked on the door. It was the same man who came regularly to check that the family was in, so Vera's parents were not alarmed. But this time it was different. The policeman insisted that the parents and children must come with him. When they came out into the street, they found a waiting bus filled with foreign Jews. Most of them were friends and neighbors.

The bus delivered its passengers to a camp near Poitiers identified as Route de Limoges. Immediately upon their arrival, the police began to call off the names of those among them who had not been born in France. For the Vogels, they called only three—Golda and Salomon, as well as Vera's brother Sammy, born in Germany in 1930. They did not call the other five children, but Golda, holding ten-month-old Berte, refused to give her up. She also grabbed Miriam, born in France in 1935, and kept her with her. Vera and her two remaining siblings, also not called, were released that same evening, along with another seventy-five to eighty children. Those not released were registered in the camp.

The following morning, Vera recalls, the rabbi of Poitiers went to the French police to plead for Miriam and Berte, both born in France and thus not eligible for arrest and deportation according to the terms of that particular roundup. He had no luck. Some 617 mostly foreign Jews arrested in and around Poitiers in October 1942 were sent to Drancy, from where most were deported to Auschwitz in November. Golda, Salomon, Sammy, Miriam, and ten-month-old Berte left for the death camp on November 6, 1942, on convoy 42.[6] They did not return.

After their parents were arrested, the same rabbi of Poitiers placed the seventy-five to eighty children with non-Jewish families throughout the city. Vera and her remaining brother and sister were sent to a local widow who lived near the school they attended. One morning in March or April 1944, Vera says, she saw French police arresting children on their way to school and in the school itself.[7] She and her siblings stayed at home with the widow that day, but they were subsequently sent to a Jewish children's home in Paris, at 16, rue Lamarck. The home was operated by the Union générale des israélites de France, the German-imposed union of all Jewish welfare organizations. Since the parents of most of the children were either at Drancy or had already been deported, it was expected that the Germans would soon come to the rue Lamarck to collect them for deportation too. Fortunately, Vera's aunt, Berte Teper Rajzman, who was living undetected in Paris with her two children, understood the danger and arranged for her nieces and nephew to leave the children's home. She placed them for a time with a woman in Brittany, who neglected them. At that point, the aunt brought the three children back to Paris, where they lived out the last months of the occupation with her.

Sigi and Vera were married in Israel and had a son, Steven. After fighting again in the 1956 war, Sigi had had enough. He explains that he wanted his child to grow up in a safe place. And so, on March 1, 1957, Sigi, Vera, and Steven arrived penniless in New York City. From there, they joined Manya in Los Angeles, where Sigi began work as a drapery installer. Life was difficult at first, but the family received what Vera describes as "tremendous help" from the Baroness Édouard de Rothschild, who had known Vera at a French orphanage after the war. In Los Angeles to visit her married daughter, the baroness visited the Harts and asked what they needed. She then provided them with an automobile, indispensable in Los Angeles, and paid the automobile insurance. With that help, Sigi was eventually able to raise ten thousand dollars to go into the manufacturing business, making boys' knit shirts. His and Vera's daughter, Carmela, was born in February 1959. Today they also have five grandchildren. Sigi is retired and works as a volunteer at Steven Spielberg's Shoah Foundation.

Willy Hart eventually joined his brother and sister in California. He married and has four children.

Boris Carmeli

Although Boris Carmeli believes that he would not have survived more than a few additional days at Bergen-Belsen without food and medical attention, his mind was still working. When the Allies who liberated him asked him where he was from, for repatriation, this Polish-born refugee from Belgium said he was French. "I never thought that my parents were still alive," he explains. "I used to look for them when the trains arrived at Auschwitz. I never saw them, but still, how could they have survived in an empty cabin in the mountains? My French was fluent. I decided I wanted to rebuild my life in Paris."

Boris arrived in Paris on May 1, 1945, European Labor Day. His train,

filled primarily with French partisans returning from deportation, was pro-
cessed quickly. All the passengers were carrying their prison garb home
with them. Thousands of French men and women met the train. Among
them were the most prominent French leaders—General Charles de Gaulle,
General Philippe Leclerc, former Prime Minister Léon Blum. Everyone was
taking photographs. Signs read, "Welcome to the French heroes!" Boris
did not feel like a hero. He weighed thirty-seven kilograms—eighty-one
pounds. With most of the others, he was taken to the Hotel Lutétia for rest,
food, and medical care.

Boris had gained ten kilograms, or twenty-two pounds, when he met
a cousin by chance in Paris. She did not recognize him, but he knew her
right away. From her, he learned that his parents were alive. After he had
been deported, they had left the mountains in the province of Cuneo and
made their way to Rome. There they were hidden by an Italian family named
Cristiani and survived. Boris does not know how they found that family.
After the liberation of Rome, Boris's brother, Peter, joined the Jewish Brigade
of the British army and eventually settled in Israel. By the early summer of
1945, his father, Hermann, had established a successful business in Rome,
but his will to live was less certain. "If my son [Boris] does not come back,"
he used to say, "I have nothing more to do with this world." But, Boris says,
"He was convinced that I was still alive."

After consulting his cousin, Boris sent two telegrams. The first went
to his brother in Tel Aviv, the second to a friend of his parents who could
break the news of his survival gradually, to ease the shock. His brother
answered first, writing, "You must come directly to Israel. Only then will
our parents agree to come too." Boris obeyed, taking a ship from Marseille.
His parents reacted just as Peter knew they would, and left for Israel. But
before they left, Boris says, his father put up posters in Rome saying, "Mio
figlio vive!"—"My son is alive!"—and inviting everyone to come to a huge
party at a local hotel. He also took a dozen poor boys to a large department
store and bought clothes for them all. "You can imagine the meeting in
Israel when they arrived," Boris says fondly.

The first years in Israel were difficult for Boris and his family. Boris
worked in a music shop and took voice and piano lessons. His big break
came in 1950, when he received two offers for specialized study abroad. The
first came from the well-known mezzo-soprano Jenny Tourel, for whom
he auditioned in Israel and who invited him to study in New York. The
second was a year's scholarship to study in Milan, won in a competition of

three hundred singers in Israel. Although deeply grateful to Jenny Tourel and reluctant to disappoint her, Boris chose the Milan option. With four hundred dollars on which to live for one year, he set out for La Scala. His father sent him off with a money pouch.

Boris worked hard in Milan, but he needed more than a year to become a professional singer. Fortunately, he was befriended by Astorre Mayer, an owner of paper mills in Italy and the honorary Israeli consul in Milan. Mayer made Boris his secretary at the consulate, a position involving three days' work a week. With the salary, Boris was able to remain in Milan, complete his studies, and embark on his operatic career. During one of his professional trips, to the United States for the first time in 1961 to perform at the San Francisco Opera, he met and married Sonja Moser, from Switzerland. Sonja, multilingual like himself, was employed in the fashion industry. The couple lives today in Rome. Boris Carmeli has overcome the Nazi attempts to extinguish not only his life but his spirit. This courageous survivor of Auschwitz has sung at most of the major opera houses throughout the world.

Boris's parents remained in Israel, where Hermann eventually established a business. Hermann died in 1975, Rachel in 1987. Boris's brother, Peter, moved to Los Angeles, where he died in 1999.

Journeys Back

ALTHOUGH BORIS CARMELI and Jacques and Paulette Samson settled in Rome and Paris, respectively, after the war, they did not revisit the old places where they had lived between 1940 and 1945. Europe for them existed in the present. The past was best forgotten, as much as possible. Boris sang professionally in Paris, Berlin, Vienna, and Warsaw but did not visit Drancy or Auschwitz. Jacques and Paulette were among the last of the group of nine families interviewed for this book to return to Saint-Martin-Vésubie, doing so only in 2003. They have never returned to the area of Borgo San Dalmazzo.

The first of the group to return to France from overseas was Lya Haberman Quitt, who traveled from Israel to Paris to see her father, Oscar, in 1955. She returned many times after that but did not visit places with emotional wartime connotations until much later. Perhaps the first to visit the city where he was born was Charles Roman, who returned to Vienna in 1964 on a business trip for the Fedders air conditioning company. He found that he had no contacts or friends left there. "Vienna," he says ambiguously, "was the same old Vienna." Then for his sixtieth birthday in 1987, his wife, Inge, gave him a trip to Vienna with herself and their daughter. Carol loved Vienna, but Charles was not comfortable until they arrived in Rome by train. "In Rome, I felt like I was home again," he recalls. "They wined and dined us."

Sigi Hart seems to have been the first to travel back to some of the places where he had lived during the war. Beginning in 1981, he and his wife, Vera, went several times to Juzet-de-Luchon to visit the people who had sheltered Sigi's family in 1942. The printer Jean Gazave, his son Clément, and their wives had all died, but Jean's grandson Jeannot and his wife, Lucette, were still there. Sigi remains in touch with them. Then in 1993, with his brother, Willy, and his friend Louis (Ludi) Goldman, Sigi traveled to Florence to visit the city where they all had hidden and been arrested and from which Sigi had been deported fifty years earlier. The three men went to the barracks where they had been held after their arrest, where Willy Hart and his father and Louis Goldman had climbed over the wall and escaped. The barracks was still a military installation with restricted public access. When they explained who they were, the soldiers let them in. While in Florence, Sigi, Willy, and Ludi also participated in a memorial ceremony marking the fiftieth anniversary of the major German roundups of Jews there.

Charles and Inge Roman also made an emotional trip in 1993. For them, the occasion was a reunion in Paris of the children who had survived with help from OSE. Three years later, they returned to France, this time to visit the Château de Chabannes, the OSE Jewish children's home where Charles's mother had placed him even before the war. They attended commemorative ceremonies at the château and also in Guéret (Creuse), the capital of the department where the château was located. They enjoyed these two trips, but they still had not been back to Saint-Martin-Vésubie or Borgo San Dalmazzo.

In 1994, one year after Sigi's trip to Florence, Sigi and Vera Hart visited Saint-Martin-Vésubie. They seem to have been the first of the nine witnesses to do so. Two years later, Sigi traveled to Auschwitz with "The March of the Living," an international educational program for Jewish teenagers. In 1997, he and Vera returned to Saint-Martin-Vésubie with Lya Haberman Quitt and her husband. The two couples then proceeded to Borgo San Dalmazzo and Valdieri.

Charles and Inge Roman did not know about Sigi and Lya's trips. At home in Teaneck, New Jersey, however, a year after those visits, the Romans read about the Cuneo region in the travel section of a February 1998 issue of *Hadassah* magazine. The article by Elin Schoen Brockman mentioned Enzo Cavaglion in connection with the Jewish community of Cuneo. From the United States, Charles called Enzo, who urged him and Inge to come for a visit. Only when they arrived in Cuneo in April 1998 did Charles realize that Enzo was the same Jewish member of Duccio Galimberti's original partisan band who had helped him and his mother at the sanctuary of the Madonna del Colletto above Valdieri in September 1943. During his April visit, Charles was asked to unveil a wooden plaque at the train station at Borgo San Dalmazzo, in memory of the Jewish refugees deported from there to Drancy on November 21, 1943. The plaque stood close to two boxcars from the war that served as a small museum to the deportation.

Charles and Inge were invited to return to Cuneo again in September of the same year to celebrate the eight-hundredth anniversary of the founding of the city and the fifty-fifth anniversary of the armistice and the arrival in Italy of the Jews from Saint-Martin-Vésubie. Also invited were William and Lottie Blye, Walter and Ellen Marx, and Harry Burger, none of whom Charles had known previously. Walter relates that he wanted to go, but thought that he should not because the ceremony was to be on the eve of Rosh Hashanah. Was there a synagogue in Cuneo? He thought not. Then he received a letter from Enzo Cavaglion, informing him not only that there was a synagogue in Cuneo but that two other ceremonies were planned for the same time as the eight-hundredth anniversary of the city. One was to celebrate the return to the synagogue of the Torah, which had been sent to Rome for restoration. The second was the unveiling of an imposing stone monument to thank the Italian people, in this anniversary year, for all that they had done during the war to help Jewish refugees in the province of Cuneo. The monument was to be in front of the remnants of the old barracks of the Italian Alpine troops where the Jews from Saint-Martin-Vésubie had been imprisoned between September 18 and November 21, 1943. Walter Marx and his mother, Johanna, and cousin Werner Isaac had been among the prisoners. How could he not attend?

Upon their arrival at Cuneo, the seven Americans first attended a formal ceremony honoring the return to the synagogue of the Torah. They proudly helped carry the scrolls through the streets "under a canopy, like a bride," Charles says. These were the same streets where, fifty-five years before, no Jew had dared to walk openly.

The following morning, the Americans participated in the unveiling of the monument in Borgo San Dalmazzo. The public square in front of the barracks is now called the Piazza Don Viale Raimondo, in honor of the intrepid rescuer-priest who stood helplessly in front of his church that terrible day in November 1943 when the victims from Saint-Martin-Vésubie were marched past on their way to the railroad station. From the steps of the church, Don Viale's associate tried to convince a young mother to leave her infant child with him, but she, not understanding, refused. Both entered the train to Nice and died at Auschwitz.[1] The little church is still there, just a short distance from the barracks on one side and the railroad station on the other.

At the unveiling of the monument, William Blye and Walter Marx were invited to speak to the assembled group, to express their gratitude to the local people for the help they and their loved ones had received during their period in hiding. In his speech, Walter evoked the young woman who had found him and his mother a room in her father's hotel in Borgo San Dalmazzo when they first arrived from Saint-Martin-Vésubie. She had then visited his mother in the prison barracks and himself in the hospital and had later taken him to join the partisans. Suddenly, a white-haired woman, no longer young but still beautiful, emerged from the crowd. It was Maddalena, or Nella, Giraudo, by then Signora Nella Giraudo Tomatis. Not only Nella and Walter were in tears. The entire crowd joined them. After the reunion, Walter invited Nella to visit him and Ellen in New York, which she did in May 2000.[2]

The celebration of the eight-hundredth anniversary of the city of Cuneo was scheduled for that afternoon. As the time for that event approached, a crowd of about two thousand gathered in the Piazza Galimberti, where Duccio Galimberti had urged Italians to oppose both the Germans and the Italian Fascists on July 26, 1943. Since Walter Marx and William Blye had spoken in Borgo San Dalmazzo that morning, Harry Burger and Charles Roman were included among the speakers for the afternoon.

"I was born in Vienna," Charles told the crowd in the Piazza Galimberti, in Italian. "With my mother, I crossed half of Europe . . . and we never found so many people willing [to help us] as here in Italy. . . . I am happy and moved to be with you today to celebrate the eight-hundredth anniversary of the foundation of Cuneo. Thank you all. Shalom and peace to all." Charles and Inge had attended earlier reunions and would enjoy still others in the future. But nothing ever quite equaled the reception they received in the Piazza Galimberti.

Since 1998, Walter and Ellen Marx have returned to Borgo San Dalmazzo every year, always in September, to visit Nella and participate in commemorations of the Italian armistice and the Jews' flight across the Alps. In addition, in 2001 they went to Saint-Martin-Vésubie, where Walter spoke at a ceremony. Sigi Hart also made two more emotional journeys to Auschwitz with "The March of the Living." In 2000, he accompanied about seven thousand youngsters on a visit of one week in Poland and one week in Israel. In 2006, when Sigi was accompanied by three of his grandchildren, the youngsters on the same trip numbered ten thousand and the adults, nearly five thousand. There was, he says, even a delegate from Cuba.

The next large event specifically for the Jews of Saint-Martin-Vésubie occurred in September 2003, on the sixtieth anniversary of the armistice and the flight over the mountains. On that occasion, Charles and Inge Roman came to Saint-Martin-Vésubie from New York, as did Lya Haberman Quitt and her daughter Anna. Miriam Löwenwirth Reuveni traveled there from Israel. Also from Israel was Menahem Marienberg with two of his grandchildren, Rakefet and Dekel. And after much encouragement from Jacky Gerhard's future wife, Annette Bulostin, who had not personally experienced the Holocaust, Jacques Samson, Paulette Samson Grunberg, and Jacky and Régine Gerhard in Paris also decided to attend. As soon as they arrived in Saint-Martin-Vésubie, they wondered why they had waited so long to go back.

While the surviving Jews of Saint-Martin-Vésubie were the guests of honor at the reunion of 2003, they were not the only participants. Local villagers eagerly attended the activities, with the old people searching for familiar faces and the young looking for confirmation of family stories of difficult times. In addition, scores of people, Jews and non-Jews alike, came from France, Germany, Italy, Poland, Israel, and the United States.

The reunion was a great success. On Saturday night, Jews and villagers and their guests enjoyed a reception at the Hôtel de Ville. The walls of the elegant room were lined with photographs of the Jews of Saint-Martin-Vésubie. Those who had lived through the period were delighted to find themselves and their families and friends in the old pictures. The next morning, participants took several buses to the sanctuary of the Madone de Fenestre, the way station on one of the two routes across the Maritime Alps that the Jews had taken in 1943. There, most of the survivors paused to chat and rest and enjoy the crisp mountain air and stunning scenery. A few climbed up toward the summit to meet a commemorative group of hikers coming up from the Italian side. Ever indomitable, seventy-four-year-old Lya Haberman Quitt startled far younger hikers by climbing well over half the distance. Jacky Gerhard, Moïse Konstadt, and some others went at least as far up the mountain as she. More numerous on the trail than the survivors, however, were the young people who had come to honor them. Strong, enthusiastic, and confident of their footing, they bounded up and down the trail just as the Jewish survivors, themselves young in 1943, had done in their turn, helping those older and younger than themselves. Among the young people were Menahem Marienberg's granddaughter Rakefet and grandson Dekel, a reserve officer in the Israeli army. Unconscious of the symbolism, they helped Lya Haberman Quitt through the steepest sections of the trail.

After the hike, lunch was served at the sanctuary. For the young, the traditional polenta with meat sauce, wine, and bread were merely delicious. For those who had lived in Saint-Martin-Vésubie during the war, the meal evoked powerful, bittersweet memories. In the afternoon, there was a concert of young singers from the area and from Nice, followed by a commemorative ceremony at a monument to the Jews of Saint-Martin-Vésubie erected in 1995. Speakers at the ceremony included the mayor, as well as departmental, national, Resistance, and Jewish spokesmen. But for the Jews themselves, the best part of the weekend was the recognizing, and sometimes the not recognizing, of old friends. Who had survived the war? Who had died, then and later? Who had come back for this and other reunions? Who was out of touch? In the reunion of old friends, Jacques Samson found Carmen Giraudi, by then Carmen Parlarieu, who had saved bread coupons for him so many years ago.

After returning to Nice on Sunday evening, the Romans, Marienbergs, and Miriam Löwenwirth Reuveni went on to Borgo San Dalmazzo. For Menahem Marienberg, this part of the trip was particularly important. He had enjoyed his visit to Saint-Martin-Vésubie. He had been delighted to show his grandchildren the house where he had lived and surprised that he could find it. But through it all, he really had one objective. He wanted to make contact with Meinardi's son Eugenio in Cuneo and lay flowers on the grave of the man who had saved his life in Italy. With Rakefet and Dekel, he did exactly that. As Rakefet later wrote, "There he could not stop his tears, feeling as if it was his father."

Walter and Ellen Marx had been unable to be in Saint-Martin-Vésubie on September 8, 9, and 10, 2003. Just a few days later, however, they were present for a series of Italian commemorations for the sixtieth anniversary of the armistice, the arrival of the Jews of Saint-Martin-Vésubie, the deportation of Jews from Borgo San Dalmazzo, and the massacre of at least twenty-three civilians at Boves. The president of Italy, Carlo Azeglio Ciampi, attended all the ceremonies. At Borgo San Dalmazzo, he laid flowers in front of the barracks that had been a prison for the Jews of Saint-Martin-Vésubie. Of this event, attended by thousands of Italians, Walter writes simply, "As one of the few survivors of the camp I . . . was honored when I was introduced to the President by the head of the Jewish community of Cuneo [Enzo Cavaglion] and the mayor of Borgo San Dalmazzo and he shook my hand and we exchanged a few words." Walter Marx richly deserves that honor, as a persecuted Jew and a partisan who fought for the liberation of Italy.

At both Saint-Martin-Vésubie and Borgo San Dalmazzo and the surrounding area, reunions and commemorative ceremonies now take place every year in September. In a moving ceremony in the synagogue of Cuneo on September 2, 2004, Don Francesco Brondello, the vice-curate of Valdieri, was honored by Yad Vashem as a Righteous Among the Nations. Present at the ceremony, in addition to Don Brondello himself, were the mayor of Cuneo, the director of the city's Jewish community, the Israeli ambassador to Italy, Enzo and Alberto Cavaglion, and thirty members of the families of Chaya Roth and Gitta Fajerstein-Walchirk, two sisters whom the priest had helped save. Chaya and Gitta had provided the testimony necessary for the award; Enzo and Alberto Cavaglion had found substantiating documents.

A large-scale event occurred again in September 2005, commemorating the sixty-second anniversary of the crossing of the Alps and the sixtieth anniversary of the end of the war. Among those present in Saint-Martin-Vésubie this time were Jacques Samson and Paulette Samson Grunberg; Charles and Inge Roman; Walter and Ellen Marx; Menahem Marienberg with his daughter Sima and son Amir Moshe; Sigi and Vera Hart with Sigi's brother, Willy, now known as Bill Hart, and his sister, Manya Breuer; Lya Haberman Quitt; and Miriam Löwenwirth Reuveni. Walter and Menahem met at that reunion for the first time since they had been in the hospital together in November 1943. The Marx and Roman couples went to Cuneo and Borgo San Dalmazzo for a few days before the reunion at Saint-Martin-Vésubie. Miriam Löwenwirth Reuveni traveled there for a short visit afterward. For Miriam, this Italian part of her trip was especially meaningful. With help from Enzo Cavaglion, she says, she was able to reconstruct her journey in the winter of 1944, when she carried fifteen false documents from Rome to the province of Cuneo to save fifteen lives. She came to realize that the village where she had delivered the documents was Demonte. She also found the trail by the cemetery where Don Raimondo Viale had escorted her family out of Borgo San Dalmazzo to a hiding place in the mountains on September 18, 1943, and the little house, now abandoned, where they had left her infant brother with a local family for a few days. But most important for her, she visited the tomb of Don Raimondo Viale, fulfilling a vow she had made many years ago.

In Borgo San Dalmazzo on April 30, 2006, a beautiful new memorial was inaugurated to honor all the Jews deported from the local barracks, including the refugees from Saint-Martin-Vésubie and the twenty-six mostly citizens arrested later. It replaced the simple wooden plaque that Charles Roman had unveiled in 1998. Three boxcars like those used for deportations now stand beside the train station. In front of the cars, embedded in a platform of white cement, metal strips the color of copper bear the names of individual deportees who did not return from Auschwitz. Very rarely a metal strip is vertical rather than horizontal. Vertical strips bear the names of those who survived.

Walter Marx and his wife attended the inauguration of the memorial, along with Enzo Cavaglion. Following the inauguration, those present walked less than a quarter mile back to the site of the barracks. They walked, in reverse, the same route the deportees had followed to the trains. In a building at the site, the Jewish community of Turin then hosted a ceremony to honor three Italian non-Jews from the area who had saved Jewish refugees. One of the three was Maddalena (Nella) Giraudo Tomatis, who helped Walter, his mother, and his cousin after September 18 and then guided Walter to the Resistance after the other two were deported. With a speech carefully prepared in the Italian that he has not often spoken in the past sixty years, Walter Marx proudly presented Nella with her award.

And so the effort to preserve the memory continues.

In examining the chronology of "journeys back," it at first seems surprising that they began so late, so long after the end of the war. There are many reasons for the delays. In the first few decades after the war, most survivors were busy with jobs and families. Many had few financial resources and little time. Historians have suggested other explanations, although these are not verified in this study. Many survivors wanted to forget or feared the psychological consequences of too much remembering. Memories were too painful to be evoked. Survivors wanted to blend in, to be like everyone else, and feared that what made them different would be misunderstood or just plain ignored. They did not want to be accused of drawing attention to their own suffering when many others had also suffered, at least in their own estimation. As survivors entered their sixties and seventies, however, their scars healed somewhat and they began to consider recording their memories for their children and grandchildren.

This study of journeys back seems to add another explanation, not of the delay, but of the frequency of ceremonies of commemoration today. Painful as their journeys back must be, most of the witnesses interviewed for this book describe them as immensely fulfilling. Perhaps that is because they have found, contrary to their fears and expectations, that others are deeply interested in what they experienced during the war. That interest has given survivors the courage and confidence to face their past, with the knowledge that they will be, if not always understood, at least respected, appreciated, and honored. It has caused them to speak publicly of their experiences and participate in a wide variety of educational activities. It has helped them to heal. If that is the case, it is a significant reason why the commemorations must continue.

Conclusion

IN BOTH FRANCE AND ITALY during the Holocaust, rates of deportation and death were proportionately higher among recent immigrant and refugee Jews than among Jewish citizens. In France, for example, there were about 195,000 French Jews and 135,000 foreign Jews in the country at the end of · 1940. Of these, about 24,500 French Jews and 56,500 foreign Jews were deported or died in France.[1] Thus, about 24.5 percent of all Jews in France were victims. When broken down into their French and foreign components, however, the percentages are quite different. About 12.6 percent of all French Jews were deported or died in France, and about 42 percent of the foreign Jews. Statistics do not distinguish between longtime resident Jewish immigrants and more recent arrivals, but examination of the events of August 1942 in unoccupied France have indicated the special focus of Vichy police on recent immigrants.

In Italy, statistics are less certain, in part because many of the foreign Jews who poured into the country from France and Yugoslavia at the time of the armistice with the Allies were never recorded. However, rough statistics indicate that there were about 38,807 Jews in German-occupied parts of Italy in mid-September 1943. The total number of Jews known to have been deported or to have been killed in Italy is 7,128. They represented about 18 percent of the 38,807. But again it is revealing to try to break down the statistics, although the results are more approximate than those of France. Very roughly, there were 30,914 Italian Jews (80 percent of the total) and 7,893 foreign Jews (20 percent) in Italy in mid-September 1943.[2] Therefore, the 4,348 Italian Jews known to have been deported or killed in Italy represented roughly 14 percent of the Italian Jews present at the time, and the 2,555 known foreign Jewish victims constituted about 32 percent of their population.[3] These rough estimates of proportionate losses are not so different from those in France, where foreign Jews were in danger of deportation for a much longer period of time.

Among the Jews who came to Italy from Saint-Martin-Vésubie, the casualty rate was probably more than 37 percent. About 350 of the roughly 950 Jews who crossed the Maritime Alps from France after September 8, 1943, were arrested on September 18. A few of these escaped deportation, but additional Jews from Saint-Martin-Vésubie were arrested after September 18, so that about 349 were sent to Auschwitz on November 21. Others were arrested and deported later, or killed in Italy. This death rate raises the question of whether flight from France to Italy was the best possible choice at the time. Would survival rates have been higher if the Jews of Saint-Martin-Vésubie had simply hidden in southeastern France, where they knew the language, had friends, and were already familiar with the mountain areas? It is a question without an answer.

Beyond statistics, other questions remain about the distinct experiences of recent immigrant and refugee Jews in France and Italy. The Vichy regime's internment and forced labor policies for foreign Jews in the unoccupied zone are not always understood, and the passage of some individuals and entire families in and out of camps can be bewildering. The subsequent fate of Jewish newcomers who escaped arrest in unoccupied France in August 1942 is not always clear. Even less known are the special hardships of foreign Jews in Italy during the German occupation. In both countries, how did men, women, and children in hiding manage to survive with no resources, no contacts, and often no language skills? Who helped them, and how did the rescue process work?

This book has attempted to answer some of these questions by examining actual cases. In France, for example, newcomers like Marianne Roman and Sigi Hart and his family were interned but then either released because of illness or able to escape, sometimes only to be interned again, to escape again. Other refugee families without resources, like that of Miriam Löwenwirth, were not interned at all. The loose, flexible nature of internment in unoccupied France in 1940 and 1941, so often misunderstood by modern readers familiar with the rigid concentration camps of the Third Reich and Poland, has become clearer. The enforcement of Vichy's internment decrees depended on individual departmental prefects or even on local village officials. However unpleasant, internment was not initially intended as punishment or as a prelude to deportation. It was, rather, a solution to the perceived social and economic problem of indigent, unwelcome Jewish refugees. The walls of French camps were consequently porous at first. When the Germans offered to take those refugees off their hands, however, many Vichy officials willingly, and without asking too many questions, accepted another, more permanent solution.

In addition to addressing French internment policies and the special circumstances of recent immigrant and refugee Jews, this book has also revealed several adaptation mechanisms that assisted many traditional Jewish families in their struggle for survival. One of these was the willingness of families to split up and go in different directions, they hoped temporarily. The mother of Charles Roman, the father of Menahem Marienberg, and the parents of Sigi Hart and Boris Carmeli, for example, all agreed to separate from their children in the hope that the children would be safer and more comfortable in Jewish children's homes. Most remarkable was the case of Sigi's mother, who insisted that her daughter, Manya, leave the dreaded camp of Gurs when the opportunity arose rather than remain to be with her. That insistence certainly saved Manya's life. And later, Sigi's father allowed Manya to leave for Rome with her boyfriend, to struggle for survival on her own rather than with her father and brothers.

Also apparent is the breakdown of traditional lines of authority within families. In some cases, men were no longer able to protect their women and children, either because they themselves had been arrested or because their skills and abilities were no longer relevant. The result was a major shift in gender and generational roles. Thus, the mothers of Charles Roman, William Blye, Miriam Löwenwirth, and Walter Marx (for only a time, tragically) assumed burdens and responsibilities that they never would have faced in normal life. Many parents also called upon their children to assume great responsibilities. Jewish children grew up quickly during their wartime odysseys. Charles Roman, Sigi and Willy Hart, Jacques and Paulette Samson, Boris Carmeli, and the Marienberg brothers traveled throughout German-occupied France alone, in the most hazardous conditions. William Blye cared for his mother after his father's arrest. Sigi Hart led his family up into the mountains to escape arrest at Aulus-les-Bains. Other youths blazed a trail from Saint-Martin-Vésubie to Italy and helped older people follow it. Charles Roman and Lya Haberman left their hiding places to shop for the group in Valdieri. And most dramatic, Miriam Löwenwirth seems to have cared for her entire family. She single-handedly reunited the family in unoccupied France, got her father out of a French prison, led the entire group into the Italian-occupied zone, refused to surrender in Valdieri when the German SS demanded it, got her mother and herself exempted from the roundup in the convent in Florence where they were hiding, escorted her siblings to Rome to join her mother there, delivered false documents from Rome to the province of Cuneo for Father Benedetto, and communicated with her father until his deportation. In normal times, Miriam would have been pampered and protected. The challenge of wartime persecution summoned all her skills and talents.

By looking at actual cases, the remarkable role of French Jewish assistance agencies in sustaining immigrant and refugee Jews has also become clear. French Jews have been criticized for their prewar discomfort with visibly foreign, unintegrated Eastern European Jewish immigrants who they feared would provoke anti-Semitism. Justly or not, French Jewish organizations have been accused of a reluctance during the war to challenge the authorities or engage in clandestine activities to protect their Jewish clients, who were often foreigners.[4] But witnesses from the nine families interviewed for this book indicate that Jewish organizations were present in their lives throughout all the years of danger.

Refugee families received subsidies for food and housing from Jewish organizations from the moment they first arrived in assigned residence in little villages in the south of France in 1940. Refugee children like Charles Roman found shelter in Jewish children's homes even before the German invasion, while others, like Boris Carmeli, Menahem and Léon Marienberg, and Sigi, Willy, and Manya Hart passed through such homes later while evading arrest. At the moment of greatest danger in August 1942 in France, Jewish boy scouts saved the lives of Menahem and Léon, while either scouts or Zionist youths did the same for Boris. A French Jewish Red Cross worker secreted Charles Roman out of Rivesaltes, while an OSE representative then protected him and employed him in the saving of other children in the same camp. Somewhat later, in Nice, the Jewish rescue agency known as the Comité Dubouchage played the most spectacular role of all. Thousands of Jewish refugees in the Italian zone, present illegally and just steps ahead of the French police, received life-saving documents from that committee, as well as the food and housing supplements that kept them alive for months. Committee activists even accompanied refugees to their places of assigned residence, to help requisition living quarters and organize economic, social, and educational activities. By this time, of course, many of these activists were foreign Jews, working side by side with their French colleagues.

In Italy, the Jewish assistance organization Delasem was also outstanding. Every one of the nine families except the two Marienberg brothers and possibly the Carmelis survived because of aid from Delasem. Without it, most of them would have been lost. Short of finding an Italian benefactor willing to support them for a year and a half, it was virtually impossible to survive in the mountains of the province of Cuneo without Delasem subsidies. Menahem and Léon Marienberg managed because of the goodness of one such benefactor, Giuseppe Meinardi. The others who stayed in hiding in the north, however—William Blye and Walter Marx until liberation, and Charles Roman and Jacques Samson for a winter—benefited from the silent goodwill of the local population but escaped starvation because of Delasem subsidies.

Similarly, newcomers who had no money and spoke no Italian could not easily strike out for Florence or Rome without some help. Charles and Marianne Roman traveled to Rome with documents supplied by Delasem, and probably with a small financial subsidy. They in March or April 1944 and Jacques and Szlama Samson the preceding January also received a referral to a safe house in Rome, operated by Settimio Sorani and Father Maria Benedetto with Delasem funds. As for Florence, Miriam Löwenwirth and her family seem to have gone there so early that social workers from a rescue committee distributing Delasem funds were not yet functioning effectively. Sigi Hart and his family also seem to have traveled to Genoa without much assistance, although they met a helpful priest there who was certainly aware of Delasem-funded groups. But both families eventually came under the protective wing of the Italian Jewish assistance agency, as seen by the places where they were hidden—the Catholic school at La Pietra, the convent of the Suore Serve di Maria Addolorata, and the convent of the Suore Francescane Missionarie di Maria. All of those locations were secured by the archbishop of Florence and his assistants, at the request of the Delasem-funded local Jewish rescue committee. Tragically, that committee was initially overwhelmed, and Sigi Hart and his father were not placed safely.

On the other hand, Lya Haberman, who traveled with her father to Florence after Yom Kippur, in mid-October 1943, benefited from help from

Delasem from start to finish. A Delasem worker contacted her father and her in the mountains to urge them to move; they traveled by train with a large group, assisted all along the way by priests working with Delasem representatives; and upon their arrival in Florence they immediately met Matilde Cassin and Monsignor Giacomo Meneghello of the Delasem-funded Jewish rescue committee. They were the beneficiaries of an impressive regionally coordinated rescue operation that saved hundreds, perhaps thousands, of lives.

After it was forced by the German occupiers of Italy to go underground and turn its funds and client lists over to local priests and prelates, of course, Delasem's rescue operations were no longer conducted exclusively by Jews. Thus the refugees from Saint-Martin-Vésubie encountered many non-Jewish rescuers: Cardinal Boetto and Don Repetto in Genoa; Cardinal Dalla Costa, Monsignor Meneghello, Don Casini, and Father Ricotti in Florence; Father Maria Benedetto in Rome; and Don Viale and Don Brondello in the province of Cuneo, to mention only a few. These supervisors of rescue networks in turn recruited other men and women of the Church, who opened the doors of their institutions to Jewish fugitives. They also recruited priests and laypersons to distribute funds and escort refugees over the frontier into Switzerland. Only a few rescuers have been encountered here, but there were many. And in addition to the Jews from Saint-Martin-Vésubie, they helped hundreds of others, both citizens and foreigners. Without their courageous cooperation, the efforts of Jewish rescue organizations would have floundered.

In addition to non-Jews who were regular participants in rescue networks, of course, there were individuals who saved Jews independently, apart from any organization. These were often individuals present on the scene by chance, who saved lives by making instant, spontaneous decisions, without time for thought or reflection about the consequences. Many subsequently continued to help the Jewish men, women, and children who had initially appealed to them as total strangers in a moment of terror. The representatives of the nine families interviewed for this book have all referred to rescuers of this type who unquestionably saved their lives. Boris Carmeli, for example, remembers a stranger he knew only as Pietro, who hid him and his family for more than three weeks after the roundup in Valdieri on September 18, 1943, and then escorted them to a safer spot. Jacques Samson tells of Signora Orselina and a local baker in Valdieri who saved the Gerhard family. For Lya Haberman, help came from an Italian woman prison guard who enabled her father in Borgo San Dalmazzo to find her after the September 18 roundup. And Walter Marx and Menahem Marienberg honor Nella Giraudo and Giuseppe Meinardi, respectively, who helped them initially almost without reflection but stayed with them over a longer period.

Nor did these quiet acts of spontaneous rescue by strangers occur only in Italy. After his father and brothers in Nice were arrested in the round-ups of recent immigrants in the unoccupied zone in August 1942, William Blye was befriended and helped by his hotelkeeper, Madame Guttin. Boris Carmeli's family was warned of the same roundup by the secretary of the mayor of Bénéjacq and was able to hide in the hayloft of total strangers until the danger had passed. Sigi Hart's family received a similar warning at the same time from a sympathetic villager in Aulus-les-Bains and escaped arrest. Paulette Samson, left behind in Saint-Martin-Vésubie when her father and brother crossed into Italy, was saved by her hotelkeeper, Fanny Vassallo, and by the Saïssi family in Monaco.

In addition to specific acts of rescue, most of the nine families interviewed for this book benefited in both France and Italy from popular attitudes that were at worst indifferent and at best benevolent. Sigi Hart and his brother, for example, were kept in a hospital in Béziers by a doctor who knew they were no longer sick but understood that conditions in the internment camp of Agde from which they had come were dangerously harsh. Later, gendarmes on bicycles passed by Sigi and his father in a rural area, although they must have known that they were outsiders, and possibly illegal. And the family with which the Harts lived in Juzet-de-Luchon became lifelong friends. Charles Roman found that most of the people in the French village of Saint-Pierre-de-Fursac were sympathetic, and he remains in touch to this day with one of the two Paillassou sisters who taught him and made him feel welcome. Jacques Samson remembers the Paris policeman who learned that he had not registered for the Jewish census and warned him to escape to the unoccupied zone. And Miriam Löwenwirth speaks of the French guard in a small internment center who let her father go. Meanwhile, on the Italian side of the border, witnesses invariably recall simple peasants who shared their meager fare and allowed them to stay in their cabins in the mountains, sometimes for many months.

Despite incidents of rescue in both countries, most of the witnesses interviewed for this book have more favorable memories of their experiences in Italy than in France. There are several reasons for this. Most spent three and a half years in wartime France, constantly harassed by Vichy authorities and often in great danger. Sigi Hart and Charles Roman spent time in dirty, disorganized internment camps. All were well aware of the more than eleven thousand foreign Jews delivered by the Vichy regime from unoccupied France to the Germans in the north, for deportation. Charles Roman, Walter Marx, Menahem Marienberg, Lya Haberman, and William Blye knew that their own loved ones had been arrested by French, not German, police. And most had mixed experiences with the French people. For every French official or common citizen who was kind in 1941 or 1942, there was someone who believed the Vichy propaganda that Jews and foreigners constituted a security threat and an economic menace. Scholars generally agree that public opinion regarding the Jews changed dramatically after August 1942, when French citizens saw whole families, including the sick, the elderly, and the mothers with their small children, mercilessly deported to what could only be their deaths.[5] But by the time many French citizens became less hostile, our witnesses were in Saint-Martin-Vésubie, dealing primarily with the Italians.

In the chaos of German-occupied Italy, the Jews of Saint-Martin-Vésubie had much less contact with Italian authorities than with the common people. They were aware that by September 1943, most Italians hated the war, the Nazis, and the Fascists who supported it and were fully sharing the shortages, the arbitrary arrests, and the massacres that were afflicting the Jews. It was easy to blame atrocities and suffering on the Germans alone, rather than on the Italians who had supported Mussolini and the war at an earlier period. But if the witnesses interviewed for this book had suffered at the hands of the French police during roundups in August 1942 and February 1943, to mention only two events, they also remember cruelty by Italians. Menahem Marienberg was arrested, imprisoned, and nearly shot by Italian militiamen. Boris Carmeli was arrested by Italian militiamen when he went into a village to buy medicine and sent to Auschwitz as a result. Walter Marx helped capture an Italian woman who was betraying Italian partisans to the Germans. And William Blye saw his young friend Marcel Futerman and his father dead under a bridge in Cuneo, shot with four other Jews from Saint-Martin-Vésubie by Italian militiamen fleeing to the north on the eve of liberation. The victims were shot merely because they were Jews.

In a prime example of what Primo Levi described as memory "incorporating extraneous features" and "fixed in a stereotype," as seen in the introduction to this book, the wartime recollections of witnesses have undoubtedly been colored by outside influences since 1945.[6] Over the years, many read about the Dreyfus Affair and other manifestations of popular anti-Semitism in France in the nineteenth century and during the 1930s. They also became painfully aware that during the first three or four decades after the war, the French were slow in acknowledging the collaboration of Vichy authorities in the persecution of the Jews. Finally, they believe that they perceive signs of anti-Semitism in France today. All of these factors have tended to reinforce witnesses' memories of unfavorable treatment during the war while obscuring those of benevolence and support. Conversely, our same witnesses after the war heard the often-repeated if oversimplified claims that anti-Semitism was virtually nonexistent in nineteenth-century Italy. Those claims reinforced positive memories of the wartime experiences of Jews there while obscuring the negative. Some witnesses are even willing to overlook the fact that many Italians have also been slow to acknowledge Fascist crimes against the Jews. Survivors have as much difficulty as the rest of us in generalizing about popular attitudes toward Jewish refugees and recent immigrants in France and Italy. However, their concrete accounts of their individual personal experiences suggest that the differences were less dramatic than stereotypes would indicate.

The wartime odysseys of the Jews of Saint-Martin-Vésubie clearly brought them into contact with the best and the worst of two countries. The memories of those who survived include many favorable impressions. Those who died were probably not so fortunate in their chance encounters. For in the final analysis, luck played an enormous role in survival. So too did each individual's personal situation, including age, health, financial resources, and family obligations. But personality was also decisive. Required were large doses of courage, imagination, intelligence, flexibility, and determination. Certainly not all who had those characteristics survived, but few managed without them. William Blye, Boris Carmeli, Lya Haberman, Sigi Hart, Miriam Löwenwirth, Menahem Marienberg, Walter Marx, Charles Roman, and Jacques and Paulette Samson had them all in good portion. All but Boris and Sigi lost a parent or two, and sometimes siblings. All lost members of their more extended families. To mention just one case, twelve members of Boris Carmeli's mother's family who remained in Poland were murdered there, as were eighteen members of his father's. But the witnesses described in this book and their surviving family members fought for life, and created new life. They also helped preserve the memory of the Jews of Saint-Martin-Vésubie.

Principal Witnesses

BLYE, WILLIAM (formerly *Wolfgang* or *Wolf Bleiweiss*)—born in Leipzig in 1924 to Maria Lustgarten and Chaim Bleiweiss, from Poland. Brothers Bernhard and Leo were born in 1923 and 1926, respectively. Chaim was a businessman. The family left Germany for Italy in 1937 and left Italy for Nice in 1939. Chaim, Bernhard, and Leo were arrested in August 1942, expelled to Drancy, and deported on September 2, 1942, to Kosel and Auschwitz. They did not return. William and Maria remained in Nice until the Italians occupied it in November 1942. They were sent to Saint-Martin-Vésubie, fled to Italy in September 1943, and hid in the mountains of the province of Cuneo until the end of the war in May 1945.

CARMELI, BORIS (formerly *Norbert Wolfinger*)—born in Poland in 1928 to Rachel Reichman and Hermann Wolfinger, a businessman. His brother, Pinkas Wolfinger, later Peter Carmeli, was born in 1921. The family immigrated to Magdeburg, Germany, in 1932, and to Brussels in 1939. In May 1940 they fled to France, where they lived in Buziet (Pyrénées-Atlantiques), Lamalou-les-Bains (Hérault), and Bénéjacq (Pyrénées-Atlantiques) until August 1942. Narrowly escaping arrest, Boris was at the OSE children's home in Moissac for a time, but then went to Nice and Saint-Martin-Vésubie with his parents. In September 1943 they fled to Italy, and although they escaped arrest on September 18, Boris was caught soon after. He was sent back to France, imprisoned briefly at Drancy, and deported from there to Auschwitz on December 7, 1943. He was liberated at Bergen-Belsen in 1945.

HABERMAN, LYA (*Quitt* by marriage)—born in Berlin in 1929 to Chana Goldberg and Oscar Haberman, who had emigrated from Poland. Her sister, Hilda, was born in 1926. Oscar, a businessman, moved to Paris in 1933. His wife and daughters joined him in 1938. The family fled from Paris in June 1940, lived for a time in Villenouvelle (Haute-Garonne), and then moved to Nice. Chana and Hilda were arrested when the Germans occupied Nice in September 1943 and deported from Drancy to Auschwitz on March 7, 1944. They did not return. Lya and Oscar were in Saint-Martin-Vésubie, the mountains of the province of Cuneo, and Florence.

HART, SIGI (formerly *Hartmayer*)—born in 1925 in Berlin to Adela Wulkan from Oświęcim, Poland, and Hermann Begleiter (later Hartmayer) from Galicia, in the Austro-Hungarian Empire until 1918. His sister, Manya, was born in 1922 and his brother, Willy, in 1928. His father was a salesman. In 1939 the family moved to Antwerp, from where they fled to France in May 1940. They were in Bagnères-de-Luchon (Haute-Garonne), in the Agde camp, in Juzet-de-Luchon (Haute-Garonne), and in Aulus-les-Bains (Ariège). Narrowly escaping arrest in August 1942, they were caught by French police in October and sent to Gurs. All but Adela got out of Gurs, went to Nice and Saint-Martin-Vésubie, and fled to the province of Cuneo in September 1943. From there Manya went into hiding in Rome. Sigi, Willy, and Hermann hid in Florence, where they were arrested in November 1943. Willy and Hermann escaped, but Sigi was deported to Auschwitz on November 9. He was liberated at Bergen-Belsen in 1945.

LÖWENWIRTH, MIRIAM LÉA (*Reuveni* by marriage)—born in 1926 in Iršava, then in Czechoslovakia, to Elena Izckovic and Eliyahu Löwenwirth, a shoe maker. Miriam had six younger brothers and sisters, one of whom died before the war. The family moved to Antwerp in 1929, from where they fled to France in May 1940. In Quarante (Hérault), they escaped arrest in August 1942 and moved to Chirac (Lozère), where Eliyahu was arrested early in 1943 but was released. The family moved to Nice and Saint-Martin-Vésubie, fled to Italy, and hid in Florence. Miriam, her mother, and her youngest brother miraculously survived the raid on the convent of the Suore Francescane

Missionarie di Maria in the Piazza Carmine on November 27, 1943. Eliyahu was later arrested and deported to Bergen-Belsen on May 16, 1944. He did not survive. The rest of the family survived in Florence and Rome.

MARIENBERG, MENAHEM—born in Brussels in 1927 to Simone Ruju-vikyet and Wolf Marienberg, from Poland. His sister, Mina, was born in 1929, brother Léon in 1933, and brother Maurice in 1938. His father was a leather worker. With his family, he fled from Brussels in May 1940, settled in Revel (Haute-Garonne), and then in Toulouse, where he remained until August 1942. Simone, Mina, and Maurice were arrested that month, expelled to Drancy, and deported on September 4, 1942, to Kosel and Auschwitz. They did not return. Menahem was then at the EIF home at Lautrec (Tarn) for a time, and Léon was at Moissac (Tarn-et-Garonne). They joined their father at Saint-Martin-Vésubie, fled to Italy in September 1943, and were arrested on September 18. Wolf was sent to Drancy, via Nice, in November 1943, and deported to Auschwitz on December 7, 1943. He did not return. Menahem and Léon escaped deportation in November because they were in the hospital. They remained in the province of Cuneo, where they were saved by Giuseppe Meinardi.

MARX, WALTER—born in Heilbronn, Germany, in 1926 to Johanna Isaac and Ludwig Marx, Germans. Ludwig was a businessman. Walter moved to Luxembourg in 1935, from where he was expelled with his parents and his cousin Werner Isaac to France by the Germans in November 1940. They lived in Montpellier, narrowly escaping arrest in August 1942, until they were moved to Lamalou-les-Bains (Hérault) in November. Ludwig was arrested there in February 1943, deported probably on March 4 or 6, 1943, and killed, probably at Majdanek. Walter and Johanna fled to Nice, were sent to Saint-Martin-Vésubie, crossed into Italy, and were arrested by the Germans in Borgo San Dalmazzo on September 18, 1943. Johanna was sent to Drancy, via Nice, in November 1943, and deported to Auschwitz on December 7, 1943. She did not return. Walter escaped deportation in November because he was in the hospital. Until the end of the war, he hid in the mountains of the province of Cuneo, where he was active in the Resistance.

ROMAN, CHARLES—born in 1927 in Vienna to Marianne Uhrmacher and Leopold Roman, Austrians. Leopold was a businessman. Charles and Marianne fled to Paris in December 1938, after the Anschluss in March and

Kristallnacht in November. Charles lived at the Château de Chabannes and the Château Montintin, OSE children's homes, until August 1942, when he joined Leopold, who had been arrested, at Rivesaltes. Leopold was expelled to Drancy and deported on September 11, 1942, to Kosel and Auschwitz. He did not return. Charles escaped. Marianne was in the camp of Agde for a time, but was then in Florac (Lozère), where her second husband Wilhelm Bauer was arrested in February 1943. He was deported to Majdanek or Sobibór, and died. Marianne moved to Nice alone, but Charles joined her in Saint-Martin-Vésubie. In September 1943, mother and son fled to the province of Cuneo, where they hid until the spring of 1944. They then hid in Rome until its liberation in June 1944.

SAMSON, JACQUES AND PAULETTE (formerly *Samsonowicz; Paulette Grunberg* by marriage)—born in Poland in 1925 and 1927, respectively, to Rywka-Rajzla Sztajman and Szlama Samsonowicz, a horse dealer. They emigrated with their father to Paris in 1937. Rajzla and two younger daughters remained in Poland, where they perished in the Holocaust. Szlama joined the Foreign Legion when war broke out and was demobilized in Marseille in the autumn of 1940. Jacques and Paulette remained in Paris but did not register in the German-decreed Jewish census in October 1940. They joined their father in Marseille in the autumn of 1942 but moved to Nice after the Italians occupied it in November 1942. Sent to Saint-Martin-Vésubie, Jacques and Szlama fled to the province of Cuneo when the Italians left after September 8, 1943, and later hid in Rome. Paulette remained in Saint-Martin-Vésubie and later hid in Monaco and France.

Abbreviations

The following abbreviations of archives, organizations, and publications are used in the text and notes.

AAF	Archivio arcivescovile di Firenze
AISRC	Archives of the Istituto storico della resistenza in Cuneo
CDEC	Centro di documentazione ebraica contemporanea, Milan
CDJC	Centre de documentation juive contemporaine, Paris
CGQ J	Commissariat générale aux questions juives
CIMADE	Comité inter-mouvements auprès des évacués
CTE	Compagnie travailleurs étrangers
Delasem	Delegazione per l'assistenza agli emigranti ebrei
EIF	Éclaireurs israélites de France
GTE	Groupements de travailleurs étrangers
ISRT	Istituto storico della resistenza in Toscano
JO	*Journal officiel de la république française: lois et décrets*
MJS	Mouvement des jeunesses sionistes
OJC	Organisation juive de combat
ORT	Organisation pour la reconstruction et le travail
OSE	Oeuvre de secours aux enfants
SSAE	Service social d'aide aux émigrants
UGIF	Union générale des israélites de France

Notes

CHAPTER ONE. JEWISH IMMIGRANTS AND POLITICAL REFUGEES
IN FRANCE, 1933–1939

1. Unless otherwise indicated, all information about Paulette and Jacques Samson throughout this book is based on interviews with Jacques in Menerbes, France, on September 15, 2003, and with Paulette in Paris on May 18, 2004; on subsequent correspondence and conversations; and on "Récit: Jacky, début–30 mai 2003," an unpublished memoir by Jacky Gerhard, who was frequently with Paulette and Jacques in the province of Cuneo in Italy and later with Jacques in Rome.

2. Another 20,000 Eastern European Jews had settled in Paris between 1880 and the First World War, for a total of 90,000. They represented 82 percent of the 110,000 Jewish immigrants to the city between 1880 and 1939. Between 1906 and 1939, roughly 150,000 to 200,000 foreign Jews entered France as a whole. See Michel Roblin, *Les juifs de Paris: Démographie, économie, culture* (Paris: A. et J. Picard, 1952), 73–74; and David H. Weinberg, *A Community on Trial: The Jews of Paris in the 1930s* (1974; Chicago: University of Chicago Press, 1977), 8.

3. Precise statistics are unclear. Roblin suggests that about 50,000 refugees from the Third Reich passed through France between 1933 and 1939, of whom more than half were Jewish. He adds that only about 10,000 of the 50,000 remained in the country (*Les juifs de Paris*, 73).

4. Unless otherwise indicated, information about Lya Haberman is based on my interview with her on August 11, 2003, and subsequent conversations.

5. From William Blye, "Surviving the War Years: A Memoir," *The New Light*,

a publication of Temple Israel, Great Neck, NY, spring 2003, 2 pp., 1. Unless otherwise noted, all discussion of William Blye throughout this book is based on the memoir, my interview with him on September 22, 2003, and subsequent correspondence and conversations.

6. In addition, this measure revoked the citizenship of all Jews who had been naturalized after January 1, 1919. Also in September, Jewish teachers and students were barred from the public schools, with the exception of students already enrolled in universities, who were allowed to complete their studies. In November 1938, other measures prohibited marriage between Jews and non-Jews, prevented Jews from owning businesses and properties over a certain value, and banned Jews from the armed forces, banks, insurance companies, and public administration. The following year, Jews were prohibited from working as notaries, and only those with special exemptions could work as journalists, doctors, pharmacists, veterinarians, lawyers, accountants, engineers, architects, chemists, agronomists, and mathematicians. Jews could not employ non-Jews as domestic servants, own radios, place advertisements or death notices in the newspapers, publish books, hold public conferences, list their names and numbers in telephone directories, or frequent popular vacation spots. These measures were thoroughly enforced. For details, see *La persecuzione degli ebrei durante il fascismo: Le leggi del 1938* (Rome: Camera dei deputati, 1998); and three works by Michele Sarfatti: *Mussolini contro gli ebrei: Cronaca dell'elaborazione delle leggi del 1938* (Turin: Silvio Zamorani, 1994); *Gli ebrei nell'Italia fascista: Vicende, identità, persecuzione* (Turin: Einaudi, 2000); and *Le leggi antiebraiche spiegate agli italiani di oggi* (Turin: Einaudi, 2002).

7. For analysis of French policies toward Jewish immigrants from Italy at this time, see Paolo Veziano, *Ombre di confine: L'emigrazione clandestina degli ebrei stranieri dalla Riviera dei Fiori verso la Costa Azzurra (1938–1940)* (Pinerolo: Alzani, 2001).

8. See, e.g., Eve Dessarre, *Mon enfance d'avant le déluge* (Paris: Fayard, 1976), esp. 172–77; and Maurice Rajfus, *Mon père l'étranger: Un immigré juif polonais à Paris dans les années 1920* (Paris: L'Harmattan, 1989).

9. Most Jews from the Third Reich were technically stateless. In 1933, Hitler's new regime denaturalized Eastern European Jewish immigrants in Germany who had become citizens after the First World War. Then in September 1935, the Nazis stripped German Jews of their citizenship as well. This measure also applied to Austria after the Anschluss in March 1938. See Vicki Caron, *Uneasy Asylum: France and the Jewish Refugee Crisis, 1933–1942* (Stanford, CA: Stanford University Press, 1999), 14, 44.

10. At least one other Jewish boy, Manfred Alter, studied at the Lycée du Parc Impérial in Nice before the war and went to Saint-Martin-Vésubie in 1943. See his name on a list in Alberto Cavaglion, *Nella notte straniera: Gli ebrei di St.-Martin-Vésubie* (1981; Dronero: L'Arciere, 2003), 91.

11. Unless otherwise noted, all information in this book about Charles Roman

is based on his taped interview at the Museum of Jewish Heritage in New York, dated November 19, 1991; my interviews with him on July 22 and December 15, 2003; and much subsequent correspondence and conversation.

CHAPTER TWO. JEWISH IMMIGRANTS AND POLITICAL REFUGEES
IN BELGIUM AND LUXEMBOURG BEFORE THE WAR

1. Unless otherwise stated, information throughout this book about Menahem Marienberg is based on my interviews with him in Nice and Saint-Martin-Vésubie on September 6, 2003, and on subsequent correspondence with him, with his granddaughter Rakefet Sherman Elisha, and with his grandson Dekel Sherman. Information about Miriam Léa Löwenwirth Reuveni is based on my interviews with her in Nice and Cuneo on September 8 and 9, 2003; on much subsequent correspondence; and on the as-yet unpublished English translation of her memoirs, entitled *Hakdasha* ("Dedication"), written in Hebrew with Miriam Dubi-Gazan after a series of 13 interviews (Raanana, Israel: Docostory, 2002). The memoirs were published in Italy as *Dedicazione* (Aosta: Le Château, 2005).

2. Information about Sigi Hart is based on my interview with him in New York City on October 30, 2003; on his interview taped for Steven Spielberg's Shoah Foundation on November 8, 1996; and on subsequent conversations and correspondence with him and his sister, Manya Breuer.

3. Marion A. Kaplan, *Between Dignity and Despair: Jewish Life in Nazi Germany* (New York: Oxford University Press, 1998), 72–73.

4. On the temporary easing of anti-Jewish measures in Germany during the Olympics, see Duff Hart-Davis, *Hitler's Games: The 1936 Olympics* (London: Century, 1986), 126–28, 138–40.

5. Ibid., 132.

6. Unless otherwise noted, information in this book about Boris Carmeli is from my interview with him in Rome on May 19, 2004, and from subsequent correspondence and conversations.

7. From Walter Marx's speech at Temple Beth Sholom of Roslyn Heights, NY, on Yom Hashoah in April 1996. Unless otherwise noted, all discussion of Walter Marx throughout this book is based on this speech; a taped interview he gave to the Jewish Partisan Educational Foundation, May 2, 2003; my interview with him on August 12, 2003; and much subsequent correspondence and conversation.

CHAPTER THREE. FLIGHT TO SOUTHERN FRANCE, MAY AND JUNE 1940

1. The number 10,000 is from Vicki Caron, *Uneasy Asylum: France and the Jewish Refugee Crisis, 1933–1942* (Stanford, CA: Stanford University Press, 1999), 259. Julian Jackson, *France: The Dark Years, 1940–1944* (Oxford: Oxford University Press, 2001), 363, puts the number at 20,000. The estimate of 40,000 is from François Delpech, *Sur les juifs: Études d'histoire contemporaine* (Lyon: Presses Universitaires de Lyon, 1983), 298; and Renée

Poznanski, *Jews in France during World War II*, trans. Nathan Bracher (1997; Hanover, NH: University Press of New England, 2001), 24.

2. Throughout this book, the place-names in parentheses following the names of French villages, towns, or cities indicate the departments in which they are located. All departments are identified on the map of France included in this book.

3. On the prefect's order, see René S. Kapel, *Un rabbin dans la tourmente (1940–1944)* (Paris: Éditions du Centre, 1985), 89.

4. For another account by a Jewish refugee in Bordeaux who also eventually went to Saint-Martin-Vésubie and Italy, see Alfred Feldman, *One Step Ahead: A Jewish Fugitive in Hitler's Europe* (Carbondale: Southern Illinois University Press, 2001), 54–56.

5. For this estimate, see Michael R. Marrus and Robert O. Paxton, *Vichy France and the Jews* (New York: Basic Books, 1981), 15. The number may have been higher. On the impossibility of knowing the exact number of refugees, see Jean Vidalenc, *L'exode de mai–juin 1940* (Paris: Presses Universitaires de France, 1957), 1–10. Vidalenc points out that many refugees deliberately avoided registration, others were counted twice, still others returned home after a few days, while some were in areas where no count was ever made. He estimates that in the country as a whole, there may have been as many as 6 million French refugees, excluding foreigners (359). He also records that according to one official count made in the unoccupied zone, there were still 2,486,500 refugees in the south on August 13, 1940 (426).

6. Caron, *Uneasy Asylum*, 224, 235.

7. See Zosa Szajkowski, *Jews and the French Foreign Legion* (New York: KTAV, 1975), 60–75.

8. See Serge Klarsfeld, *Le calendrier de la persécution des juifs en France, 1940–1944* (Paris: Les Fils et Filles des Déportés Juifs de France, 1993), 11–12; and Szajkowski, *Jews and the French Foreign Legion*, 66. By special agreement with the French government in the autumn of 1940, Czech and Polish immigrants in France could enlist with the military forces of the Czech and Polish governments in exile. Many Czech Jews did so, but the Polish forces did not welcome Jews. Despite its disadvantages, most Polish Jews preferred the French Foreign Legion.

9. Exceptions were made for former French female citizens who had lost their nationality by marrying Germans; German mothers of French children; pregnant women and mothers of children younger than 16; the mothers, wives, or daughters of men in a military or labor unit attached to the French army; and those judged too ill to endure internment. After the armistice in June 1940, many of these internees, especially non-Jews, were released or escaped, but several thousand Jews languished in camps until they were deported to Germany, usually in August 1942. See Caron, *Uneasy Asylum*, 240–67; and Anne Grynberg, *Les camps de la honte: Les internés juifs des camps français (1939–1944)* (Paris: La Découverte, 1991), 64–83. For the expe-

riences of some arrested and interned immigrants, see Lion Feuchtwanger (German and Jewish, at Les Milles), *The Devil in France: My Encounter with Him in the Summer of 1940*, trans. Elisabeth Abbott (New York: Viking, 1941); Lisa Fittko (German and Jewish, at Gurs) *Escape through the Pyrenees*, trans. David Koblick (Evanston, IL: Northwestern University Press, 1991); Arthur Koestler (Hungarian and Jewish, at Le Vernet), *Scum of the Earth* (New York: Macmillan, 1941); Leo Lania (Austrian and Jewish, at the Stade de Colombes and Rolande Garros in Paris, and Meslay-du-Maine and Audierne), *The Darkest Hour: Adventures and Escapes*, trans. Ralph Marlowe (Boston: Houghton Mifflin, 1941); and Louis Lecoin (French non-Jewish pacifist, at Gurs), *De prison en prison* (Antony, Seine: Louis Lecoin, n.d.).

10. Klarsfeld, *Le calendrier*, 14, 16. Klarsfeld also points out that although the total number of internees at any given time is difficult to determine, the German Kundt Commission, created at the time of the armistice, found about 32,000 Jewish and non-Jewish individuals in some 50 camps throughout France in the summer of 1940. Of these, about 7,500 were Germans and about 5,000 of the 7,500 were Jews (20).

11. The Compagnies travailleurs étrangers had been created as a result of the decree law of April 12, 1939. They were intended as a vehicle for national service in peace or war for foreigners who could not or would not serve in the military.

12. Jean-Louis Crémieux-Brilhac, "Engagés volontaire et prestataires (1939–1940)," in Karel Bartosek, René Gallissot, and Denis Peschanski, eds., *De l'exil à la résistance: Refugiés et immigrés d'Europe Centrale en France, 1933–1945* (Saint-Denis: Presses Universitaires de Vincennes, 1989), 95–100, at 97. For a personal memoir by an interned German Jewish woman who knew many prestataires, see Lisa Fittko, *Solidarity and Treason: Resistance and Exile, 1933–1940*, trans. Roslyn Theobald (Evanston, IL: Northwestern University Press, 1993).

13. See Klarsfeld, *Le calendrier*, 51.

14. Ibid., 49; Claude Laharie, *Le camp de Gurs, 1939–1945: Un aspect méconnu de l'histoire du Béarn* (Biarritz: Société Atlantique d'Impression, 1985), 173; Michael R. Marrus and Robert O. Paxton, *Vichy France and the Jews* (New York: Basic Books, 1981), 10–11. Within the prewar borders of France, the Germans also expelled 3,000 Jews still remaining in Alsace and Moselle westward in July and August 1940 and sent 1,400 German Jews from the area of Bordeaux into the unoccupied zone in the autumn. See Poznanski, *Jews in France during World War II*, 27, 172.

CHAPTER FOUR. JEWISH REFUGEES IN THE UNOCCUPIED ZONE, MAY 1940–AUGUST 1942

1. In addition to the German-occupied, Italian-occupied, and unoccupied zones, the French departments of Moselle, Bas-Rhin, and Haut-Rhin in Alsace and Lorraine that had been German between 1871 and 1918 were

annexed to the Third Reich, and the departments of the Nord and the Pas-de-Calais in northeastern France were placed under the administration of a German military governor based in Belgium.

2. About 70 Communist senators and deputies had been expelled in January 1940, and 27 others from several parties, including Édouard Daladier and Georges Mandel, had sailed to North Africa in June 1940 in the hope of continuing the war from there.

3. The figure for French Jewish citizens includes naturalized adults and the children of immigrants who were born in France and declared by their parents at birth to be French citizens. The statistics also include those believed not to have registered in the Jewish censuses in the occupied and unoccupied zones. See Serge Klarsfeld, *Vichy-Auschwitz: Le rôle de Vichy dans la solution finale de la question juive en France: 1942* (Paris: Fayard, 1983), 24–25; and Serge Klarsfeld, *Le calendrier de la persécution des juifs en France, 1940–1944* (Paris: Les Fils et Filles des Déportés Juifs de France, 1993), 1091.

4. Within the next three years, the resulting commission reviewed the cases of 13,839 Jews, revoking the citizenship of 7,055, and made it clear that its work was not complete. See CDJC, XXVII-47, report of Maurice Gabolde, keeper of the seals, to Fernand de Brinon, recorded by Brinon, September 8, 1943. The commission also reviewed grants of citizenship to non-Jews.

5. See the text of these laws in JO, September 4, 1940, and October 1, 1940. A circular on November 28, 1941, defined "en surnombre dans l'Économie Nationale" as those who did not have the means of supporting family members in their charge or who did not receive support from their closest relatives.

6. See the report prepared by the Comité de Nîmes, a coordinating committee of Jewish and non-Jewish assistance organizations, for Vichy officials in October 1941, reprinted in Joseph Weill, *Contribution à l'histoire des camps d'internement dans l'Anti-France* (Paris: Éditions du Centre, 1946), 167–71; and Gérard Gobitz, "Les déportations de l'été 1942," in Monique-Lise Cohen and Éric Malo, eds., *Les camps du sud-ouest de la France, 1939–1944: Exclusion, internement et déportation* (Toulouse: Privat, 1994), 173–80.

7. For the text of the two Statuts des Juifs, see JO, October 18, 1940, and June 14, 1941. According to the first statute, anyone with three grandparents "of the Jewish race" was to be considered Jewish regardless of possible conversion, as well as anyone with two grandparents of the same "race" who had a Jewish spouse. The second statute made the same provisions for any person with three grandparents "of the Jewish race" but stipulated that anyone with two grandparents "of the Jewish race" would be considered Jewish if he or she was married to someone similarly half Jewish. It then added that a person with two Jewish grandparents was, despite his or her spouse, also to be considered Jewish unless he or she could produce a baptismal certificate dated before June 25, 1940. For evidence that the Vichy statutes were not imposed by the Germans, see Susan Zuccotti, *The Holocaust, the French, and the Jews* (New York: Basic Books, 1993), 56.

8. The number 140,000 is from CGQ J to the Controleur général d'armée, December 2, 1941, CDJC, CXCIII-86. It apparently does not include the several thousand foreign Jews in internment camps in the unoccupied zone. According to Klarsfeld, of the 109,983 Jews over age 15 included in the census, 59,344 were French and 50,639 were foreigners (*Vichy-Auschwitz: 1942*, 22).

9. For the text of the law, see JO, October 18, 1940. Internment statistics can be found in Anne Grynberg, *Les camps de la honte: Les internés juifs des camps français (1939–1944)* (Paris: La Découverte, 1991), 12; and Georges Wellers, *L'étoile jaune à l'heure de Vichy: De Drancy à Auschwitz* (Paris: Fayard, 1973), 99. About 3,000 Jews died of exposure, disease, and malnutrition in French internment camps, many of them in the terrible first winter of the war. The names of 2,000 are recorded in Serge Klarsfeld, *Memorial to the Jews Deported from France, 1942–1944* (New York: Beate Klarsfeld Foundation, 1983), 612–40.

10. See CDJC, CCXIII-125, "Internement des Israelites," for a copy of the order. It is also printed in Klarsfeld, *Le calendrier*, 94.

11. For discussion of these measures, see Renée Poznanski, *Jews in France during World War II*, trans. Nathan Bracher (1997; Hanover, NH: University Press of New England, 2001), 177.

12. On Agde, see esp. Michaël Iancu, *Spoliations, déportations, résistance des juifs à Montpellier et dans l'Hérault: 1940–1944* (Avignon: A. Barthélemy, 2000), 93–98. Some 20,000 Indochinese laborers came to France in 1939 and 1940 to work in war production. After the armistice, when their labor was less essential but they were unable to return home, many were interned in camps like Agde and Rivesaltes. See www.travailleurs-indochinois.org. I am grateful to Diane Afoumado at the CDJC for her help on this issue.

13. For the local and Jewish populations at the time, see René S. Kapel, *Un rabbin dans la tourmente (1940–1944)* (Paris: Éditions du Centre, 1985), 89.

14. For accounts by other Jews released from internment camps, see Karl Elsberg, *Come sfuggimmo alla Gestapo e alle SS*, intro. Klaus Voigt (Aosta: Le Château, 1999); and Alfred Feldman, *One Step Ahead: A Jewish Fugitive in Hitler's Europe* (Carbondale: Southern Illinois University Press, 2001), 86–96. Karl Elsberg, a German Jewish refugee in Belgium who was expelled to France with 1,100 other men regarded as spies in May 1940 and interned in Saint-Cyprien and then Gurs, was released to supervised residence when a local priest whom his wife had come to know vouched for him. Alfred Feldman's German Jewish father, a war refugee from Belgium, was interned at Agde in June 6, 1941, because he was unemployed but was released to supervised residence soon after because he was ill. Feldman declares that the town of Agde was accessible even to internees in the loosely guarded camp (95). Apparently, internees often went there to shop and talk at the cafés.

15. OSE was founded in Russia in 1912 to provide health care to Jewish adults and children. Its offices were moved to Berlin in 1923 and to Paris in 1933. By the spring of 1941, OSE had two children's homes in the occupied zone

and seven in the unoccupied zone. In June 1941, it was caring for 752 children in the unoccupied zone, of whom 202 had been released from internment camps. A few months later, it had places for 1,340. Grynberg, *Les camps de la honte*, 231. For more on OSE, see esp. Sabine Zeitoun, *L'oeuvre de secours aux enfants (OSE) sous l'occupation en France: Du légalisme à la résistance, 1940–1944* (Paris: L'Harmattan, 1990); and Vivette Samuel, *Rescuing the Children: A Holocaust Memoir*, trans. Charles B. Paul (1995; Madison: University of Wisconsin Press, 2002).

16. For the testimony of Renée and Irène Paillassou, see *The Children of Chabannes*, a film produced and directed by Lisa Gossels and Dean Wetherell, 1999, 92 mins.

17. Félix Chevrier was honored as a Righteous Among the Nations at Yad Vashem in 2001. Renée and Irène Paillassou had been similarly honored in 1983. Renée died in 2000, but Charles is still in contact with Irène, now in her nineties and living in Cannes. For more on Chevrier and the Paillassou sisters, see Limore Yagil, *Chrétiens et juifs sous Vichy (1940–1944): Sauvetage et désobéissance civile* (Paris: Cerf, 2005), 440–42.

18. On Montintin, see Ernst Papanek, *Out of the Fire*, written with Edward Linn (New York: William Morrow, 1975).

CHAPTER FIVE. ARRESTS IN THE OCCUPIED ZONE, 1941–1942

1. For the text of this ordinance and a second one on October 18, 1940, concerning the registration of Jewish businesses, see Serge Klarsfeld, *Le calendrier de la persécution des juifs en France, 1940–1944* (Paris: Les Fils et Filles des Déportés Juifs de France, 1993), 23–24, 31. The first German ordinance defined as a Jew anyone with more than two Jewish grandparents or anyone who adhered to the Jewish religion. For the first anti-Jewish statements and actions in German-occupied Paris, see the diary of A. Honig, *Métamorphose du juif érrant* (Paris: La Pensée Universelle, 1978,) esp. the entry for July 30, 1940, 164–65.

2. Prefect of police to Militärbefehlshaber in Frankreich (MBF; the German Military Administration), October 26, 1940, CDJC, LXXIXa-10. The statistics are for the department of the Seine; about 20,000 Jews lived in the rest of the occupied zone in 1940. Renée Poznanski, *Jews in France during World War II*, trans. Nathan Bracher (1997; Hanover, NH: University Press of New England, 2001), 33, puts the number of foreign Jews at 65,070. She also points out that some 3,000 additional Jews in the Paris area registered later.

3. For details, see David Diamant (who received but did not heed the summons), *Le billet vert: La vie et la résistance à Pithiviers et Beune-la-Rolande [sic], camps pour juifs, camps pour chrétiens, camps pour patriotes* (Paris: Renouveau, 1977); and Serge Klarsfeld, *Vichy-Auschwitz: Le rôle de Vichy dans la solution finale de la question juive en France: 1942* (Paris: Fayard, 1983), 15.

4. See Klarsfeld, *Vichy-Auschwitz: 1942*, 25–27.

5. Of the 74 major convoys that carried 73,853 Jews to camps in Poland be-

tween March 27, 1942, and August 17, 1944, 62 left from Drancy, two from Compiègne, six from Pithiviers, two from Beaune-la-Rolande, one from Angers, and one from Lyon. In addition, at least 815 Jews in the departments of the Pas-de-Calais and the Nord were deported to Poland from Malines, Belgium; about 400 wives and children of Jewish prisoners of war were delivered to Bergen-Belsen in 1944; roughly 360 from Toulouse were sent to Ravensbruck and Buchenwald on July 30 or 31, 1944; at least 63 from Clermont-Ferrand were shipped to Auschwitz on August 22, 1944; and at least 230 were deported as resistants. Of the total of at least 75,721 Jewish deportees from France, about 2,800 survived. See Serge Klarsfeld, *Memorial to the Jews Deported from France, 1942–1944* (New York: Beate Klarsfeld Foundation, 1983), xxvii.

6. Roger Gompel, *Pour que tu n'oublies pas . . .* (Paris: Mme. S. de Lalène Laprade [private printing], 1980), 89. Gompel was released because a family member was employed by UGIF, the same coordinating organization of French Jewish social agencies that helped Walter Marx's family in August 1942, as seen in chapter 6.

7. For the number who died by November 1941, see Nöel (Nissim) Calef, *Drancy 1941: Camp de représailles: Drancy la faim* (Paris: Les Fils et Filles des Déportés Juifs de France, 1991), xix. Serge Klarsfeld states that only about 100 Jews escaped from Drancy during the three years of its existence (*Le calendrier*, 138). He also indicates that of 39,411 entering prisoners between August 20, 1941, and December 31, 1942, 2,454 were released (711). Also on Drancy, see Maurice Rajsfus, *Drancy: Un camp de concentration très ordinaire, 1941–1944* (Levallois-Perret: Manya, 1991).

8. For accounts of this roundup by survivors, see Gompel, *Pour que tu n'oublies pas;* Jean-Jacques Bernard, "Le camp de la mort lente: Choses vécues," *Les oeuvres libres,* vol. 227 (Paris: Fayard, 1944), 87–127; and Georges Wellers, *L'étoile jaune à l'heure de Vichy: De Drancy à Auschwitz* (Paris: Fayard, 1973). See also Klarsfeld, *Vichy-Auschwitz: 1942,* 32.

9. See Klarsfeld, *Memorial,* 1–79. From surviving transport manifests of convoys carrying Jews from France to "the East," Klarsfeld is able to list the names of nearly all deportees.

10. Foreign Jews exempted from wearing the star included those from enemy countries such as the United States and Britain; from neutral countries such as Spain and Switzerland; and, for a time, from German-allied nations that had not imposed a similar ordinance, such as Italy, Hungary, and Bulgaria. For personal testimony about the forced wearing of the star, see Claude Bochurberg, *Mémoire et vigilance* (Paris: Le Lisère Bleu, 1986), 152, 188; Ginette Hirtz, *Les hortillonnage sous la grêle: Histoire d'une famille juive en France sous l'occupation* (Paris: Mercure de France, 1982), 59; Annette Muller, *La petite fille du Vel' d'Hiv': Récit* (Paris: Denöel, 1991), 76; Maurice Rajfus, *Jeudi noir: 16 juillet 1942: L'honneur perdu de la France profonde* (Paris: L'Harmattan, 1988), 23–25; Claudine Vegh, *I Didn't Say Goodbye,* trans.

Ros Schwartz (1979; Hampstead, Eng.: Caliban Books, 1984), 39, 109, 143, 150; and Wellers, *L'étoile jaune à l'heure de Vichy*, 136–37. See also Léon Poliakov, *L'étoile jaune* (Paris: Éditions du Centre, 1949); and Serge Klarsfeld, *L'étoile des juifs* (Paris: L'Archipel, 1992).

11. Klarsfeld, *Vichy-Auschwitz: 1942*, 25.

12. On this roundup, see esp. Klarsfeld, *Vichy-Auschwitz: 1942*; Claude Lévy and Paul Tillard, *Betrayal at the Vel d'Hiv*, trans. Inéa Bushnaq (1967; New York: Hill and Wang, 1969); Rajsfus, *Jeudi noir*; and Adam Rayski, *Nos illusions perdues* (Paris: Balland, 1985).

13. Klarsfeld, *Memorial*, 125–32. On the transport manifest for the convoy of August 5, 1942, most names are clear and correct, but some are not. Three of the Biners—Chaya (Rywka), Chana (Annie), and Abram (Albert)—are listed as Bined, while the father, Lipza, is identified as Biner.

14. Klarsfeld, *Le calendrier*, 711.

15. Paulette has those documents today.

16. Klarsfeld, *Le calendrier*, 721. According to Poznanski, *Jews in France during World War II*, 373, 600 of the Jews arrested in Marseille were French citizens, hitherto usually spared unless they had broken specific laws. Also on arrests in Marseille, see Donna Ryan, *The Holocaust and the Jews of Marseille: The Enforcement of Anti-Semitic Policies in Vichy France* (Urbana: University of Illinois Press, 1996).

17. Klarsfeld, *Memorial*, 410.

CHAPTER SIX. ARRESTS IN THE UNOCCUPIED ZONE, AUGUST 1942

1. For discussion of negotiations and preparations for this action, see Serge Klarsfeld, *Vichy-Auschwitz: Le rôle de Vichy dans la solution finale de la question juive en France: 1942* (Paris: Fayard, 1983), 63–162; and Klarsfeld, "La livraison par Vichy des juifs de zone libre dans les plans SS de déportation des juifs de France," in Monique-Lise Cohen and Éric Malo, eds., *Les camps du sud-ouest de la France, 1939–1944: Exclusion, internement et déportation* (Toulouse: Privat, 1994), 133–54. For a copy of the order of August 5, see *Vichy-Auschwitz: 1942*, 318–19.

2. Klarsfeld, *Vichy-Auschwitz: 1942*, 158. Most of those already interned in unoccupied France were deported from Drancy on convoys 17 through 21, between August 10 and 19, 1942. Forced laborers were deported on convoys 24, 25, and 26, between August 26 and 31. There were of course individual exceptions, who were deported later. These convoys, with lists of victims' names, are described in Serge Klarsfeld, *Memorial to the Jews Deported from France, 1942–1944* (New York: Beate Klarsfeld Foundation, 1983), 140–235.

3. For copies of orders to that effect, issued on August 18 and 22, 1942, see Klarsfeld, *Vichy-Auschwitz: 1942*, 339–40, 348–53.

4. Ibid., 159. Most recent immigrant and refugee Jews arrested in the unoccupied zone between August 26 and mid-September 1942 were deported on convoys 27 to 33 and convoys 37, 40, and 42, between September 2 and No-

vember 6, 1942. See Klarsfeld, *Memorial*, 236–343, for descriptions and lists of names.

5. This German presence was unusual. Arrests of foreign Jews in the unoccupied zone in August 1942 were generally carried out by French police alone, acting on orders from the Vichy regime.

6. For a description of the train from Nice to Drancy, see Gérard Gobitz, *Les déportations de réfugiés de zone libre en 1942* (Paris: L'Harmattan, 1996), 100–101. For description of convoy 27 from Drancy to Kosel to Auschwitz, see Klarsfeld, *Memorial*, 236–42. William's father and brothers were listed on the deportation manifest composed at Drancy as Chaim, Bernard, and Lea (sic) Blajwajs, the Polish spelling of their last name. See ibid., 237.

7. Ludwig Greve, *Un amico a Lucca: Ricordi d'infanzia e d'esilio*, ed. Klaus Voigt, trans. Loredana Melissari (Rome: Carocci, 2006), 195. Ernst Papanek, an OSE activist at the time, confirms that there was a large raid at Montintin on August 26, 1942. He claims that 69 children taken from several OSE homes that night died at Auschwitz. See his *Out of the Fire* (New York: William Morrow, 1975), 250, 294. After being imprisoned at Sachsenhausen following Kristallnacht, Ludwig Greve's father, Walter, took his wife, Johanna, and their two children, Ludwig and Evelyn, on the passenger ship *Saint Louis*, bound for Havana. Refused admission to Cuba along with 900 other passengers, they were granted asylum in France, where Walter was interned for a time as an enemy alien when war broke out. After many harrowing experiences, they eventually made their way to Saint-Martin-Vésubie and then to Italy.

8. According to an OSE report dated May 17, 1945, about 200 children were taken from its institutions, of whom 134 were expelled to Drancy in the occupied zone and deported. The others were rescued from various French internment camps before expulsion. Of the 134 deportees, 28 were under the age of ten, 31 were between ten and 14, and 75 were over 14. The report estimated that some 300 to 350 children were taken from homes operated by EIF and other Jewish organizations. See CDJC, CCXV-38a, "Note sur les enfants déportés."

9. On conditions at Rivesaltes before August 1942, see Vivette Samuel, *Rescuing the Children: A Holocaust Memoir* (Madison: University of Wisconsin Press, 2002), 36–56. Twenty-two-year-old Vivette Samuel was an OSE social worker there at the time.

10. Catherine Lewertowski, *Morts ou juifs: La maison de Moissac, 1939–1945* (Paris: Flammarion, 2003), 174, states that rumors were circulating among recent immigrant and refugee Jews at the end of August 1942 that families with children would not be expelled from the unoccupied zone and that some Jewish social workers tried to convince them that the rumors were false. It is not clear if these rumors originated with the police or with the Jews themselves.

11. Serge Klarsfeld, *Les transferts de juifs du camp de Rivesaltes et de la région de*

Montpellier vers le camp de Drancy en vue de leur déportation, 10 août 1942–6 août 1944 (Paris: Les Fils et Filles des Déportés Juifs de France, 1993), 23, 28.

12. For information about convoy 31 to Kosel and Auschwitz, see Klarsfeld, *Vichy-Auschwitz: 1942,* 159; and Klarsfeld, *Memorial,* 260–73. Leopold Roman is listed in *Memorial,* 271.

13. Solange Zitlenok is mentioned in Sabine Zeitoun, *L'Oeuvre de secours aux enfants (O.S.E.) sous l'occupation en France* (Paris: L'Harmattan, 1990), 153.

14. For an account by a representative of another organization, the Secours suisse aux enfants, who was in Rivesaltes in August 1942 and also succeeded in getting some children out, see Friedel Bohny-Reiter, *Journal de Rivesaltes, 1941–1942* (Carouge-Geneva: Éditions Zoé, 1993).

15. Salomon's report is printed in full in Samuel, *Rescuing the Children,* 78–82.

16. For evidence of their presence at Noé, see Hélène Regnier, "La déportation des juifs en Haute-Garonne de 1942 a 1944" (thesis, University of Toulouse, 1989–90), 54. For more on Noé, see Éric Malo, "Le camp-hôpital de Noé, antichambre d'Auschwitz (août–septembre 1942)," in Cohen and Malo, *Les camps du sud-ouest de la France,* 193–205; Éric Malo, "1942: Les camps, antichambres d'Auschwitz," in Jean Estèbe, *Les juifs à Toulouse et en Midi toulousain au temps de Vichy* (Toulouse: Presses Universitaires du Mirail, 1996), 131–43; and Anne Grynberg, *Les camps de la honte: Les internés juifs des camps français (1939–1944)* (Paris: La Découverte, 1991), 207–10.

17. On the convoy from Toulouse to Drancy, see Klarsfeld, *Vichy-Auschwitz: 1942,* 159. For a description and manifest of convoy 28 from Drancy to Kosel and Auschwitz, see Klarsfeld, *Memorial,* 243–50. The three Marienbergs are listed at 248. Mina is listed as Malka.

18. For more on the EIF, see Alain Michel, *Les Éclaireurs israélites de France pendant la seconde guerre mondiale, septembre 1938–septembre 1944: Action et évolution* (Paris: Éditions des EIF, 1984). Accounts by those personally involved include three by Isaac Pougatch: *Charry: Vie d'une communauté de jeunesse* (Paris: Chant nouveau, 1946); *Un batisseur Robert Gamzon dit "Castor soucieux," 1905–1961* (Paris: Service Technique pour l'Éducation, 1971); and *À l'écoute de son peuple: Un éducateur raconte* (Neuchatel: À la Baconnière, 1980); Frederic Chimon Hammel, *Souviens-toi d'Amalek: Témoignage sur la lutte des juifs en France, 1938–1944* (Paris: CLKH, 1982); Gérard Israël, *Heureux comme Dieu en France: 1940–1944* (Paris: Robert Laffont, 1975); and Robert Gamzon, *Les eaux claires: Journal, 1940–41* (Paris: Éditions des EIF, 1982).

19. On the home in Moissac, see the testimony of its directors, Shatta and Bouli Simon, n.d., but postwar, CDJC, DLXXII-46, 16 pp.; and Lewertowski, *Morts ou juifs: La maison de Moissac.*

CHAPTER SEVEN. NARROW ESCAPES AND SUBSEQUENT ARRESTS IN THE UNOCCUPIED ZONE, AUGUST–NOVEMBER 1942

1. Michaël Iancu, *Spoliations, déportations, résistance des juifs à Montpellier et dans l'Hérault: 1940–1944* (Avignon: A. Barthélemy, 2000), 107.

2. Miriam speculates that the commander was able to remove her father's name from the list of those arrested that day, which no one else had yet seen.

3. Only Pinkas (Peter) Wolfinger, born in 1921, is included on the list of refugees registered in Saint-Martin-Vésubie to receive ration cards. The list, known to be incomplete, is printed in full in Alberto Cavaglion, *Nella notte straniera: Gli ebrei di St.-Martin-Vésubie* (1981; Dronero: L'Arciere, 2003), 48–51.

4. For descriptions of Le Vernet in 1939 and 1940 by men there at the time, see Arthur Koestler, *Scum of the Earth* (New York: Macmillan, 1941); and Bruno Frei, *Die Männer von Vernet: Ein Tatsachenbericht* (Berlin: Deutscher Militärverlag, 1961). Koestler described a camp where deliberate murder was not the norm, as in the German camps he had seen, but where food, accommodations, and hygiene were inferior to those in the Third Reich.

5. For convoys from Gurs to Drancy, see Claude Laharie, *Le camp de Gurs, 1939–1945: Un aspect méconnu de l'histoire du Béarn* (Biarritz: Société Atlantique d'Impression, 1985), 236; and Serge Klarsfeld, *Vichy-Auschwitz: Le rôle de Vichy dans la solution finale de la question juive en France: 1942* (Paris: Fayard, 1983), 158–59. The convoys on August 6, 8, and 24, 1942, included at least 1,660 recent immigrant and refugee Jews who had already been interned in the camp or had been recalled from forced labor brigades. The fourth train, on September 1, 1942, included 502 recent immigrant and refugee Jews arrested for purposes of expulsion on or about August 26. For children from Aulus-les-Bains included in the convoys, see Serge Klarsfeld, *French Children of the Holocaust: A Memorial* (New York: New York University Press, 1996), 223–24; and Klarsfeld, *Memorial to the Jews Deported from France, 1942–1944* (New York: Beate Klarsfeld Foundation, 1983), 247–48.

6. Laharie, *Le camp de Gurs,* 184.

7. The phrase is from Nina Gourfinkel, a Russian Jewish social worker who worked with him, in her *L'autre patrie* (Paris: Seuil, 1953), 240. For more on Abbé Glasberg and the centres d'accueil, see Gérard Gobitz, *Les déportations de réfugiés de zone libre en 1942* (Paris: L'Harmattan, 1996), 258; and Susan Zuccotti, *The Holocaust, the French, and the Jews* (New York: Basic Books, 1993), 71–80. The agencies supporting the centres d'accueil worked together, coordinated by the Comité de coordination pour l'assistance dans les camps, informally called the Comité de Nîmes. The Jewish agencies included the American Jewish Joint Distribution Committee, OSE, ORT, and EIF, as well as individual French rabbis. Non-Jewish agencies included the CIMADE, the YMCA, the Quakers, various national branches of the Red Cross, the Secours suisse, the SSAE, the Unitarian Service Committee, the Rockefeller Foundation, and representatives of Pierre Cardinal Gerlier, the archbishop of Lyon, and Pastor Marc Boegner, president of the French Protestant Federation. Early in 1942, Catholics and Protestants working to help Jews created L'Amitié chrétienne, which worked closely with Glasberg.

8. For an account of this event, with further documentation, see Anne

Grynberg, *Les camps de la honte: Les internés juifs des camps français (1939–1944)* (Paris: La Découverte, 1991), 327–32; and Zuccotti, *The Holocaust, the French, and the Jews,* 130–32. On Glasberg's success elsewhere, see Gobitz, *Les déportations de réfugiés de zone libre,* 259–60; and Lucien Lazare, *L'Abbé Glasberg* (Paris: Cerf, 1990), 47–61. On tragedies in other institutions, see Gourfinkel, *L'autre patrie,* 263, 267–68; and CDJC, CCXVII-41a, "Rapport sur l'activité de la Direction des centres d'accueil (DCA), (1941–1944)," 8 pp., signed by Abbé Alexandre Glasberg, Lyon, September 15, 1944, 4–5.

9. Serge Klarsfeld, *Vichy-Auschwitz: Le rôle de Vichy dans la solution finale de la question juive en France: 1943–1944* (Paris: Fayard, 1985), 31–36; and Klarsfeld, *Memorial,* 392–94.

10. Limore Yagil, *Chrétiens et juifs sous Vichy (1940–1944): Sauvetage et désobéissance civile* (Paris: Cerf, 2005), 345.

11. For documents describing the trains from Gurs to Drancy, see Klarsfeld, *Vichy-Auschwitz: 1943–1944,* 34–35. Contrary to German orders that the 2,000 victims should be men specifically arrested for this particular reprisal, the 1,727 sent north from Gurs included some who were already in internment. For details about convoy 50 from Drancy to Sobibór and Majdanek, see Klarsfeld, *Memorial,* 392–409; and Klarsfeld, *Vichy-Auschwitz: 1943–1944,* 33–36. Wilhelm Bauer's name appears on the manifest for convoy 50, reproduced in Klarsfeld, *Memorial,* 398. Charles Roman still has Wilhelm Bauer's last note to his mother.

12. The Compagnons de France were organized in August 1940 to help reconstruct the country and indoctrinate boys with the values of the new Vichy regime. Some 25,000 boys completed its training program. According to one source, the new director Guillaume de Tournemire toned down pro-Vichy propaganda and eliminated anti-Semitic rhetoric in the organization's official publication in 1942. After the roundups in August of that year, some group leaders knowingly allowed Jewish youths to participate under false names. See P. A. Brooke, "Introduction," in Joseph Joffo, *Un sac de billes* (London: Routledge, 1989), 1–69, at 7–8. The Germans dissolved the Compagnons de France in January 1944.

13. Iancu, *Spoliations,* 100–101, from reports by Vichy officials.

14. Many non-Jewish citizens in Montpellier seem to have been uncomfortable with the roundups of August 1942, and denunciations were not common. According to a prefect report on September 1, "Although certain sectors of the population agree that the Jews are responsible for many of our troubles, [the Jews] benefit from a certain sympathy from a public that now considers them only innocent victims of the occupation authorities. . . . Everyone, however, agrees in placing the responsibility for these measures on the German authorities, much more than on the French government." The report is cited in ibid., 102.

15. Walter has a document from the office of the mayor of Montpellier, indicating the dates of his arrival in and departure from that city.

16. Serge Klarsfeld, *Les transferts de juifs du camp de Rivesaltes et de la région de Montpellier vers le camp de Drancy en vue de leur déportation, 10 août 1942–6 août 1944* (Paris: Les Fils et Filles des Déportés Juifs de France, 1993), 17. The Vichy government had directed the refugees to Lamalou in 1940.

17. The names of the 233 appear on a prefect list, dated December 31, 1942, and printed in full in Iancu, *Spoliations*, 107–12. The names of Johanna, Ludwig, and Walter Marx appear on the list, as does Werner Isaac. All four are listed as *apatride,* or stateless. Werner is listed as having moved to Lamalou-les-Bains, but the Marx family is mentioned as having "left without a known address."

18. For the raid in the rue Sainte-Catherine, see Klarsfeld, *Vichy-Auschwitz: 1943–1944,* 29; and Serge Klarsfeld, *La rafle de la rue Sainte-Catherine à Lyon le 9 février 1943* (n.p.: pub. by Klarsfeld, n.d. but after 1986). For roundups elsewhere in France in April and May 1943, see Michael R. Marrus and Robert O. Paxton, *Vichy France and the Jews* (New York: Basic Books, 1981), 308.

19. For the order from the prefect of Hérault to his police agents, reproduced in full, see annex XVI in Carol Iancu, *Les juifs à Montpellier et dans le Langue-doc à travers l'histoire du Moyen Age à nos jours* (Montpellier: CREJH, 1986), 398. For the number of men arrested in the Hérault, see the editor's note attached to the police order. Concerning the arrest of his father, Walter has a document from the office of the mayor of Lamalou-les-Bains, dated July 26, 1945, stating that two local witnesses confirmed the fact and the date of the arrest of Ludwig Marx. The witnesses signed the document.

20. For information and lists from both convoys, see Klarsfeld, *Memorial,* 392–409.

CHAPTER EIGHT. SAINT-MARTIN-VÉSUBIE, NOVEMBER 1942–
SEPTEMBER 1943

1. According to Jean-Louis Panicacci, "L'occupazione italiana delle Alpi Marit-time," *Notiziario* (June 1978), 7–35, 7, an estimated 70 percent of the rural portion of the present commune, or township, of Saint-Martin-Vésubie was in Italy until 1945.

2. Ralph Schor, "Les Italiens dans les Alpes-Maritimes, 1919–1939," in *Les Italiens en France de 1914 à 1940,* ed. Pierre Milza (Rome: École française de Rome, 1986), 577–607, at 577.

3. The departments were Alpes-Maritimes, Haute-Savoie, Savoie, Hautes-Alpes, Basses-Alpes, Var, and parts of Ain, Drôme, Isère, and Vaucluse. The Germans maintained control of both sides of the mouth of the Rhône, as well as the cities of Marseille, Aix-en-Provence, and Toulon, although Italian-occupied territory completely surrounded Toulon. Further north, the Germans also occupied Avignon and Lyon. The demarcation line be-tween the two zones was not always clear or heavily guarded. For details, see Daniel Carpi, *Between Mussolini and Hitler: The Jews and the Italian*

Authorities in France and Tunisia (Hanover, NH: University Press of New England, 1994), 80.

4. On these events in December and in the months that followed, see Carpi, *Between Mussolini and Hitler*, 79–192; Serge Klarsfeld, *Vichy-Auschwitz: Le rôle de Vichy dans la solution finale de la question juive en France: 1943–1944* (Paris: Fayard, 1985), 36–37; Michael R. Marrus and Robert O. Paxton, *Vichy France and the Jews* (New York: Basic Books, 1981), 315–21; Paniccaci, "L'occupazione italiana delle Alpi Marittime," 18–20; Léon Poliakov, "The Jews under the Italian Occupation in France," in Léon Poliakov and Jacques Sabille, *Jews under the Italian Occupation* (Paris: Éditions du Centre, 1955), 19–128; Jonathan Steinberg, *All or Nothing: The Axis and the Holocaust, 1941–1943* (London: Routledge, 1990), 105–16; and Klaus Voigt, *Il rifugio precario: Gli esuli in Italia dal 1933 al 1945*, vol. 2, trans. Loredana Melissari (Scandicci: La Nuova Italia, 1996), 302–7.

5. For details on what Italian diplomats knew about the genocide, see Carpi, *Between Mussolini and Hitler*, 107; and Voigt, *Il rifugio precario*, 309–10.

6. The statistics for March 1942 are from Voigt, *Il rifugio precario*, 2:296. Voigt estimates that no more than 5,000 Jews moved from German-occupied to Italian-occupied France after November 1942 (2:306). Most other estimates of new arrivals are much higher. See, e.g., Alberto Cavaglion, *Nella notte straniera: Gli ebrei di St.-Martin-Vésubie* (1981; Dronero: L'Arciere, 2003), 35.

7. Alfred Feldman describes this process, as it happened to him, in his memoirs *One Step Ahead: A Jewish Fugitive in Hitler's Europe* (Carbondale: Southern Illinois University Press, 2001), 119–20.

8. Official French policy toward Jewish refugees in the department of Alpes-Maritimes finally softened in May 1943, when Prefect Marcel Ribière was replaced by Jean Chaigneau. After informing leaders of the Jewish community in Nice, "I shall not leave to the Italians the noble privilege of being the sole defenders of the tradition of tolerance and humanity, which is really the role of France," Chaigneau legalized the situation of foreign Jews who had entered the department without permission. See Poliakov, *Jews under the Italian Occupation*, 30; and Jean-Louis Panicacci, "Les juifs et la question juive dans les Alpes-Maritimes de 1939 à 1945," *Recherches Régionales* 4 (1983), 266–67, at 315.

9. French Jewish organizations initially received funds directly from the office of the American Jewish Joint Distribution Committee in Lisbon, but such help became virtually impossible after December 7, 1941. The "Joint" then borrowed money from French Jews, with a guarantee of reimbursement at specified exchange rates after the war. When that source also dried up toward the end of 1943, money was funneled into France by Saly Mayer, the head of the Swiss Jewish Community and director of the "Joint" in that country. For details, see Yehuda Bauer, *American Jewry and the Holocaust: The American Jewish Joint Distribution Committee, 1939–1945* (Detroit, MI: Wayne State University Press, 1981), 243–44; and Isabelle Goldsztejn, "Au

secours d'une communauté: American Jewish Joint Distribution Committee en France (1933–1950)" (thesis, University of Paris I: Panthéon Sorbonne, 1992).

10. See doc. F-2, allegato no. 6, Nice 1943, Questione ebraica, extract from Lospinoso's defense before the Commissione di epurazione, 1946, from the Lospinoso papers and reproduced in Joseph Rochlitz, "The Righteous Enemy: Document Collection" (manuscript, Rome, 1988), 58. In a letter for the commission on March 6, 1946, notarized by the chief rabbi of Rome, Angelo Donati confirmed Lospinoso's account of his activities on behalf of the Jews. See doc. F-4 in ibid., 62; Voigt, *Il rifugio precario*, 2:307–18; and Steinberg, *All or Nothing*, 115–30.

11. For the July statistics, see Lospinoso report, 1946, in Rochlitz, "The Righteous Enemy," 59. SS First Lieutenant Heinz Röthke, chief of the Gestapo's Jewish Office in France, reported to his superior in June 1943 that 2,200 Jews had left for the interior by May 25 but that 400 more were scheduled to leave the following month. See Röthke to Knochen, doc. 21, in Poliakov and Sabille, *Jews under the Italian Occupation*, 95; and Carpi, *Between Mussolini and Hitler*, 145. For statistics for Megève and Saint-Gervais, see Christian Villermet, *A noi Savoia: Histoire de l'occupation italienne en Savoie: Novembre 1942–septembre 1943* (Montmélian: La Fontaine de Siloé, 1999), 75.

12. For statistics for April and the end of August, see doc. F-12, rabbi of Nice, "Rapporto morale e religioso sulla situazione dei assegnati alla residenza di St. Martin Vésubie," April 9, 1943, and doc. F-25, "Note pour Monsieur Lo Spinoso [sic]," August 30, 1943, from the Comité Dubouchage file, both in Rochlitz, "The Righteous Enemy," 76, 94; and Voigt, *Il rifugio precario*, 2:317. Because documents were destroyed when the Germans occupied Nice and the hinterland, there is no complete list of all the Jews of Saint-Martin-Vésubie. The longest list, from files of the Comité Dubouchage and reproduced in Rochlitz, has 369 names (98–102). Among individuals mentioned in this book, members of the Feldman, Gorges, Greve, Hartmayer (Hart), Löwenwirth, Neumann, Samsonowicz (Samson), Wolfinger (Carmeli), Blum, and Halpern families are included. Another list, this time of 141 Jews in Saint-Martin-Vésubie registered to receive ration cards, is printed in Cavaglion, *Nella notte straniera*, 48–51. Here the familiar names include Hartmayer, Marienberg, Thorn, and Wolfinger. However, many refugees, deeply suspicious of the authorities, did not register for ration cards, registered under a false name, or registered only a few family members.

13. For details on Italian arrests of political suspects, see Voigt, *Il rifugio precario*, 2:296–300. For an account by another Jewish internee in Sospel, see Harry Burger, *Biancastella: A Jewish Partisan in World War Two* (Niwot: University of Colorado Press, 1997), 71–77. Harry Burger was later assigned to Saint-Martin-Vésubie and made his way from there to Italy in September 1943. For a suggestion that Italians did not force legally resident foreign

Jews to move, see point 6 in doc. F-25, "Note pour Monsieur Lo Spinoso [sic]," August 30, 1943, from the Comité Dubouchage file, reproduced in full in Rochlitz, "The Righteous Enemy," 94.

14. Paula, Edith, Hella, and Jenny were interned in Rivesaltes and expelled to the German-occupied zone on September 4, 1942. They were on the same convoy as Leopold Roman, which Charles Roman so narrowly escaped. They were deported to Auschwitz on convoy 31 on September 11, also with Leopold Roman. They did not return. See Serge Klarsfeld, *Les transferts de juifs du camp de Rivesaltes et de la région de Montpellier vers le camp de Drancy en vue de leur déportation, 10 août 1942–6 août 1944* (Paris: Les Fils et Filles des Déportés Juifs de France, 1993), 23; and Klarsfeld, *Memorial to the Jews Deported from France, 1942–1944* (New York: Beate Klarsfeld Foundation, 1983), 268.

15. Alfred Feldman to Alberto Cavaglion, in Cavaglion, *Nella notte straniera,* 43.

16. Ibid.

17. For the colorful account of one French smuggler, see Danielle Baudot Laksine, *La pierre des juifs,* vol. 1 (Châteauneuf: Éditions de Bergier, 2003), 157–70.

18. Frederick Thorn is cited in Cavaglion, *Nella notte straniera,* 44. Information about Werner Isaac, including the number of patients at the home for the elderly at Berthemont, is from my interview with him in the spring of 2004.

19. National prisoner-of-war statistics are from Pierre Ayçoberry, *The Social History of the Third Reich, 1933–1945,* trans. Janet Lloyd (New York: New Press, 1999), 284. Departmental labor statistics are from Panicacci, "L'occupazione italiana delle Alpi Marittime," 21. In September 1942, Prime Minister Pierre Laval instituted a program known as the *relève,* by which one French prisoner of war in Germany was to be released for every three French skilled workers who volunteered to go to the Third Reich. When this program failed to satisfy German labor demands, Laval was obliged in February 1943 to introduce the Service du travail obligatoire (STO), in which entire age groups of French men were drafted for labor in Germany.

20. David Blum, memorandum to the office of the mayor of Saint-Martin-Vésubie, 1987, kindly made available to me by Danielle Baudot Laksine.

21. For other Jewish organizations in Saint-Martin-Vésubie, see an anonymous report by one of their representatives, dated October 6, 1943, printed in Cavaglion, *Nella notte straniera,* 121–26. On the carabiniere, see Burger, *Biancastella,* 76.

22. The list from the Comité Dubouchage, printed in Rochlitz, "The Righteous Enemy," 98, mentions three members of the Gorges family in Saint-Martin-Vésubie.

23. In northwestern Czechoslovakia, Theresienstadt was primarily a transit camp for Jews and Gypsies from the Protectorate of Bohemia and Moravia. Many prominent and elderly German Jews were also sent there, in an attempt to disguise the true meaning of deportation "to the East." Many Jews

died in the camp from starvation and disease, but most were sent on to be murdered elsewhere.

24. Feldman, *One Step Ahead*, 122, 124. The story of two escapees who went to Nice is told in Annie Latour, *The Jewish Resistance in France (1940–1944)*, trans. Irene R. Ilton (1970; New York: Holocaust Library, 1981), 150–51; and Klarsfeld, *Memorial*, 413. According to Klarsfeld, they were named Honig and Haim Salomon, escaped from Auschwitz in 1942, and reached Nice in 1943.

25. Feldman, *One Step Ahead*, 123.

26. Thorn, cited in Cavaglion, *Nella notte straniera*, 44. According to Danielle Baudot Laksine in a letter to me of May 15, 2006, the beautiful and elegant Lady Hélène Butler was not English at all but the French-born daughter of Jewish immigrants from Poland, in assigned residence like the others. There were, nevertheless, some non-Jewish immigrants and refugees in assigned residence in Saint-Martin-Vésubie, who also had to report to the Italian authorities.

27. Baudot Laksine, *La pierre des juifs*, 179, 190–91, for testimony of René Gasiglia and Carmen Parlarieu (née Giraudi). According to Moïse Konstadt, a young refugee in Saint-Martin-Vésubie, there was an evening curfew but it was not strictly enforced. See his testimony to Danielle Baudot Laksine in her "La veillée du 6 septembre 2003 à Saint-Martin-Vésubie," *Pays Vésubien* [Musée de Saint-Martin-Vésubie] 6 (2005), 70.

28. See Baudot Laksine, *La pierre des juifs*, 175–223, for additional testimony.

29. For lists from the municipal archives of 12 children born in Saint-Martin-Vésubie in the spring and summer of 1943, and two marriages, see Cavaglion, *Nella notte straniera*, 45–48. Suggestive of omission, the list of births record none after July 31, 1943. The couples married were Isidor Gottlieb and Ruth Mendelsberg, on August 9, and Pinchas Apelbaum and Ruth Galant, on August 11. Isidor Gottlieb joined the Resistance after his arrival in Italy, was captured along with six other partisans during a confrontation on March 17, 1944, and was executed. His wife, Ruth, was arrested soon after, was deported to Auschwitz on April 5, 1944, and survived (ibid., 106).

30. From Bronka Halpern, *Keren Or Bachoschechà* (Jerusalem: Rubin Mass, 1967), 39. Written in Hebrew, this phrase is translated and cited in Cavaglion, *Nella notte straniera*, 42.

CHAPTER NINE. CROSSING THE ALPS AFTER SEPTEMBER 8, 1943

1. This story is told in Danielle Baudot Laksine, *La pierre des juifs*, vol. 1 (Châteauneuf: Éditions de Bergier, 2003), 109–10.

2. Philippe Erlanger, *La France sans étoile: Souvenirs de l'avant-guerre et du temps de l'occupation* (Paris: Plon, 1974), 278.

3. For details, see the testimony of Lucio Ceva in *8 settembre: Lo sfacelo della IV Armata: Relazioni, testimonianze, studi attuali* (Turin: Istituto Storico della Resistenza in Piemonte, 1978), 99–105; and Christian Villermet, *A noi*

Savoia: Histoire de l'occupation italienne en Savoie: Novembre 1942–septembre 1943 (Montmélian: La Fontaine de Siloé, 1999), 28–30.

4. For details on this confused period, see Daniel Carpi, *Between Mussolini and Hitler: The Jews and the Italian Authorities in France and Tunisia* (Hanover, NH: University Press of New England, 1994), 169–80; and CDJC, CCXVIII-22, "Exposé de Monsieur Donati," 5 pp. Part of this document is translated and published in Léon Poliakov and Jacques Sabille, *Jews under the Italian Occupation* (Paris: Éditions du Centre, 1955), 40–42. In the exposé, Donati explains that the Italians had reassured Jewish leaders in Nice that they would resist the German advance into Italy and protect the Jews, but the premature announcement of the armistice prevented them from doing so. For more on Donati, see Madeleine Kahn, *Angelo Donati: De l'oasis italienne au lieu du crime* (Paris: Bénévent, 2004); and Alberto Cavaglion, "Foreign Jews in the Western Alps (1938–1943)," *Journal of Modern Italian Studies* 10, no. 4 (December 2005), 426–46.

5. "Exposé de Monsieur Donati," 5; Stefan Schwamm, "L'oeuvre du Père Benoît Marie et du Comité de Secours à Rome," CDEC, 8—"Opera di soccorso e di assistenza ai perseguitati," written in December 1945 and printed in full in *Le Monde Juif* 149 (September–December 1993), 95–102; and, in ibid., Claude Kelman, "L'activité des organizations juives dans la zone italienne en 1943," 90–94. Kelman, a member of the political commission of the Comité Dubouchage, explains that there was some disagreement about the decision to bring refugees from Megève and Saint-Gervais back to Nice just before September 8, 1943. He would have preferred sending them to the Swiss frontier and trying to get them into Switzerland.

6. On the incident in Nice, see Jean-Louis Panicacci, "L'occupazione italiana delle Alpi Marittime," *Notiziario* (June 1978), 7–35, at 33. On action around Fréjus and Albertville, see Villermet, *A noi Savoia*, 47.

7. Adriana Muncinelli, *Even: Pietruzza della memoria: Ebrei, 1938–1945* (Turin: Gruppo Abele, 1994), 161.

8. See Schwamm, "L'oeuvre du Père Benoît Marie," 95–102. Schwamm himself accompanied this group as far as Rome, where most of them survived.

9. Karl Elsberg, *Come sfuggimmo alla Gestapo e alle SS*, intro. Klaus Voigt (Istituto Storico della Resistenza in Valle d'Aosta; Aosta: Le Château Edizioni, 1999). For more description of the various escape routes, see Klaus Voigt, *Il rifugio precario: Gli esuli in Italia dal 1933 al 1945*, 2 vols., trans. Loredana Melissari (Scandicci: La Nuova Italia, 1996), 2:414. Voigt estimates that from 1,300 to 1,500 Jews fled to Italy from Italian-occupied France immediately after the armistice (413). Since roughly 950 left from Saint-Martin-Vésubie, those from other parts of the occupied zone may have numbered 350 to 550.

10. David Blum, memorandum to the office of the mayor of Saint-Martin-Vésubie, 1987, kindly made available to me by Danielle Baudot Laksine.

11. Bronka Halpern, quoted in Alberto Cavaglion, *Nella notte straniera: Gli ebrei di St.-Martin-Vésubie* (1981; Dronero: L'Arciere, 2003), 51.

12. See Raimondo Luraghi, *Eravamo partigiani: Ricordi del tempo di guerra* (Milan: RCS Libri, 2005), 17–18.

13. Information that the Italian soldiers often provided food and water from their various barracks in the mountains is confirmed by Alfred Feldman, *One Step Ahead: A Jewish Fugitive in Hitler's Europe* (Carbondale: Southern Illinois University Press, 2001), 132; Raimondo Luraghi, "Dalla GAF alla Resistenza," in *8 Settembre*, 268; and Antonio Bruno, "Relazione sui fatti che si sono verificati nel sottosettore di Valdieri alla data dell'8/9/1943," 4, unpublished written testimony dated March 29, 1974, and signed by Bruno, available at AISRC. Lieutenant Colonel Antonio Bruno was the commander of subsector II/B, which included the Col de Fenestre and the Col de Cerise.

14. Luraghi, *Eravamo partigiani*, 17–18. Cavaglion, *Nella notte straniera*, 60, also states that the Italian soldiers were ordered first to stop the refugees and later to release them.

15. For Feldman, see his *One Step Ahead*, 132. The unidentified refugee report is from the archives of OJC, printed in David Knout, *Contribution à l'histoire de la résistance juive en France, 1940–1944* (Paris: Éditions du Centre, 1947), 44–46, 44.

16. Grete Uhrmacher Edelschein, born in 1903 in Austria, was probably taken to Rivesaltes after her arrest. She is listed on the manifest of convoy 33 that left Drancy for Auschwitz on September 16, 1942. Of the 1,003 passengers, 38 are known to have survived. Grete did not survive. See Klarsfeld, *Memorial*, 283–86. After the war, Marianne returned to Vienna and had her half sister's name inscribed on her father's tombstone.

17. Marianne and Charles Roman's photographs have been published in Cavaglion, *Nella notte straniera;* and Susan Zuccotti, *Under His Very Windows: The Vatican and the Holocaust in Italy* (New Haven and London: Yale University Press, 2000), as well as in this book.

18. Feldman, *One Step Ahead*, 130.

19. Conversation with Werner Isaac, spring 2004.

20. Refugee report in Knout, *Contribution à l'histoire de la résistance juive en France*, 44; and Kelman, "L'activité des organizations juives dans la zone italienne en 1943," 92. Kelman writes that on September 9, 1943, he accompanied a busload of 58 foreign Jews, who had been in assigned residence elsewhere, from Nice to Saint-Martin-Vésubie. Presumably he and the committee believed they would be safer there.

CHAPTER TEN. THOSE WHO STAYED BEHIND

1. Report by an unnamed activist with the Nice rescue committee who was present in Saint-Martin-Vésubie on September 9, 1943, dated October 6, 1943, and printed in full in Alberto Cavaglion, *Nella notte straniera: Gli ebrei di St.-Martin-Vésubie* (1981; Dronero: L'Arciere, 2003), 122–26.

2. Léon Poliakov, *L'auberge des musiciens: Mémoires* (Paris: Mazarine, 1981),

124–25. Poliakov later became an eminent historian of the Holocaust and anti-Semitism.

3. Dr. A. Drucker testimony, February 15, 1946, CDJC, CCXVI-66, 8–10.

4. Serge Klarsfeld, *Vichy-Auschwitz: Le rôle de Vichy dans la solution finale de la question juive en France: 1943–1944* (Paris: Fayard, 1985), 124; and Klarsfeld, *Memorial to the Jews Deported from France, 1942–1944* (New York: Beate Klarsfeld Foundation, 1983), 455–526.

5. Klarsfeld, *Memorial*, 508–26. Chana and Hilda Haberman are listed at 521.

6. The statistic is from Cavaglion, *Nella notte straniera*, 52.

7. Paulette nominated Fanny Vassallo and Henriette and Paul Saïssi for the designation of Righteous Among the Nations at Yad Vashem. They received the honor posthumously at ceremonies commemorating the sixty-second anniversary of the Jews' crossing of the Alps and the sixtieth anniversary of the end of the war, in Saint-Martin-Vésubie in September 2005. Three other residents of Saint-Martin-Vésubie, Joseph and Victorine Raibaut, posthumously, and their daughter Marguerite Raibaut-Franco, were honored at the same time. Paulette's more recent nominations of Simone Saïssi (Tengelin by marriage) and Jeannine Boin are pending. Information from my interview with Paulette is supplemented here by her sworn testimony for those two recent nominations, kindly made available to me, with Paulette's permission, by Danielle Baudot Laksine. Part of that testimony is printed in Baudot Laksine, *Les grands visiteurs*, vol. 2 (Châteauneuf: Éditions de Bergier, 2005), 109–15; more of Paulette's story is told at 209–24 and 229–46.

8. This phrase is taken from Denis Torel, "Réflexions sur le traitement particulier de la 'question juive' en Principauté de Monaco durant la seconde guerre mondiale," *Le Monde Juif* 116 (October–December 1984), 175–92, at 176.

9. Ibid., 184–85; David Knout, *Contribution à l'histoire de la résistance juive en France, 1940–1944* (Paris: Éditions du Centre, 1947), 46–47.

10. For details about Le Chambon-sur-Lignon, see esp. the film *Weapons of the Spirit* by Pierre Sauvage, who was born to Jewish parents hiding in the village in 1944. See also Philip P. Hallie, *Lest Innocent Blood Be Shed: The Story of the Village of Le Chambon and How Goodness Happened There* (1979; New York: Harper Colophon Books, 1980); Pierre Fayol, *Le Chambon-sur-Lignon sous l'occupation: Les résistances locales, l'aide interalliée, l'action de Virginia Hall (OSS)* (Paris: L'Harmattan, 1990); and Mordecai Paldiel, *The Path of the Righteous: Gentile Rescuers of Jews during the Holocaust* (Hoboken, NJ: KTAV, 1993), 27–30.

11. See Klarsfeld, *Memorial*, 462, 468. On the list of deportees on convoy 61, Jacques Weintraub's name appears as Jacques Wajntrob.

12. Ernst Appenzeller is listed as a deportee on convoy 79, August 17, 1944, in ibid., 599. For more on the train, see Jean-François Chaigneau, *Le dernier wagon* (Paris: Julliard, 1981); René S. Kapel, *Un rabbin dans la tourmente (1940–1944)* (Paris: Éditions du Centre, 1985), 149–75; and Georges Wellers,

Un juif sous Vichy (Paris: Éditions Tiresias Michel Reynaud, 1991), 182. Another of these last deportees from Drancy, 12-year-old Georges-André Kohn, whose father had been the director of the Rothschild Hospital in Paris, was among roughly 20 Jewish children from all over Europe subjected to horrible medical experiments at Neuengamme. On April 20, 1945, these children were hanged in the basement of a school in Hamburg. For details, see Günther Schwarberg, *The Murders at Bullenhuser Damm: The SS Doctor and the Children,* trans. Erna Baber Rosenfeld with Alvin H. Rosenfeld (1980; Bloomington: Indiana University Press, 1984).

13. For more on Blum's activities in the Resistance, see his interview with Cavaglion, described in *Nella notte straniera,* 53; and Michaël Iancu, *Spoliations, déportations, résistance des juifs à Montpellier et dans l'Hérault: 1940–1944* (Avignon: A. Barthélemy, 2000), 139–40.

14. On hiding in the area of Saint-Martin-Vésubie, see Claude Kelman, "L'activité des organizations juives dans la zone italienne en 1943," *Le Monde Juif* 149 (September–December 1993), 90–94. For the testimony of a French woman who took several elderly Jews by taxi to Limoges, at great risk, see Jean-Louis Panicacci, "Les juifs et la question juive dans les Alpes-Maritimes de 1939 à 1945," *Recherches Regionales* 4 (1983), 271. In three works, *La pierre des juifs,* vol. 1 (Châteauneuf: Éditions de Bergier, 2003), 232–46; *Les grands visiteurs,* 106; and "Le Groupe Franc-Tireur Vésubie," *Pays Vésubien* [Musée de Saint-Martin-Vésubie] 6 (2005), 16–17, Danielle Baudot Laksine cites several other examples.

15. For Alfred Feldman's recollection, see his *One Step Ahead: A Jewish Fugitive in Hitler's Europe* (Carbondale: Southern Illinois University Press, 2001), 127. Chinka Feldman is listed as a deportee on convoy 60, October 7, 1943, in Klarsfeld, *Memorial,* 457.

CHAPTER ELEVEN. THE FIRST WEEK IN ITALY, SEPTEMBER 11–17, 1943

1. Bronka Halpern, *Keren Or Bachoschechà* (Jerusalem: Rubin Mass, 1967), 44. Written in Hebrew, this observation is from the portion translated into Italian and cited in Alberto Cavaglion, *Nella notte straniera: Gli ebrei di St.-Martin-Vésubie* (1981; Dronero: L'Arciere, 2003), 63–64.

2. To provide some perspective, a male prisoner at the Italian internment camp of Ferramonti in mid-1942 received a subsidy of eight lire a day to buy his meals and supplies. A woman received four lire, and a child, three. The subsidy was inadequate. A cooked meal prepared in the camp cost six or seven lire. See CDEC, f. Israel Kalk, VII-I, testimony of internee Mirko Haler, 7–8.

3. Parts of Don Giordanengo's diary are published in M. Ristorto, *Valdieri centro turistico della Valle Gesso* (Cuneo: SASTE, 1973), 100–103. This extract is at 101. During the first half of the twentieth century, the title "don," as it is usually written in Italian, or "Don" in English usage, usually indicated a priest in the secular clergy who had a parish. The term "Father" or "Padre"

referred to a priest of the regular clergy, a member of a religious order who had been ordained. I have kept this distinction, to indicate what various priests were called during the war.

4. See the report of the Commissario prefettizio of Borgo San Dalmazzo to the prefect of Cuneo, September 15, 1943, in CDEC, b. 5F, f. Borgo San Dalmazzo.

5. On Italian prisoners of war, see Charles F. Delzell, *Mussolini's Enemies: The Italian Anti-Fascist Resistance* (Princeton, NJ: Princeton University Press, 1961), 277. On the fighting between Italians and Germans in Rome after the armistice, see Robert Katz, *The Battle for Rome: The Germans, the Allies, the Partisans, and the Pope, September 1943–June 1944* (New York: Simon and Schuster, 2003), 33–45. Meanwhile at Salerno, General Don Ferrante Gonzaga refused to surrender his weapon to the Germans and was immediately shot down. Violence was still greater in Italian-occupied Greece. On the islands of Cephalonia and Corfu, several thousand Italian officers and men were massacred when they resisted German demands to surrender.

6. Giordanengo's diary in Ristorto, *Valdieri centro turistico della Valle Gesso,* 101. The number of deserters is from Nuto Revelli, *Il mondo dei vinti* (Turin: Einaudi, 1977), cxvii.

7. For the number arrested, see Revelli, *Il mondo dei vinti,* cxxii. On Leonardo Bagni, see Michele Calandri, Mario Cordero, and Stefano Martini, eds., *Valle Stura in guerra, 1940–1945* (Cuneo: Tecnograf Piasco, [c. 1994]), 16.

8. Enzo and Riccardo Cavaglion stayed with the group until October 1943, when they had to leave to help their own families escape arrest in Cuneo. Enzo is the father of Alberto Cavaglion, who has done so much to record the story of the Jews of Saint-Martin-Vésubie. Enzo Cavaglion lives today in Cuneo. His brother, Riccardo, lives in Israel. Ildo Vivanti fought as a partisan until he was shot on April 21, 1944. The eight other founders of this partisan band were Livio Bianco, Arturo Felici, Leonardo Ferrero, Dino Giacosa, Ugo Rapisarda, Leandro Scamuzzi, Edoardo Soria, and Giancarlo Spirolazzi. Two others present on September 12, Ettore Rosa and Ezio Aceto, left to organize Resistance units elsewhere. The names of the 14 are listed on a monument at the Madonna del Colletto.

9. After greatly enlarging his original partisan formation, Galimberti, born in Cuneo in 1906, participated in several military actions. He was badly wounded in a skirmish on January 12, 1944, and was treated by Bronka Halpern from Saint-Martin-Vésubie, who was hiding in the area. Galimberti was arrested in Turin on November 28, 1944, and executed near Cuneo on December 4. For details, see Antonino Repaci, *Duccio Galimberti e la resistenza italiana* (Turin: Bottega d'Erasmo, 1971).

10. See Faustino Dalmazzo, "La ricostruzione dei fatti di Boves attraverso il processo in Germania," *Notiziario* 12 (December 1977), 5–8; and Don Raimondo Viale, "Le figure più indimenticabili tra le vittime: Don Mario Ghibaudo," *Bollettino Parrocchiale* 3 (September–October 1946), in Elena Giuliano and

Gino Borgna, *Cella n. zero: Memorie di un prete giusto e resistente* (Cuneo: AGA, 1994), 90.

11. For arrests and atrocities in Merano, Novara, and the area around Lago Maggiore, see Liliana Picciotto Fargion, *Il libro della memoria: Gli ebrei deportati dall'Italia (1943–1945)* (1991; Milan: Mursia, 2002), 44, 818–19, 868. For more on the Lago Maggiore massacres, see *La strage dimenticata: Meina settembre 1943: Primo eccidio di ebrei in Italia,* intro. Roberto Morozzo della Rocca (Novara: Interlinea, 2003). On December 17, 1944, men from the same First SS Panzer Division Leibstandarte Adolf Hitler were responsible for the Malmedy massacre, the murder of some 70 to 80 American prisoners of war during the Battle of the Bulge. By-then Colonel Joachim Peiper and 72 of his men were later tried for that crime by an American war-crimes military tribunal sitting in Dachau. Forty-three of the accused, including Peiper, were sentenced to death, but the sentences were commuted to prison terms. Peiper served 11 years and was released in December 1956.

CHAPTER TWELVE. THE ROUNDUP IN VALDIERI AND BORGO SAN DALMAZZO, SEPTEMBER 18, 1943

1. Alberto Cavaglion, *Nella notte straniera: Gli ebrei di St.-Martin-Vésubie* (1981; Dronero: L'Arciere, 2003), 67. According to Klaus Voigt, *Il rifugio precario: Gli esuli in Italia dal 1933 al 1945,* 2 vols., trans. Loredana Melissari (Scandicci: La Nuova Italia, 1996), 2:415, Müller's first name has not been determined.

2. The exact number of people arrested on September 18 is not certain. A list of the names, birth dates, and birthplaces of deportees from Borgo San Dalmazzo back to France on November 21 indicates that they numbered about 349 people, but a few of these, like Boris Carmeli (Norbert Wolfinger), had been arrested later. Some of the prisoners arrested on September 18 escaped before November 21, while others, like Walter Marx and Menahem and Léon Marienberg, were not deported because they were in the hospital in Cuneo on that day. The list also contains some errors and omissions. For the list of deportees, see Cavaglion, *Nella notte straniera,* app. 3, 132–58.

3. Leopold Neumann survived the war and lives today in Antibes.

4. Serge Klarsfeld, *Memorial to the Jews Deported from France, 1942–1944* (New York: Beate Klarsfeld Foundation, 1983), 399. Leopold Gerhard is listed as Adler Gerhard, but his identity is confirmed by his place and year of birth, Dukla, Czechoslovakia, 1907.

5. This account is by Jacky Gerhard, in his unpublished memoir, "Récit: Jacky, début–30 mai 2003," and confirmed by Jacques Samson. Rosa Eller's father, Salomon, was deported on March 4, 1943, on convoy 50 to Sobibór and Majdanek, along with Wilhelm Bauer and Leopold Gerhard, his brother-in-law. See ibid., 399. I found no listing for Rosa'a mother, Malka.

CHAPTER THIRTEEN. DEPORTATION FROM BORGO SAN DALMAZZO

1. On September 28, 1943, at least 37 of the 182 Jewish citizens living in Cuneo were arrested, not by Germans but by Fascist militia and carabinieri, and taken to the barracks in Borgo San Dalmazzo. They were released without explanation on November 9, 1943. For these arrests, see "Quarantacinque giorni nel campo di concentramento di Borgo S. Dalmazzo (Cuneo), diario di Rosetta Scotti Douglas," in *Gli ebrei in Italia durante il fascismo: Quaderni della Federazione giovanile ebraica d'Italia* (1961; Milan: Arnaldo Forni, 1981), 78–89.

2. On the list of deportees from Borgo San Dalmazzo, Johanna's name appears as Giovanni Marx, born in Germany on April 29, 1900. The compiler of the list tended to give an Italian version of first names, although Giovanni is the male counterpart of Giovanna. Werner Isaac's name follows Johanna's. Their birthplaces are given as Merzig, a bigger town than Fremersdorf, but also in the Saarland, about five kilometers to the north. See the list printed in full in Alberto Cavaglion, *Nella notte straniera: Gli ebrei di St.-Martin-Vésubie* (1981; Dronero: L'Arciere, 2003), app. 3, 132–58, prisoners 226 and 227 (150). In her list of the names of nearly all Jewish deportees from Italy, Liliana Picciotto Fargion, *Il libro della memoria: Gli ebrei deportati dall'Italia (1943–1945)* (1991; Milan: Mursia, 2002), 351, also cites Johanna Isaac, born in Fremersdorf on April 29, 1900. The date of arrest, September 18, 1943, is correct, but the date of deportation, December 10, 1943, is not. Picciotto Fargion does not mention Werner.

3. For information on convoy 64, see Serge Klarsfeld, *Memorial to the Jews Deported from France, 1942–1944* (New York: Beate Klarsfeld Foundation, 1983), 477–83. Johanna Marx is listed at 481. For a list of 12 survivors of deportation from the group of about 349, 11 of whom were on convoy 64 to Auschwitz, see Cavaglion, *Nella notte straniera*, 134–35.

4. Hospital affidavit, in the possession of Menahem Marienberg.

5. The list of prisoners on convoy 64 is in Klarsfeld, *Memorial*, 477–83. The younger Menahem, our Menahem's cousin, is listed at 481 by his French name of Michel. For the Marienberg family members on the list of prisoners deported from Borgo San Dalmazzo on November 21, see Cavaglion, *Nella notte straniera*, prisoners 272 and 273 (153) and prisoners 302–5 (155). Isaac and Eva Marienberg and their children Menahem and Simone had disguised their real names, and were listed as Giovanni, Marianna, Michele, and Simona Idkowiacz, "of the Aryan race." The dates and places of birth are correct.

6. Boris Carmeli is recorded by his name at that time, Norbert Wolfinger (Volfinger on the list), in the list of prisoners deported from Borgo San Dalmazzo, reproduced in Cavaglion, *Nella notte straniera*, prisoner 342, (158).

7. Norbert Wolfinger is on the list of deportees on convoy 64 printed in full in Klarsfeld, *Memorial*, 483.

CHAPTER FOURTEEN. HIDING IN THE PROVINCE OF CUNEO

1. Cuneo is at the confluence of the Gesso and the Stura di Demonte Rivers. Borgo is on the Gesso, but it is also at the opening of the Stura valley, just a few kilometers south of the Stura di Demonte River.

2. Francesco Repetto, "La consegna della Medaglia dei Giusti fra le Nazioni," *Liguria* 49, no. 3 (May–June 1982), 27–30, at 29. The story of Valobra's visit to Cardinal Boetto is also told by Alexander Stille, *Benevolence and Betrayal: Five Italian Jewish Families under Fascism* (New York: Summit, 1991), 223–78. Founded with Mussolini's permission in 1939 to facilitate the emigration of foreign Jews from Italy, Delasem also aided impoverished Jews within the country. See Settimio Sorani, *L'assistenza ai profughi ebrei in Italia (1933–1947): Contributo alla storia della "Delasem"* (Rome: Carucci, 1983); and Sandro Antonini, *Delasem: Storia della più grande organizzazione ebraica italiana di soccorso durante la seconda guerra mondiale* (Genoa: De Ferrari, 2000).

3. Testimony of Don Viale in Nuto Revelli, *Il prete giusto* (Turin: Einaudi, 1998), 119. For the story of cooperation between several Italian prelates in efforts to help Jews, see Susan Zuccotti, *Under His Very Windows: The Vatican and the Holocaust in Italy* (New Haven and London: Yale University Press, 2000), 233–64. Although Bishop Rosso's role in assisting Jewish refugees is not clear, there is evidence that he firmly defended his priests in difficulties with the Germans and Fascists. See Giuseppe Griseri and Aldo Benevelli, eds., *Voi Banditen!: Preti e religiosi vittime della violenza e dell'odio* (Milan: Nicola, 1995), 38–39.

4. Alberto Cavaglion, "Ebraismo e Cuneesità (1943–1945)," *Caratteri della resistenza cuneese* (Cuneo: Cassa di Risparmio di Cuneo, 1994), 119.

5. See Elena Giuliano and Gino Borgna, *Cella n. zero: Memorie di un prete giusto e resistente* (Cuneo: AGA Editrice, 1994), 17–53. According to a report from the office of the prefect of Cuneo, in his speech on June 2, 1940, Don Viale simply pointed out that Pius XII wanted peace, just as Benedict XV had during the First World War. See the report in Emma Mana, ed., "Mondo cattolico e potere politico nel Cuneese durante la 2ª guerra mondiale: Documenti," *Notiziario dell'ISRC* 16 (December 1979), 29–30.

6. Don Viale is quoted in Revelli, *Il prete giusto*, 55. For a description of one trip and of the archival evidence of it, see Alberto Cavaglion, *Nella notte straniera: Gli ebrei di St.-Martin-Vésubie* (1981; Dronero: L'Arciere, 2003), 96, 109. There is no evidence that the funds received in Genoa and distributed by local priests to Jewish refugees in the province of Cuneo came from sources other than Delasem and the Italian Jewish community itself.

7. For security reasons, Don Viale's lists before the end of the war usually did not refer to families by name. Only in May 1945 do names and details about the families appear. For the lists, see AISRC, fasc. 5, Carte di Don Raimondo Viale. This folder also contains many letters from refugees, written after the war, to thank Don Viale for his assistance. In 2000 at Yad Vashem in Israel,

Don Viale was honored as Righteous Among the Nations. The priest who recruited him, Don Repetto, was similarly honored in 1976. The names of most of the equally valiant priests who helped distribute Delasem funds have been lost.

8. Don Giuseppe Giordanengo, the parish priest of Valdieri, noted in his diary in November 1943 that an American plane had been shot down by two German fighters near the Madonna del Colletto, that five American flyers had been killed, and that five others either were captured or escaped. See excerpts from his diary in Maurizio Ristorto, *Valdieri: Centro turistico di Valle Gesso* (Cuneo: SASTE, 1973), 101.

9. See AISRC, fasc. 5, Carte di Don Raimondo Viale.

10. Ludwig and Johanna eventually traveled to Lucca, where they were saved by priests and nuns. Soon after Johanna was wounded, Ludwig's father, Walter, and sister, Evelyn, were arrested and imprisoned with 24 other recently seized Jews, mostly Italian citizens from nearby Saluzzo and Mondovì, in the same barracks at Borgo San Dalmazzo that had been emptied on November 21. All 26 prisoners were sent to the central Italian concentration camp of Fossoli in Carpi, near Modena, on February 15, 1944, and deported from there to Auschwitz at the end of the month. Two survived, but Walter and Evelyn did not. Walter and Evelyn Greve are listed as Peter and Evelina Gimpel in Liliana Picciotto Fargion, *Il libro della memoria: Gli ebrei deportati dall'Italia (1943–1945)* (1991; Milan: Mursia, 2002), 322. On their arrests, see Ludwig Greve, *Un amico a Lucca: Ricordi d'infanzia e d'esilio*, ed. Klaus Voigt, trans. Loredana Melissari (Rome: Carocci, 2006), 198. On this second group of mostly citizen Jews held in the barracks at Borgo San Dalmazzo, see Adriana Muncinelli, *Even: Pietruzza della memoria: Ebrei, 1938–1945* (Turin: Gruppo Abele, 1994), 167–80; and Cavaglion, "Ebraismo e Cuneesità (1943–1945)," 111–30.

11. Walter Marx still has his discharge papers from the hospital in Cuneo.

12. The date is from the hospital affidavit, in the possession of Menahem Marienberg.

13. Menahem's second stay in the hospital in Cuneo is confirmed by an affidavit, as is that of Léon.

CHAPTER FIFTEEN. RESISTANCE

1. By the summer of 1944, these bands were incorporated into brigades and divisions. Walter's military discharge papers show that by the end of the war, he belonged to the First Alpine Division "Giustizia e Libertà," Valle Stura Brigade "Carlo Rosselli." The commander who signed his papers called himself simply "Renato." The division commander was Aldo Quaranta, formerly a captain in the Italian army in occupied France. The commander of the Carlo Rosselli Brigade was Nuto Revelli, who later wrote several books about the partisan experience and its impact on the local population in the province of Cuneo.

2. Statistics regarding partisans are elusive. The number 220 is from the commemorative plaque at the Madonna del Colletto. The statistic of 600 is from Nuto Revelli, *La guerra dei poveri* (Turin: Einaudi, 1962), 286. The provincial statistic is from Revelli, *Il mondo dei vinti* (Turin: Einaudi, 1977), cxxii.

3. Harry Burger was born in Vienna in 1924, where his father, Elias, owned a textile company. Like William Blye but a year later, Harry and his family entered France illegally from Italy, where they had gone after Kristallnacht in 1938. Elias Burger was arrested by the French in Nice in October 1941 for buying false visas. Imprisoned for a time in Le Vernet, he was sent to Drancy, probably in August 1942. He was deported to Auschwitz on September 4, 1942, from where he did not return. Harry and his mother, Maria Theresia Pories, went to Saint-Martin-Vésubie in April 1943, from where they entered Italy in September. See Harry Burger's memoirs, *Biancastella: A Jewish Partisan in World War Two* (Niwot: University of Colorado Press, 1997). Elias Burger is listed among the deportees to Auschwitz in Serge Klarsfeld, *Memorial to the Jews Deported from France, 1942–1944* (New York: Beate Klarsfeld Foundation, 1983), 245.

4. Revelli, *Il mondo dei vinti*, cxv–cxix, explains that peasants in the province of Cuneo, disgusted with the war, Fascism, and the Germans and demoralized by their own losses of loved ones especially on the Russian front in the winter of 1942–1943, usually sympathized with the partisans, although their enthusiasm tended to wane after German offensives when they realized how much a partisan presence in their area endangered them. Spies and informers among the peasants were rare.

5. Peasant claims for reimbursements after the war, based on receipts like those Walter distributed, may be found in the Archivio di Demonte at AISRC. Peasants were often victimized by outlaws and mavericks operating on the fringes of partisan bands. Partisan leaders sometimes found it difficult to prevent their men from taking similar advantage of the peasants, but Nuto Revelli has written from his own experience that "our own partisans who broke the rules, who threatened the people, who behaved like bandits, ended up against the wall. At Paralup we shot two young men guilty of theft." See ibid., cxix–cxx.

6. Theresia Burger and her son are listed among the recipients of Delasem funds distributed by Don Viale's network. See AISRC, fasc. 5, Carte di Don Raimondo Viale. For description of the rare winter forays by German and Fascist troops, see Bronka Halpern, *Keren Or Bachoschechà* (Jerusalem: Rubin Mass, 1967), 44. Written in Hebrew, her chapter about her time in the province of Cuneo has been translated into Italian. See AISRC, d.b.40, 30 pp.

7. For fighting around Vinadio in July and August 1944, see Michele Calandri, Mario Cordero, and Stefano Martini, eds., *Valle Stura in guerra, 1940–1945* (Cuneo: Tecnograf Piasco, [c. 1994]), 23–24, 64.

8. Ibid., 64. On Harry Burger's concern for his mother, see his *Biancastella*, 95. On Walter's stipend, see AISRC, fasc. 5, Carte di Don Raimondo Viale, where his name is mentioned, although for a somewhat later date.

9. Calandri, Cordero, and Martini, eds., *Valle Stura in guerra, 1940–1945*, 18–19. In a related incident at about the same time, German troops arrested men and women alike from the mountain village of Desertatto, near Valdieri, and sent them to prison in Cuneo. They also burned the hamlet of Tetti Fré. See excerpts from the diary of Don Giuseppe Giordanengo, parish priest in Valdieri, in Maurizio Ristorto, *Valdieri: Centro turistico di Valle Gesso* (Cuneo: SASTE, 1973), 102.

10. See the account by Viale's assistant parish priest, Don Luigi Picinoli, in Giuseppe Griseri and Aldo Benevelli, eds., *Voi Banditen! Preti e religiosi vittime della violenza e dell'odio* (Milan: Nicola, 1995), 52–53.

11. In her memoirs of her war experience, *Keren Or Bachoschechà*, Bronka Halpern frequently complained of the monotony and lack of activity. Halpern, who later became a pediatrician in Israel, hid in the mountains around Demonte until April 1944, when she and her family went to Rome. Although she suffered from a lack of intellectual stimulus and social intercourse, however, her life was hardly boring. She was in great demand among the local peasants and partisans because of the medical training she had received in Warsaw before the war. As seen, she even treated the partisan commander Duccio Galimberti.

12. This incident is related, with reference to Cuneo prison records, in Alberto Cavaglion, *Nella notte straniera: Gli ebrei di St.-Martin-Vésubie* (1981; Dronero: L'Arciere, 2003), 107, 112. Bernardo Futerman is identified as Marcel's father, and Armando Appelbaum, as Bernardo's brother-in-law, in the lists of Don Raimondo Viale, in AISRC, fasc. 5, Carte di Don Raimondo Viale. Hugo Korbel and Siegfried Schwartz's names appear on a list of those registered for ration cards in Saint-Martin-Vésubie during the period when Jews were living there. The list, though incomplete, is reproduced in ibid., 48–51. Schwartz is also mentioned by Harry Burger in *Biancastella*, 76, 80, 112.

CHAPTER SIXTEEN. TRAVELING TO AND HIDING IN FLORENCE,
SEPTEMBER AND OCTOBER 1943

1. My interview with Don Brondello, Boves, September 12, 2003. Don Brondello explained that he was not one of Don Viale's regular couriers and gave out money on only one occasion, on Yom Kippur, described below.

2. Looking back on this incident years later, Lya decided that her visitor must have been Raffaele Cantoni, a prominent Delasem activist discussed below. This is not certain. Although Cantoni did visit Don Viale at a later date, there is little evidence that he came to the mountains above Valdieri during the first month of the German occupation. For evidence of Cantoni's later visit with Don Viale, see his letter to the priest on June 26, 1945, where he writes, among other things, "I am pleased to be able to go back in my

thoughts to those days when I knocked on your door, and you comforted me with your advice and your precious assistance." The letter is reproduced in full in Elena Giuliano and Gino Borgna, *Cella n. zero: Memorie di un prete giusto e resistente* (Cuneo: AGA, 1994), 95. This visit probably occurred after Cantoni escaped from a deportation train in December 1943, when he made his way to Genoa to warn Cardinal Boetto and Don Repetto that the Germans had arrested many members of the Refugee Assistance Committee in Florence that had received Delasem funds from them.

3. Louis Goldman, a refugee from Saint-Martin-Vésubie who was a close friend of Lya and Sigi, also thinks that the man who came to the mountains around Valdieri in October 1943 to convince Jewish refugees to move to Florence was Raffaele Cantoni. He wrote in his memoirs that his family made the trip with Cantoni's help and that Cantoni put the Goldmans in touch with the same Refugee Assistance Committee in Florence that helped Lya. See Louis Goldman, "Friends for Life" (manuscript, 1983), 33–50, translated into Italian by Anna Cursi Li Volsi and published as *Amici per la vita* (Florence: Edizioni SP44, 1993). Although Cantoni was a member of the Refugee Assistance Committee, however, there is little other evidence to confirm that he actually traveled to the area of Valdieri in October.

4. About the visitor from Florence, see excerpts from the Viale diary in Giuliano and Borgna, *Cella n. zero*, 60. The authors identify the man as De Angeli. Cantoni's letter to Viale, June 26, 1945, in ibid., 95, also indicates that De Angeli occasionally visited the priest. Brondello's testimony is from my interview with him.

5. On the founding of the Refugee Assistance Committee, its relation to Delasem, and its funding, see CDEC, b. 13-B—Comunità ebraiche in Italia, f. Firenze, "Consiglio di amministrazione della Comunità israelitica di Firenze," signed by Eugenio Artom, May 10, 1945, 8 pp. For Cassuto and Cantoni's role, see CDEC, b. 8-A-1, f. Materiale per una storia della Delasem, "Testimonianza del Sig. Giorgio Nissim," Pisa, March 2, 1969, 2 pp. Nissim was a Delasem representative in Pisa.

6. CDEC, b. 13-B, f. Firenze, Artom report, 2. See also Liliana Picciotto Fargion, "Le retate del novembre 1943 a Firenze," *La Rassegna Mensile di Israel* 67 (January–August 2001), 243–63, at 243.

7. For discussion of exactly who first went to the cardinal, see Susan Zuccotti, *Under His Very Windows: The Vatican and the Holocaust in Italy* (New Haven and London: Yale University Press, 2000), 252. For more details and the date of September 20, as well as Cassin's statement on her work with Father Riccoti, see Massimo Longo Adorno, *Gli ebrei fiorentini dall'emancipazione alla Shoà* (Florence: La Giuntina, 2003), 105–6. For Ricotti's statement to Paola Pandolfi, see her *Ebrei a Firenze nel 1943: Persecuzione e deportazione* (Florence: Università di Firenze, Facoltà di Magistero, 1980), 36–37, 77. Father Ricotti was honored as a Righteous Among the Nations by Yad Vashem in 1972.

8. Don Casini recorded that he became involved around the end of October, because too many Jews were coming to the archbishop's palace to see Meneghello, as Lya Haberman did in middle of that month. Dalla Costa feared they would attract attention. See Don Leto Casini, "Assistenza prestata agli ebrei in Firenze nel momento più cruciale della discriminazione razziale," in ISRT, Archivio Dalla Costa, Carteggio Ebrei, fasc. 6, 2 pp. Don Casini was honored as a Righteous Among the Nations at Yad Vashem in 1966.

9. Goldman, "Friends for Life."

10. AAF, fondo Dalla Costa, b. 8, doc. 117, "Pio Istituto delle Suore Serve di Maria SS Addolorata, Via Faentina 195," bill submitted to the archbishop's office. This particular bill does not make clear who supplied the funds for payment. In another case, however, Mother Sandra at the Franciscan convent at the Piazza del Carmine understood and wrote clearly that the expenses of the women she sheltered were paid "by the synagogue." See her report to Cardinal Elia Dalla Costa, printed in full in Emanuele Pacifici, *Non ti voltare: Autobiografia di un ebreo* (Florence: La Giuntina, 1993), 103. Don Leto Casini also testified after the war that he had distributed 720,000 lire to refugees, given to him on three different occasions by Raffaele Cantoni of Delasem. See his *Ricordi di un vecchio prete* (Florence: La Giuntina, 1986), 50.

11. Fifty-five years later, in 1998, Miriam Löwenwirth Reuveni's testimony was instrumental in the granting of an award as a Righteous Among the Nations to the head of the school of the Suore Serve di Maria Addolorata, Mother General Maddalena Cei.

12. Those two nuns were Mother Superior Benedetta Vespignani and Sister Marta Folcia. They were honored as Righteous Among the Nations in 1994. Among those testifying on their behalf was Emanuele Pacifici, who, with his brother, Raffaele, was also sheltered at the Collegio di Santa Marta during the German occupation. This account of the school is based on my interview with Emanuele Pacifici, Rome, October 29, 1996. Emanuele and Raffaele were the sons of Chief Rabbi Riccardo Pacifici of Genoa, arrested in Genoa on November 3, 1943, and Wanda Abenaim Pacifici, arrested at the convent of the Suore Francescane Missionarie di Maria in the Piazza Carmine in Florence on November 27, 1943. Riccardo and Wanda were deported to Auschwitz on December 6, 1943, where they both died.

13. Mother Sandra (Ester Paola Busnelli) confirmed this hall as their place of lodging, describing it as "il salone del teatro." She wrote that other refugees were in the convent's "pensionato," a place for outside guests. See her report, printed in full in Pacifici, *Non ti voltare*, 103–9. Mother Sandra was honored as a Righteous Among the Nations in 1995.

14. Goldman, "Friends for Life," 52–53.

15. Ibid., 54, 87–89.

CHAPTER SEVENTEEN. ARRESTS AND NARROW ESCAPES IN FLORENCE,
NOVEMBER 1943

1. Sigi believes that the raid was in the early morning of November 7. If it had occurred on November 8, he says quite logically, the men at the movie theater would have heard of arrests known to have occurred elsewhere on the night of November 6–7 and been warned. Apart from Sigi Hart and Ludi Goldman, now deceased, there are no other known testimonies or records of the raid.

2. Louis (Ludi) Goldman, "Friends for Life" (manuscript, 1983), 85–86, translated into Italian by Anna Cursi Li Colsi and published as *Amici per la vita* (Florence: Edizioni SP44, 1993). After the war, Harry Goldman moved to Israel with his family. He joined the Israeli army and was killed on June 11, 1948. He was 20 years old.

3. Ibid., 73.

4. Ibid., 76–83, for Goldman's version of the escape. According to Liliana Picciotto Fargion, *Il libro della memoria: Gli ebrei deportati dall'Italia (1943–1945)* (1991; Milan: Mursia, 2002), 45, the train left Florence and Bologna on November 9, 1943. Because Sigi Hart thinks that he was arrested on November 7, however, and since he knows he was detained for only about 24 hours, a statement with which Goldman concurs, he believes that the deportation train left Florence on November 8. He recalls that the train stopped in Bologna for a couple of hours, and he believes that one prisoner escaped there.

5. Picciotto Fargion, *Il libro della memoria*, 45, 58–59, 340, 885. According to Picciotto Fargion, only 83 of the victims have been identified. She also states that one person returned but lists Sigi Hart, or Sigfried Hartmeier, as having died in deportation. This he decidedly did not do.

6. Ibid., 46, 58–59, 182, 236, 364, 386, 884–87. Arrested and deported with Cassuto were Luciana and Wanda Lascar, Hans Kahlberg, and Joseph Ziegler. Kahlberg and Ziegler returned. Joseph Ziegler was arrested with the others on November 26 but was mysteriously released, only to be re-arrested with his entire family on December 8 and deported with them and with Cassuto, the Lascars, and Kahlberg on January 30. Cassuto's wife, Anna Di Gioacchino, was arrested on November 29 and also deported on January 30. She survived Auschwitz, only to be killed during an attack on a busload of civilians in Jerusalem during the 1948 war. For more on the persecution of Jews in Florence, see Massimo Longo Adorno, *Gli ebrei fiorentini dall'emancipazione alla Shoà* (Florence: La Giuntina, 2003), 103–50; Paola Pandolfi, *Ebrei a Firenze nel 1943: Persecuzione e deportazione* (Florence: Università di Firenze, Facoltà di Magistero, 1980); and Liliana Picciotto Fargion, "Le retate del novembre 1943 a Firenze," *La Rassegna Mensile di Israel* 67 (January–August 2001), 243–63.

7. Madre Sandra (Ester Busnelli), report to Cardinal Elia Dalla Costa, printed in full in Emanuele Pacifici, *Non ti voltare: Autobiografia di un ebreo* (Florence: La Giuntina, 1993), 103–9, at 107.

8. Walter and Richard are included in the list of all known Jewish deportees from Italy in Picciotto Fargion, *Il libro della memoria*, 586. Edith is listed as Edith Hahn, her maiden name, at 338. Walter and Edith are also named on the monument at the synagogue of Florence to non-Florentine Jews arrested in Florence and deported, although Richard is not. Elena is also mentioned on the monument, but according to Miriam, she died in a hospital in Florence.

9. Ibid., 46.

10. The order for the arrest of Jews was broadcast over the radio on the evening of November 30 but sent to prefects and police on December 1. Known as police order number 5, it included Jews previously granted exemptions from persecution under the Italian racial laws of 1938 and 1939 but excluded individuals born of mixed marriages. Ten days later, Jews who were gravely ill, over age 70, or married to non-Jews were also excluded, although these exemptions were often ignored, especially toward the end of the war. Jews with citizenship in certain countries, including, to mention only Europe, Spain, Portugal, Switzerland, Hungary, Romania, Sweden, Finland, and Turkey, were also exempt. See Longo Adorno, *Gli ebrei fiorentini dall'emancipazione alla Shoà*, 116.

11. Leonilda (Ilda) Pancani was honored as a Righteous Among the Nations by Yad Vashem in 1999.

12. In the last months of 1943, money to support Jews in hiding in Florence and Rome came from Delasem in Genoa, where Valobra had turned over the organization's funds to Cardinal Boetto. By January 1944, however, this source was no longer available, in part because Raffaele Cantoni of the Florentine Rescue Assistance Committee, who had acted as the principal courier, had been arrested but escaped to Switzerland. At this point, Settimio Sorani, head of Delasem in Rome, and Father Benedetto began to send money to Florence from funds raised in Rome. Since the American Jewish Joint Distribution Committee could no longer transfer dollars to Italy because of the war, Sorani and Benedetto sought contributions from wealthy Jews in Rome. They also borrowed lire from Italian non-Jews, with the promise to repay in dollars after the war. With help from the American and British representatives to the Holy See, they obtained two letters of credit to assure Roman lenders that the "Joint" had already deposited money for repayment in a British bank in London, from where it would become available as soon as the war ended. The first letter of credit for $20,000 was received at the end of March 1944; the second, for $100,000, arrived just before the liberation of Rome on June 4, 1944. See Archives of the American Joint Distribution Committee, AR 33/44, file 716, "1943–1945; 1961–1962—Reports on the Situation of Jews in Italy," Settimio Sorani to Harold Tittman, Florence, January 22, 1962. Father Benedetto made it clear after the war that despite claims to the contrary by spokesmen for Pope Pius XII, he and Sorani did not receive money from the Vatican.

See "Alcune precisazioni di Padre Benedetto," *Israel* 46, no. 36, July 6, 1961, 5.

13. Picciotto Fargion, *Il libro della memoria*, 417. Eliyahu is listed as Elia Loewenwirth. His two companions were also deported, Hermann Brender, born in a town near Eliyahu's in Czechoslovakia, to Bergen-Belsen on May 16, 1944; and Enrico Rathaus, born in Leipzig, according to Leah, who knew him, but listed as Henri Rataud, born in Lunéville, France, to Auschwitz on April 5, 1944. Neither man returned. See ibid., 160, 523.

14. Ibid., 50–51, for the trains from Fossoli to Auschwitz and Bergen-Belsen on May 16, 1944. There were no gas chambers at Bergen-Belsen for the extermination of Jews upon arrival, as at Auschwitz, Bełzec, Majdanek, Sobibór, and Treblinka. Bergen-Belsen became most deadly during the last weeks of the war, when it was overcrowded and inadequately supplied.

15. For the transfer to Biberach, see Picciotto Fargion, *Il libro della memoria*, 51. For more on the Kaufering system, see Edith Raim, "Concentration Camps and the Non-Jewish Environment," in Michael Berenbaum and Abraham J. Peck, *The Holocaust and History: The Known, the Unknown, the Disputed, and the Reexamined* (Bloomington: Indiana University Press, 1998), 401–8.

CHAPTER EIGHTEEN. TRAVELING TO AND HIDING IN ROME,
JANUARY–JUNE 1944

1. See Settimio Sorani, *L'assistenza ai profughi ebrei in Italia (1933–1947): Contributo alla storia della "Delasem"* (Rome: Carucci, 1983), 142; Stefan Schwamm, "L'oeuvre du Père Benoît Marie et du Comité de Secours à Rome," CDEC, 8B—"Opera di soccorso e di assistenza ai perseguitati," written in December 1945 and printed in full in *Le Monde Juif* 149 (September–December 1993), 95–102, 98, 100; and Father Maria Benedetto, "Report on the activity of the DELASEM by Father Benedetto," in Renzo De Felice, *The Jews in Fascist Italy: A History*, trans. Robert L. Miller and Kim Englehart (1961; New York: Enigma Books, 2001), 758.

2. See, e.g., Wilhelm Reiter to Don Viale, April 4, 1944, in AISRC, fasc. 5, Carte di Don Raimondo Viale.

3. For details about this roundup, see esp. Robert Katz, *Black Sabbath: A Journey through a Crime against Humanity* (Toronto: Macmillan, 1969); and Liliana Picciotto Fargion, *Il libro della memoria: Gli ebrei deportati dall'Italia (1943–1945)* (1991; Milan: Mursia, 2002), 877–84.

4. Picciotto Fargion, *Il libro della memoria*, 30–31, 58–60, 882. The figure of 671 Jews arrested in Rome after October 16, 1943, represents the difference between the total of 1,694 Jews arrested there during the entire German occupation and deported and the 1,023 arrested on October 16 and deported two days later. The figure does not include those arrested in Rome but subsequently released.

5. See Sorani's account of the transfer of Delasem operations in his *L'assistenza ai profughi ebrei*, 145; and Benedetto's in "Report on the activity of the

DELASEM," 756–58. The Delasem office was close to the central office of the Unione delle comunità israelitiche italiane at 9, Lungotevere Sanzio. The higher statistics, usually cited, of 4,000 Jews helped, including 1,500 foreigners, are provided by Benedetto in the same report (757). The statistics of "more than 2,000, of whom 1,000 were foreigners," are given by Sandro Antonini, *Delasem: Storia della più grande organizzazione ebraica italiana di soccorso durante la seconda guerra mondiale* (Genoa: De Ferrari, 2000), 280. Father Benedetto, or Pierre Peteul by birth, was honored as a Righteous Among the Nations at Yad Vashem in Israel in 1966. For a description of Father Benedetto's rescue activities in France as well as in Italy, see Mordecai Paldiel, *The Path of the Righteous: Gentile Rescuers of Jews during the Holocaust* (Hoboken, NJ: KTAV, 1993), 56–59.

6. Sorani, *L'assistenza ai profughi*, 145–46. Sorani writes that 62 beneficiaries of Delasem assistance in Rome were caught, mostly after May 1, 1944, but it is not clear how many of them were arrested at the Albergo Salus or the Pensione Heslin. See also Antonini, *Delasem*, 236, 282. Aron Kastersztein, born in 1901, was sent to Fossoli and deported to Auschwitz on June 26, 1944. He was transferred to Buchenwald and survived. See Picciotto Fargion, *Il libro della memoria*, 366. Her statement that Kastersztein was arrested on April 1, 1944, is probably a mistake.

7. Alberto Cavaglion, *Nella notte straniera: Gli ebrei di St.-Martin-Vésubie* (1981; Dronero: L'Arciere, 2003), 105–6. Abraham Goldemberg is buried in the tiny cemetery in Valdieri.

8. De Felice, *The Jews in Fascist Italy*, 754. De Felice prints a list of the names of Catholic convents and monasteries in Rome that hid Jews during the German occupation, along with the numbers hidden in each (751–55). He explains that he obtained the list from the German Father Robert Leiber, S.J., private secretary to Pope Pius XII during most of his papacy (609). Elsewhere, Leiber explains that the list was compiled by Father Beato Ambord, S.J., at an undeclared date, and confirmed in 1954 by unknown researchers. See Robert Leiber, "Pio XII e gli ebrei di Roma: 1943–1944," *La Civiltà Cattolica*, 1961, vol. 1, quad. 2657, March 4, 1961, 449–58, 451.

CHAPTER NINETEEN. AUSCHWITZ

1. Sigfried Hartmeier (sic; Sigi Hart) and Pinkus Goldmann (sic) are listed as deportees to Auschwitz on November 9, 1943, in Liliana Picciotto Fargion, *Il libro della memoria: Gli ebrei deportati dall'Italia (1943–1945)* (1991; Milan: Mursia, 2002), 326, 340.

2. Norbert Wolfinger (Boris Carmeli) is on the list of deportees on convoy 64, printed in full in Serge Klarsfeld, *Memorial to the Jews Deported from France, 1942–1944* (New York: Beate Klarsfeld Foundation, 1983), 483.

3. Picciotto Fargion, *Il libro della memoria*, 45.

4. "Relazione supplettiva sui campi di concentramento ebrei di Borgo San Dalmazzo," signed by the mayor, June 12, 1945, in AISRC, Borgo San Dal-

mazzo, Fondo-Ebrei, fasc. E/1. The names of the five Rudnitzkys are on the
list of prisoners sent from Borgo San Dalmazzo to Drancy, printed in full in
Alberto Cavaglion, *Nella notte straniera: Gli ebrei di St.-Martin-Vésubie* (1981;
Dronero: L'Arciere, 2003), 135–58. They are also on the list of convoy 64
from Drancy to Auschwitz, in Klarsfeld, *Memorial*, 482; and listed in Picciotto Fargion, *Il libro della memoria*, 544, 546. Elena Rudnitzky appears on
Klarsfeld's list as Hélène Roth. In November 1943 she was engaged to Noël
(Natale) Roth, who was arrested with her in Italy and deported to Drancy
and Auschwitz, where he died. After liberation from Auschwitz, Elena married Noël's cousin, Aron Roth, who, with his first wife, Berthe, and son,
Sylvain, had been arrested in Italy at the same time as the Rudnitzkys and
deported with them. Berthe and Sylvain died at Auschwitz.

5. The statistic is from Raul Hilberg, *The Destruction of the European Jews*,
   vol. 3 (New York: Holmes and Meier, 1985), 984–85. The prisoners went to
   Buchenwald, Sachsenhausen, Gross Rosen, Mauthausen, Dachau, Dora-
   Mittelbau, and Ravensbruck. Since many of these camps were full, others
   continued on to Bergen-Belsen.
6. Donald Niewyk and Francis Nicosia, *The Columbia Guide to the Holocaust*
   (New York: Columbia University Press, 2000), 199.
7. Kramer's testimony for the week of April 4–13 is cited in Hilberg, *The
   Destruction of the European Jews*, 986.
8. Niewyk and Nicosia, *The Columbia Guide to the Holocaust*, 196.

CHAPTER TWENTY. AFTER THE WAR

1. Miriam Léa Löwenwirth Reuveni's memoirs, entitled *Hakdasha*, were writ-
   ten in Hebrew with Miriam Dubi-Gazan (Raanana, Israel: Docostory, 2002).
   They were translated into Italian and published under the title *Dedicazione*
   (Aosta: Le Château, 2005). This quotation is taken from *Dedication*, the
   as-yet unpublished English translation, with the permission of Miriam
   Löwenwirth Reuveni and Miriam Dubi-Gazan.

CHAPTER TWENTY-ONE. AFTER THE WAR

1. Demonte and Borgo San Dalmazzo had been liberated on April 28, but the
   war continued for a few more days.
2. Serge Klarsfeld, *Memorial to the Jews Deported from France, 1942–1944* (New
   York: Beate Klarsfeld Foundation, 1983), 220. Regarding Josef Appel's expulsion from Belgium as a German enemy alien in May 1940, we have seen
   that Charles Roman's father, Leopold, and Karl Elsberg (not associated with
   Saint-Martin-Vésubie) had the same experience.
3. For the story of their rescue in Florence and elsewhere in Italy, see Louis
   Goldman, "Friends for Life," (unpublished manuscript, 1983), translated
   into Italian by Anna Cursi Li Volsi and published as *Amici per la vita*
   (Florence: Edizioni SP44, 1993).
4. My interview with three nuns at the convent, October 22, 1996; Federica

Barozzi, "I percorsi della sopravvivenza (8 settembre '43–4 giugno '44): Gli aiuti agli ebrei romani nella memoria di salvatori e salvati" (thesis, Università degli studi di Roma "La Sapienza," 1995–96), 121.

5. Ruth Gruber, *Haven: The Unknown Story of One Thousand World War II Refugees* (New York: Coward-McCann, 1983), 57, 63. Gruber, a young assistant to Secretary of the Interior Harold Ickes during the war, traveled to Italy to meet the group, accompanied them to Oswego, and assisted them during their internment. Manya's story is told throughout the book.

6. Klarsfeld, *Memorial*, 343. Miriam is listed as Marie, and Sammy, as Lomi.

7. On January 27, 1944, the Germans ordered the regional prefect of Poitiers to arrest French and foreign Jews in his area. After receiving authorization from his French superiors, he obeyed, launching a major roundup on January 31. From a list of 633 Jews, 484 were seized—a high percentage. An additional 60 Jews were arrested in the Poitiers area in April. This is the raid Vera remembers. See Serge Klarsfeld, *Vichy-Auschwitz: Le rôle de Vichy dans la solution finale de la question juive en France: 1943–1944* (Paris: Fayard, 1985), 150–51, 155, 372.

CHAPTER TWENTY-TWO. JOURNEYS BACK

1. Story told by Don Viale in an interview with Nuto Revelli, printed in Revelli, *Il prete giusto* (Turin: Einaudi, 1998), 53.

2. See "From a Wartime Escape to a Stateside Reunion," *New York Times*, May 7, 2000, 54.

CONCLUSION

1. Serge Klarsfeld, *Vichy-Auschwitz: Le rôle de Vichy dans la solution finale de la question juive en France: 1943–1944* (Paris: Fayard, 1985), 179–81. The statistic for French Jews includes about 8,000 foreign-born Jews who had been naturalized, as well as about 8,000 children born in France to foreign Jews and legally French by parental declaration. The deportation figures include 2,800 who returned.

2. These calculations are based on Liliana Picciotto Fargion, *Il libro della memoria: Gli ebrei deportati dall'Italia (1943–1945)* (1991; Milan: Mursia, 2002), 28, 32, 854–57. The deportation figures include the 837 Jews who returned.

3. Ibid., 28, and 32. Of the 6,806 Jews deported from Italy, 4,148 were Italian, 2,444 were foreigners, and 214 were of unknown nationality. Of the 322 killed in Italy, 200 were Italian, 111 were foreigners, and 11 were of unknown nationality.

4. For discussion of this issue, see Jacques Adler, *The Jews of Paris and the Final Solution: Communal Response and Internal Conflicts, 1940–1944* (New York: Oxford University Press, 1987); Richard I. Cohen, *The Burden of Conscience: French Jewry's Response to the Holocaust* (Bloomington: Indiana University Press, 1987); and Maurice Rajsfus, *Des juifs dans la collaboration: L'U.G.I.F., 1941–1944* (Paris: Études et Documentation Internationales, 1980).

5. See, e.g., Serge Klarsfeld, *Vichy-Auschwitz: Le rôle de Vichy dans la solution finale de la question juive en France: 1942* (Paris: Fayard, 1983), 163–92; and Michael R. Marrus and Robert O. Paxton, *Vichy France and the Jews* (New York: Basic Books, 1981), 270–79.
6. Primo Levi, *The Drowned and the Saved* (1986; New York: Simon and Schuster, 1988), 23–24.

Index

10